THE HEART OF THE YALE LECTURES

THE HEART OF THE
YALE LECTURES

BY

BATSELL BARRETT BAXTER

BAKER BOOK HOUSE
Grand Rapids, Michigan

PHOTOLITHOPRINTED BY CUSHING - MALLOY, INC.
ANN ARBOR, MICHIGAN, UNITED STATES OF AMERICA
1975

TO

MY WIFE

WANDA ROBERTS BAXTER

Introduction

Batsell Barrett Baxter (1916-   )
The Heart of the Yale Lectures

The author of this book deserves to be widely known
for his ministry. After serving congregations from
1938-51, he served as the Chairman of the Department
of Speech and Homiletics, David Lipscomb College,
Nashville, Tennessee. Since 1957 he has served as
Chairman of the Bible Department at the same insti-
tution. From 1951-70, he was minister of the Hills-
boro Church of Christ in Nashville. He is the author
of several books on preaching and has added the responsibility of being the speaker on the nationwide
Herald of Truth radio and television programs.

The Yale Lectures began in 1871 and in this cen-
tenary year it is a distinct service to reissue this volume. The attempt is made and achieved to sift the
lectures up to 1944 to discover what they have to say
about preaching. The revealing of personalities and
the qualities possessed, the style and delivery of the
sermon, and the special approach to the art of preaching — all this and more is covered.

The Preacher, The Sermon, The Congregation —
here is a broad coverage of every significant ideal as
related to the practical ends of the ministry. Because
few possess a complete set of the Yale Lectures, and
not many may have read all the volumes as issued,
this book reports what is the best said and written.
Both content and technique are discussed by one who
is involved in that field by teaching and preaching.
Under his skilled guidance the reader will find in this
material a unique text for the study and amplification
of Homiletics.

While it is true that the principles underlying all

public speech are the same, nevertheless the preacher is called to a divine task of ministry and communication of the Gospel and this demands a high standard. Character is the foundation, but spirit and method are also demanded. In this area this book will give to student and pastor a rewarding experience of a postgraduate course not given anywhere else. To "preach the word" in the Pauline exhortation requires a knowledge of the art of preaching as commended by Baxter's unique book.

RALPH G. TURNBULL

PREFACE

The most outstanding contribution to the field of homiletics yet produced in America has been made at the Divinity School of Yale University. This contribution consists of the world-renowned Lyman Beecher Lectureship on Preaching. The plans for the series of lectures originated in the mind of Henry Ward Beecher, the famous preacher of Plymouth Church in Brooklyn, and were made possible by Henry N. Sage, a member of the same church. In the Records of the Corporation of Yale College for April 12, 1871, this paragraph is to be found:

> *Voted,* To accept the offer of Mr. Henry N. Sage, of Brooklyn, of the sum of ten thousand dollars, for the founding of a lectureship in the Theological Department, in a branch of Pastoral Theology, to be designated, "The Lyman Beecher Lectureship on Preaching," to be filled from time to time, upon the appointment of the Corporation, by a minister of the Gospel, of any evangelical denomination, who has been markedly successful in the special work of the Christian ministry.[1]

Henry Ward Beecher, who had been instrumental in planning the lectureship and who had given it the name of his father, Lyman Beecher, was the natural choice to begin the series. So well received were his first lectures that he was called to deliver the lectures a second year and a third. He remains the only man who has spoken on more than two occasions.

Begun in 1871, the lectures have been delivered each year through the seventy-seven-year period until the present date, with the exception of four widely separated years. On several

[1] Phillips Brooks, *Lectures on Preaching* (New York: E. P. Dutton & Company, 1898), recto page following title page.

vii

other occasions the lectures were delivered but never published. There are in existence at the present time sixty-six volumes of the famous series.

Because of the eminence of the preachers who have been called to appear before the Divinity School of the university, this particular lectureship has achieved a distinction unequaled by other lectureships in the field of homiletics. It is natural, therefore, that the published volumes of the Yale lectures are highly esteemed wherever they are to be found.

In spite of the high quality and vital nature of the material contained in the Yale lectures, few preachers in the present busy world can find time to read more than a few scattered volumes. For some time there has been a need for someone to gather the choicest of the fruits of these many volumes into a single volume which can be mastered in a much briefer period of time, and which at the same time will be more readily accessible to the thousands of interested ministers. In undertaking this task I have conceived my responsibility to be that of faithfully reporting what the Yale lecturers have said. In this volume I have not undertaken to endorse or, on the other hand, to condemn the various expressions of these eminent men, but rather to report them so that the reader may judge them for himself.

The pages which follow are filled with an unusual number of quotations, some of which are longer than is ordinarily acceptable in books of our time. This practice was followed for three reasons: (1) the lectures were often given in a style which could not be paraphrased without the loss of much of the speaker's force; (2) the numerous quotations will enable the reader to draw his own conclusions concerning the matters discussed and will assist him in evaluating the conclusions included in the final chapter; and (3) the inaccessibility of many volumes of the Yale lectures makes generous quotation in a book such as this a service to the reader.

The lectures fall into two distinct classes—one group dis-

cussing the content of preaching; the other the technique of
preaching. Those lectures on the content of preaching lay beyond the scope of this volume, for, although even in them
there were found scattered suggestions on the technique of
preaching, they dealt primarily with theological concepts
rather than with the factors which determine skill in preaching. The material in this present book is restricted to a study
of homiletics; this is a volume dealing with the *art of preaching.*

As is readily apparent, this book is divided into three parts,
in order that special emphasis may be placed upon the three
major elements in the art of preaching: the *preacher,* the
sermon, and the *congregation.* In failing to list the preacher's
message as one of the most important elements in the art of
preaching, I do not imply that it is less important than the
elements just named. Rather, the message is simply beyond the
consideration of this book, as is indicated above.

In order that the reader may compare the precepts set forth
in the Yale lectures concerning effective pulpit speaking with
the precepts set forth by the world's outstanding rhetoricians
concerning effective secular speaking, a final chapter of
summary and evaluation has been included. The comparison
is careful, though necessarily brief. The reader will be impressed with the similarity of the rules of success in religious
and in secular speaking.

It is inevitable in such a work as this that the reader may
occasionally fail to find one of his favorite passages. At such a
moment I beg you to remember the vastness of the entire series
of lectures and the limitations of a single volume. Only the
choicest of contributions could be included. While we may
regret that some things had to be left behind, we can approach
the reading of the pages which follow with a confidence that
the path ahead will be strewn with nuggets. To say that the
Yale lectures are a gold mine of instruction and inspiration in
the field of homiletics is not overstatement.

I should like to express appreciation to the following for permission to quote from their published volumes: Abingdon-Cokesbury Press; D. Appleton-Century Company, Inc.; G. Bell & Sons, Ltd.; Brown University; F. S. Crofts & Co.; Dodd, Mead & Company; Harper & Brothers, Publishers; Hodder & Stoughton, Limited; Houghton Mifflin Company; The International Council of Religious Education; The Macmillan Company; The Newton Company; Fleming H. Revell Company; Charles Scribner's Sons; A. P. Watt & Son; and Yale University Press. In addition, I should also like to express appreciation to the following persons who have given permission for the use of their materials: Charles Reynolds Brown, Raymond Calkins, Albert Edward Day, W. H. P. Faunce Estate, Mrs. James E. Freeman, Mrs. George P. Hyde, C. Frederic Jefferson, William Pierson Merrill, Francis Greenwood Peabody Estate, and Ralph Sockman. In the appendix of the book the reader may find a listing of the volumes from which contributions were made by each of the above copyright holders. In addition, proper credit has been given in footnotes for the quotations used throughout the book.

Finally, I should like to acknowledge a debt of gratitude to the late Ray Keeslar Immel, recent Dean of the School of Speech of the University of Southern California, for valuable assistance in the planning of this book.

BATSELL BARRETT BAXTER

Nashville, Tennessee

CONTENTS

xi

PART III

THE CONGREGATION

CHAPTER I

INTRODUCTION

Some years ago George A. Buttrick had under his care several young men who were preparing themselves for the ministry. On one occasion he discussed with these young ministerial students the elements which are essential to success in preaching. Later, he described this meeting in one of his lectures before the Yale University Divinity School as follows:

> What is the secret of real influence in a preacher?—
> we asked. Is it physical vitality? That is a factor, we
> agreed; it gives red blood to a sermon, and infects the
> listener with health and cheer. Is it mental keenness?
> That also is an asset: a sharp intellectual scythe is better
> in the time of harvest than a dull blade. But these ques-
> tions left us still on the circumference of the quest. Two
> men of equal energy and equal mind might be imagined
> preaching the same sermon: in the one case it might fall
> dead at his feet, and in the other flame like a torch. Char-
> acter, then—is that the answer? Not in any obvious mean-
> ing of the word: two preachers might be of equally good
> character, so far as eye could judge, and one carry con-
> viction and the other leave his congregation almost
> inert.[1]

The question of that day's discussion is the question which the Yale lecturers have sought to answer. What is the secret of real influence in the pulpit? What are the elements which give a man power when he stands before a congregation, and what are the factors which render him impotent? These

[1] George A. Buttrick, *Jesus Came Preaching* (New York: Charles Scribner's Sons, 1931), p. 170.

questions are most vital to every preacher, for the degree to which he succeeds in his life work is limited by the degree to which he finds the answers to them. To a few supremely gifted men the search for answers to these questions seems unnecessary. They succeed with but little effort; but to most ministers the learning of the art of preaching is a lifelong task.

In the first lecture of the first series, Henry Ward Beecher spoke of the magnitude of the task of learning to preach:

> Young man, when you get a parish, don't be discouraged for the first ten years, no matter how poor your work. There is no trade that requires so long an apprenticeship as preaching; and yet there is no trade to which they admit a man so soon, or in which he learns so fast. It is easier to study law and become a successful practitioner, it is easier to study medicine and become a successful practitioner, than it is to study the human soul all through,—to know its living forms, and to know the way of talking to it, and coming into sympathy with it. To make the truths of God and the Divine influences a part of your daily, enthusiastic experience, and to bring to bear out of your treasury what is needed here or there,—that requires a great deal of experience, and a great deal of study.[2]

The Yale lectures were designed to give experienced and successful ministers an opportunity to tell young men who are entering the ministry some of the things they will so soon and so desperately need to know. It is an effort upon the part of older men to save younger men from the necessity of learning the difficult technique of preaching through trial and accidental success.

DEFINITION OF PREACHING

In order that all may understand the scope of this study alike, it seems wise to present at this point several of the

[2] Henry Ward Beecher, *Yale Lectures on Preaching* (New York: Fords, Howard, & Hulbert, 1892), I, 12–13.

definitions of preaching which are to be found interspersed among the lectures. Since Beecher's definition was presented first in point of time, it deserves the first position here:

> Eloquence has been defined, sometimes, as the art of moving men by speech. Preaching has this additional quality, that it is the art of moving men from a lower to a higher life. It is the art of inspiring them toward a nobler manhood.[3]

The definition George Wharton Pepper gave was, "Preaching, in its strictest sense, is the public use of speech with intent to reveal God to man." [4]

Of all the definitions of preaching appearing in this series, the most widely quoted has been the one given by Phillips Brooks in the sixth annual presentation of the lectures:

> What, then, is preaching, of which we are to speak? It is not hard to find a definition. Preaching is the communication of truth by man to men. It has in it two essential elements, truth and personality. Neither of those can it spare and still be preaching. The truest truth, the most authoritative statement of God's will, communicated in any other way than through the personality of brother man to men is not preached truth.[5]

Not content to define the term "preaching" alone, the Yale lecturers extended their definitions to cover the general functions of the preacher. James Edward Freeman gave a rather extended analysis of the exact position which the preacher occupies as a special servant of God:

> "We are ambassadors for Christ," declared the great apostle. What the ambassador is, to and for his country, implies first of all, the imposition of authority. He is what

[3] Beecher, *op. cit.*, I, 29.
[4] George Wharton Pepper, *A Voice from the Crowd* (New Haven: Yale University Press, 1915), p. 28.
[5] Phillips Brooks, *Lectures on Preaching* (New York: E. P. Dutton & Company, 1898), p. 5.

he is by reason of his credentials; he is vested with a
power that, conferred upon him by his government, guarantees to him a place of recognition and distinction. He
has a prescribed and definite duty, and the success of his
mission is conditioned, on the one hand by his sense of authority, and on the other, by his unfailing fidelity and
utter devotion to the cause to which he is committed. As
a minister plenipotentiary he has his assignment, his prescribed sphere of influence, and the success of his administration will be determined by his fitness, his loyalty,
his equipment, his technique, and the recognition of his
perils. . . .

. . . .

The office of the Christian minister, rightly conceived
and exercised, carries with it powers and responsibilities
not less worthy and important.[6]

So significant did Freeman consider this explanation of the
minister's relationship to God that he called his volume of
Yale lectures by the name, *The Ambassador*. Almost exactly
the same description of the preacher's work was given by L. P.
Jacks:

I conceive of the preacher as essentially a man under
orders, a man not his own master, a man whose leadership, if he claim to be a leader, is based throughout on his
obedience to the Power whose ambassador he is. Such a
man will naturally have a strain of heroism in his composition. The quality of a good soldier will never be
wholly absent from his work. He will carry his life in
his hand. To such a man one may talk freely of difficulties and dangers without fearing they will depress him.[7]

J. H. Jowett warned that the preacher does well to remain
in his own field:

When the preacher becomes economist there are men
outside who can surpass him in his office. His influence

[6] James Edward Freeman, *The Ambassador* (New York: The Macmillan
Company, 1928), p. 25.

[7] L. P. Jacks, *Elemental Religion* (New York: Harper & Brothers, 1934),
pp. 2-3.

in these secondary realms is comparatively small. . . .
It is for him to keep a clean, clear, true insight into the
things that matter most, to explore the wonderful love
of God, to delve and mine in the treasures of redemption,
"to know nothing among men save Jesus Christ and Him
crucified." [8]

After mentioning that the preacher has a number of responsibilities, Beecher pointed to his work in the pulpit as his chief
obligation:

. . . he is an administrator, or more like what in civil
government is termed an executive. But besides this, he
is to teach and inspire men from the platform or pulpit;
and that is what we mean distinctively by Preaching. . . .
I believe that it is the wish and purpose of this Institu-
tion to send out *preachers,*—not merely good managers,
good pastors, but good *preachers.* [9]

John Watson thought it wise to echo this same sentiment
when he delivered the lectures some years later:

It lies upon the minister of Christ to care for the souls
of his people from house to house; to spare no pains that
divine service be beautiful and reverent; to afford to the
young every useful means of religious culture; to move
his congregation unto such good works as lie to their
hand: but it is well for him to remember that the most
critical and influential event in the religious week is the
sermon. . . . No power in human experience has
wrought such mighty works as the spoken word: it has
beaten down impiety, taught righteousness, given freedom to the oppressed, and created nations. [10]

THE CALL

Closely related to the subject of the functions which the
Christian minister is to perform is the subject of who the

[8] J. H. Jowett, *The Preacher: His Life and Work* (New York: Hodder &
Stoughton, 1912), p. 86.

[9] Beecher, *op. cit.,* I, 1-2.

[10] John Watson [Ian Maclaren], *The Cure of Souls* (New York: Dodd, Mead
& Company, 1896 and Hodder & Stoughton, Ltd.), pp. 3-4.

minister should be. Of all the thousands of young men in our country, which ones should determine to make the public preaching of the gospel of Christ their life work? Through many generations, this problem has been discussed under the heading of "the call to preach." "What constitutes a valid call to preach?" has been the question most often phrased.

Obviously, the answer which a given individual makes to this question is determined in large measure by his particular theology. So it was among the lecturers at Yale. The emphasis was sometimes placed upon the part that God plays in the call, sometimes upon the part played by the natural qualifications of the candidate, and sometimes upon both these elements.

Although some of the speakers passed by the discussion of the call entirely, or mentioned it only slightly, others discussed the matter at length. Since Nathaniel J. Burton, in the series of 1884, discussed this subject more fully than any of the others, it is fitting that his views be presented somewhat fully. He lists first what he terms the natural elements in the call, then proceeds to speak of the supernatural elements which enter into the call:

> First, then. If a man has gifts, he may be a minister—and examining committees always feel bound to start the question of gifts. Has the candidate any intellect, and has the moral region of his head any size? Can he think? And when he thinks does he produce anything, ordinarily? Is there any ethical sound to the movement of his mind? Does he know anything? Can he tell to other people what he knows? Can he tell it in an engaging manner, so that if we start him out as a preacher, somebody will be likely to want to hear him.
>
> And then passing from his mind to his exterior make-up, what physical gifts has he? Is he a person whom one can look at with any comfort? What sort of a voice has he? Has he lungs, and a degree of digestion, and an affirmative physique all around, rather than a physique negative and peeping. . . .
>
> At the same time, in order that we may not be too

knowing in this matter, and may not fall into the delusion that God is shut up to ten-talented people, for the accomplishment of his works, behold what mighty men some weak men are, in his kingdom and work-field. . . .

The second sign of a real ministerial call is found in a certain convergence of the man's circumstances towards the work ministerial. . . .

The third indication of a young man truly called, is the united advice of judicious friends.[11]

About the supernatural element of the call, Burton adds:

My brethren, having now stated the different particulars of a valid call, as partly natural and partly supernatural, and having spent some time on the naturals, I desire to put in an energetic testimony in behalf of God's direct and explicit part in the calling of his servants and ambassadors. Of course our natural gifts are his gift— and our circumstances are of his providing and our good advices are his messages—and therefore there is a sense in which these natural things are all supernatural, and that sense of things we need to bear in mind, with reverence and gratitude; but over and beyond all that, God may serve a notice on a man in wonderful ways—in ways that force the man to say, "Lo! God is here with me— in me—all through me—through and through—calling me—pressing me—making me seven times willing, expectant, and self-consecrate." [12]

Matthew Simpson had preceded Burton by five years in the lectures with an explanation of the call to the ministry which, though more brief, traveled the same path as the explanation by Burton:

In the ordinary call, they teach that the young man arrives at the conviction that he should preach, from the consideration of his qualifications, mental tendencies, and surrounding circumstances; that the same influences lead him to enter the ministry, which, with some changes,

11 Nathaniel J. Burton, *In Pulpit and Parish* ([New York: The Macmillan Company, 1925]), pp. 36–39.
12 *Ibid.*, p. 42.

would have led him to enter the profession of medicine or law, or to engage in some special secular pursuit. He simply follows the indications of Providence manifested in his own nature and in the world around him. These are found in his physical power, intellectual capacity, fondness for study, readiness of utterance, benevolent tendency, and religious life. He beholds around him a world lying in wickedness. Men are going astray. He has felt in his own heart the love of God, with an accompanying desire to do all the good he can, and looks upon the work of the ministry as a work of benevolence and love. He believes that he could be useful in teaching the ignorant, and in elevating the aspirations of the young; in holding the attention of congregations, and in persuading them to believe the word of the Lord.[13]

Later, Simpson spoke of the supernatural element:

But I believe the true call to the ministry contains a supernatural element not embraced in this description of an ordinary call.

The extraordinary call of such writers, or what I deem the true call to the ministry, does not consist in any audible voice, in any vision or dream, or in any extraordinary external circumstances. The message which God sends is spiritual. Like a still, small voice, it influences the inner nature, and is extraordinary only in that it is a special divine communication. In its slightest form it is a persuasion that he who receives it *ought* to preach the Gospel; in its strongest form, that God requires him to do this work at the peril of his soul. . . .[14]

Charles H. Parkhurst left room for the inclusion of both of the above-mentioned elements in his explanation of a valid call:

. . . whether God communicates to me his thought concerning me, and his purpose respecting me, through the counsel of a friend, through the shaping of circumstances, or by a dream, a vision, a burning bush, a great

[13] Matthew Simpson, *Lectures on Preaching* (New York: Phillips & Hunt, 1879), pp. 42-43.
[14] *Ibid.,* p. 45.

light, or less startlingly, but more in consonance with the usual method of divine procedure, by the drawing of my own temperament and the peculiar fitness natively inherent in me, my calling in the latter case, equally as in the former ones, is a calling from the Lord.[15]

After one of Beecher's lectures the matter of a proper call to the ministry was introduced by a member of his audience in the form of a question. In his reply upon the following day, Beecher plainly left no room for the supernatural element mentioned by several of the other lecturers:

Some one asked me yesterday, What was to be regarded as a proper call to the ministry? I reply, the possession of those qualities which make a good minister,—good sense, good nature, good health, and downright moral earnestness.[16]

Jowett spoke more of the intensity of the call than of its nature:

Now I hold with profound conviction that before a man selects the Christian ministry as his vocation he must have the assurance that the selection has been imperatively constrained by the eternal God. . . . The candidate for the ministry must move like a man in secret bonds. "Necessity is laid" upon him. His choice is not a preference among alternatives. Ultimately he has no alternative: all other possibilities become dumb: there is only one clear call sounding forth as the imperative summons of the eternal God.[17]

The completeness with which the minister is to give himself to his work was mentioned by Jacks when he said, "The preacher of the Gospel who is not enlisted for life is neither a disciple nor an apostle, but a hired mercenary. The Gospel has no use for such." [18] In recent years, Morgan Phelps Noyes

[15] Charles H. Parkhurst, *The Pulpit and the Pew* (New Haven: Yale University Press, 1913), p. 16.
[16] Beecher, *op. cit.*, I, 39–40.
[17] Jowett, *op. cit.*, pp. 12–13.
[18] Jacks, *op. cit.*, p. 31.

added, "A minister is not likely to be a preacher of the Word of God unless that is his highest ambition." [19]

THE CHALLENGE

Sixty generations after Jesus the people of the world are still unable to live together in peace. The trend of civilization has been unmistakably upward, but the summit is still far ahead. The forces of evil are so well entrenched that many are discouraged with the prospect of remaking the nations into one Christian world. Progress has been so slow, and sometimes nullified by a later retreat, that many are wondering if the Christians of the world are really a force after all. It was something of this feeling which William Fraser McDowell expressed in his lectures which were delivered in the midst of the first World War:

> Men are wondering, as they have in other periods, whether Christianity is a living or a spent force in the world. The faith of many is in eclipse. Many walk in despair and darkness. They feel that one world is dead, they are not sure that a better has any power to be born. Into such an era you come.[20]

Almost a generation later, in the midst of the second World War, Elmore McNeill McKee turned the spotlight upon the men who preach Christ to the world and wondered whether their preaching were really a force:

> Is preaching a FORCE? One wonders. We have one or more pulpits in nearly every village, and in every town and city in the land, and what is the result? . . .
> . . . We may be tolerated simply because we do not count; tolerated because we are a relatively impotent minority in a society which has ceased to be Christian.

[19] Morgan Phelps Noyes, *Preaching the Word of God* (New York: Charles Scribner's Sons, 1943), p. 26.

[20] William Fraser McDowell, *Good Ministers of Jesus Christ* (New York: The Abingdon Press, 1918), p. 20.

. . . If we had preached better we might have produced a better society, or have been locked up for trying to do so.[21]

None of these eminent men seriously doubted that preaching is a great power for good, but their doubts seemed to say that preaching is not yet the force that it is capable of becoming. It was Brooks who expressed the conviction, or perhaps it was only a hope, that, "The world has not heard its best preaching yet." [22] When Charles Reynolds Brown came to the end of his 1922 series of lectures he concluded them with the same hopeful, challenging sentence: "The world has not heard its best preaching yet." [23]

THE JOY

When one dedicates himself to the proclaiming of the Christian gospel what may he expect in return? No better answer has been given than that of Beecher:

I have seen a great deal of life, and on all of its sides. I have seen the depths of poverty, and I have seen competency. I have seen the extremity of solitariness, and the crowds of a city, both at home and abroad. I have seen what art has done, and whatever is to be seen in the wilderness. I have had youth and middle age, and now I am an old man. I have seen it all, and I bear witness that, while there are single moments of joy in other matters that, perhaps, carry a man up to the summit of feeling, yet for steadfast and repetitious experience there is no pleasure in this world comparable to that which a man has who habitually stands before an audience with an errand of truth, which he feels in every corner of his soul and in every fiber of his body, and to whom the Lord has given liberty of utterance, so that he is pouring out the

[21] George Arthur Buttrick and others, *Preaching in These Times* (New York: Charles Scribner's Sons, 1940), pp. 79–80.
[22] Brooks, *op. cit.*, p. 33.
[23] Charles Reynolds Brown, *The Art of Preaching* (New York: The Macmillan Company, 1922), p. 248.

whole manhood in him upon his congregation. Nothing in the world is comparable to that.[24]

Much of the faithful minister's reward comes in the happiness that is his in this life, but there is even more in the life beyond. Beecher devoted one of his most inspiring paragraphs to that beyond:

> And, young gentlemen, it matters but very little what titles you get here, what emoluments, what confidence, and what pleasure; for when you shall stand at the coming of the Lord, in the gateway of heaven, saying to him, "Here am I, and these whom I have brought," one greeting, one look, from him will repay you for every groan, for every sorrow, for every sadness, and for all the waiting that you ever knew upon earth. You are sons of God walking in disguise. What you do now you know not.[25]

SUMMARY

When the chemist works out a formula involving only two or three elements, his task is relatively simple. When, however, he must blend a number of elements into a formula which will perform a delicate and specific operation, his task is infinitely greater. The art of preaching involves the careful selection and skillful blending of a multitude of elements. It requires much experimentation and study. He who gives himself to preaching must be willing to dedicate his best efforts through all his lifetime to the learning and perfecting of the art.

Preaching has as its objective the lifting of mankind from a lower to a higher plane. The truth of God is most effective in accomplishing this task when it comes through the personality of a consecrated man of God. A man may assume that he is "called to preach" when his natural qualifications are such as are needed by the minister, when he feels certain that God

[24] Beecher, op. cit., I, 192-93.
[25] Ibid., III, 189-90.

desires him as a public proclaimer of the gospel, and when he himself desires to preach to such a degree that he could never be quite conscience-free should he decline the opportunity to preach.

No matter into what generation a minister may come, the condition of the world provides a never-ending challenge to him. The forces of evil are so powerful and the representatives of God are so few that there is always room for another in the ranks. Having once entered upon the work of preaching, the minister begins immediately to reap the rewards for his service. These rewards, while not always paid in the coin of the realm, never cease to be found in the supreme joy that comes to the preacher as he sees his humble efforts succeed in lifting his fellow-men to that higher realm of God.

PART I

THE PREACHER

Chapter II

POWER OF PERSONALITY

There is at least one major difference between the priest and the preacher. The priest has no great demand for personality, inasmuch as a great portion of his duties is entirely ritualistic. To the validity of sacraments he can add nothing by his own virtues and efforts, and from such validity his vices and negligences can withdraw nothing.[1] With the preacher, however, such is not the case. More important than almost anything else is the man himself. The widespread emphasis placed upon the preacher's personality in the Lyman Beecher Lectures indicated that there was a high degree of unanimity of feeling that this element deserves recognition of the highest order.

Brooks set the matter forth:

Truth through Personality is our description of real preaching. The truth must come really through the person, not merely over his lips, not merely into his understanding and out through his pen. It must come through his character, his affections, his whole intellectual and moral being. It must come genuinely through him. I think that, granting equal intelligence and study, here is the great difference which we feel between two preachers of the Word.[2]

Earlier, Beecher had said:

A Bible alone is nothing. A Bible is what the man is who stands behind it,—a book of hieroglyphics, if he be

[1] H. Hensley Henson, *The Liberty of Prophesying* (New Haven: Yale University Press, 1910), pp. 1–2.
[2] Brooks, *op. cit.*, p. 8.

17

nothing but a spiritual Champollion; a book of rituals, if he be nothing but a curiosity-monger, or an ingenious framer of odds and ends of things; and a valuable guide, full of truth and full of benefit for mankind, if he be a great soul filled with living thought.[3]

After discussing this personal element in preaching at some length, William Jewett Tucker concluded that, "The law is, the greater the personality of the preacher, the larger the use of his personality, the wider and deeper the response of men to the truth." [4] A. J. F. Behrends added, "We preach to persuade men, and the secret of persuasion is the impact of soul upon soul. . . ." [5] Beginning at quite a different point of view, but coming to the same conclusion, was John Kelman:

> All art is essentially self-expression, the outgoing of a man's own personality upon others. Of no art is this so true as of the art of preaching. The deepest secret of its power, humanly speaking, is the letting loose of the preacher's personality upon his hearers.[6]

Simpson expressed the same feeling as did the others just mentioned:

> The word of God is the constant quantity, the preacher the variable. If this be true, then that preaching is best which, on the one hand, is most full of the divine message, and which, on the other, has the greatest personality of the preacher.[7]

Ralph W. Sockman went so far as to say, "Not what is said, but who says it—that is the consideration which gives weight to what we hear." [8] A little later he added, "Preaching and

[3] Beecher, *op. cit.*, III, 8.

[4] William Jewett Tucker, *The Making and the Unmaking of the Preacher* (Boston: Houghton Mifflin and Company, 1898), p. 124.

[5] A. J. F. Behrends, *The Philosophy of Preaching* (New York: Charles Scribner's Sons, 1890), pp. 57-58.

[6] John Kelman, *The War and Preaching* (London: Hodder and Stoughton, [1919]), p. 165.

[7] Simpson, *op. cit.*, pp. 166-67.

[8] Ralph W. Sockman, *The Highway of God* (New York: The Macmillan Company, 1942), p. 111.

personality are inextricably intertwined." [9] Freeman said that
". . . the ministry of one personality to another has an indescribable value." [10] Pepper, the only layman to deliver a
series of lectures, said from his own point of view that, "The
message invariably comes to the man in the pew tinged with
the personality of the man in the pulpit." [11]

Although many another Yale lecturer spoke of the importance of the preacher's personality, these are sufficient authorities to cite to indicate the high degree of emphasis placed
upon the matter. No better summary has been given than
that set forth by McDowell when he said, "What one personality can do with another we have not begun to measure." [12]

The Lyman Beecher lecturers were not content to announce
the principle that personality is important in preaching, but
were quick to point out examples of this truth in history.
Naturally, the first example mentioned was that of Christ:

> It was as Man that Christ led men to God. It must be
> as men that we carry on the work of Christ and help
> men's souls to Him. This truth seems to me to lie at the
> bottom of all the best successes, and the forgetfulness of it
> at the bottom of all the worst failures of the ministry. [13]

McDowell called attention to the same illustration:

> Certain men do illustrate what can be accomplished in
> the ministry by a maximum of personality. Why multiply
> illustrations? Why go beyond that one figure ever be-
> fore us as we study our task? And why miss the supreme
> lesson that his life brings for our personal lives as well as
> for our world-philosophy—the supreme value of person-
> ality? Wealth can be matched with equal or larger wealth;
> splendor of plant can be equaled or surpassed; elaborate
> organization can be met and overcome in kind. The

9 *Ibid.*, p. 113.
10 Freeman, *op. cit.*, p. 75.
11 Pepper, *op. cit.*, p. 176.
12 McDowell, *op. cit.*, p. 281.
13 Brooks, *op. cit.*, p. 85.

enemy of the ministry is very rich, very fertile, very enter-
prising and resourceful in all these ways. . . . But the
one thing he cannot imitate, nor duplicate, nor match,
nor conquer is a Christlike personality. He knows that
such a personality cannot be resisted, that it draws men
across all barriers of race, creed, and condition. . . .[14]

Beecher pointed out the early disciples of Christ as further
examples of the power of personality:

This living force, then, of the human soul, brought to
bear upon living souls, for the sake of their transforma-
tion, being the fundamental idea, I think it will be interesting to you for me to state more at large the fact that not
only was this the Apostolic idea of preaching, but it was
the secret of the power of the first Christian Church for
many hundred years. It is historically true that Christianity did not in its beginning succeed by the force of
its doctrines, but by the *lives* of its disciples. . . .
    It was not by doctrinal subtleties that they overcame
philosophy. . . . It was the beauty of Christian life that
overcame philosophy, and won the way for Christian
doctrine.[15]

Freeman took in still further territory:

It is safe to say that there has been no great preacher
who has given men an inspiration to live, who has not
infused into his every utterance something of his own
divinely gifted personality.[16]

Henry van Dyke was no less inclusive in his view of the power
of personality:

The world moves by personality. All the great currents
of history have flowed from persons. Organization is powerful; but no organization has ever accomplished anything until a person has stood at the centre of it and filled
it with his thought, with his life. Truth is mighty and

14 McDowell, *op. cit.*, pp. 123-24.
15 Beecher, *op. cit.*, I, 13.
16 Freeman, *op. cit.*, p. 108.

must prevail. But it never does prevail actually until it gets itself embodied, incarnated, in a personality.[17]

During the various periods of great inventive progress in the world's history, such as the period when the invention of printing made it possible for books and printed matter of all kinds to be widely and cheaply distributed, there have been those who have arisen to predict the downfall of the pulpit. At the introduction of printing it was argued that men would no longer bestir themselves to hear a local preacher when they could remain at home and enjoy a superior sermon from the printed page. Simpson made answer to such predictions in the following way:

> Some tell us that the press has superseded the pulpit; that men need no longer be hearers, because they are readers. The Bible is in their hands; and if they need expositions or explanations, they have the works of great commentators. Why should they hear sermons, or listen to preachers of little experience, and of only average mental strength and culture? But they forget the human element: the power of man over his fellow-men; the force derived from experience; the visible embodiment of ideal truth. Preaching is not merely . . . the delivery of the message, but the delivery of the message by a man who professes to have felt its power, and who testifies to its truth in his own experience.[18]

In the present century radio made its debut, and again the prophesy was made that church attendance would decline sharply. Jacks took notice of the prediction:

> . . . whereas there are other forms of truth which may be conveyed by impersonal means, such as the printed book or the radio, the truth of the Living God cannot be so conveyed, but always demands, in the last resort, and behind whatever other means may be employed, the personal presence of the revealer. Its vehicle

[17] Henry van Dyke, *The Gospel for an Age of Doubt* (New York: The Macmillan Company, 1897), p. 59.
[18] Simpson, *op. cit.*, pp. 32–33.

is always a person—and a person not hidden, not anonymous, but known, felt and even loved as a person by those to whom his word is addressed. . . . In this revelation of God the ultimate force of the appeal will always reside, not so much in the word spoken as in the man who speaks.[19]

David H. Greer added a word on the same subject:

The distinctive power of the pulpit is its personality. Not primarily what it says, though that, of course, is important, but who says it; otherwise a phonograph or a telephone would do.[20]

In the 1940 lectures, Sockman was qualified to speak on the same subject after having observed radio's effect upon preaching for more than fifteen years. He concluded that, "Despite the depersonalizing influence of mechanical means of communication, the personality behind the words is becoming ever more important." [21]

In the opening paragraphs of his first lecture, Parkhurst spoke of the limitations placed upon preaching by the men who do the preaching:

Every man is the measure of his work and the measure of his word. He cannot do a work that outmeasures his own proportions, nor speak an effective word that is more eloquent than his own personality. Upon whatever line of service therefore a man enters, the prime question turns on stature.[22]

In a somewhat fuller discussion some three years earlier, Charles E. Jefferson had already pointed out the need for developing character as a prerequisite of effective preaching:

Most Christian congregations know this. They are caring less and less for scholastic attainments, academic

[19] Jacks, op. cit., pp. 38–39.
[20] David H. Greer, The Preacher and His Place (New York: Edwin S. Gorham, 1904), p. 79. Used by permission of Charles Scribner's Sons.
[21] Sockman, op. cit., pp. 110–11.
[22] Parkhurst, op. cit., p. 1.

degrees and titles, denominational affiliations, even creedal loyalties—what they want is a man. Things that men pick up in the schools have their value, but they can never take the place of the one thing essential in a preacher—character. Two men go from the same seminary, in the same year, with the same education and the same creed. One succeeds from the beginning, and his successes increase with the seasons. The other fails from the start, and his entire career is a disappointment. It is not a difference in rhetoric, ideas, or training, but a difference in men. They take their texts out of the same Bible, preach the same scheme of doctrinal truth, make use in general of the same ideas and illustrations, but they do not preach the same gospel, for the gospel is truth moulded and vivified by the soul of the man who preaches it. . . . When words do not penetrate, it is because there is a feeble man behind them. When ideas do not kindle, it is because there is no divine fire in the lips that speak them. Bullets may be of equal size and like material, but the distance to which they travel depends upon the gun. Sermons are bullets. How far they go does not depend upon the text or upon the structure of the sermon, but upon the texture of the manhood of the preacher. The building of the preacher becomes, then, a matter of tremendous moment to everyone interested in the building of the church.[23]

Earlier still, Brooks had mentioned the importance of building men for the ministry.

But this . . . decrees for us in general what the preparation for the ministry is. It must be nothing less than the making of a man. It cannot be the mere training to certain tricks. It cannot be even the furnishing with abundant knowledge. It must be nothing less than the kneading and tempering of a man's whole nature till it becomes of such a consistency and quality as to be capable of transmission.[24]

[23] Charles E. Jefferson, *The Building of the Church* (New York: The Macmillan Company, 1911), pp. 276–77.
[24] Brooks, *op. cit.*, p. 9.

When it came to analyzing this personal power of the preacher and enumerating its constituent parts, there was a general feeling among the Lyman Beecher lecturers that such a task was impossible. For example, in discussing the differences in effectiveness of various preachers, Simpson said, "The element which gives success is termed ministerial power. It is so subtle and spiritual in its character as to be beyond the reach of clear definition or explanation." [25] "Personal attraction or magnetism is of course a thing quite beyond the reach of definition," [26] agreed Kelman.

In discussing the power of an unnamed friend, Greer said:

> . . . there was a great and helpful attractiveness in his preaching which I perceived and felt, as did everybody else who heard him; but what that attractiveness really was, or in what it consisted, I could not say then, and cannot say now. Personality, perhaps, would express it as much as anything else. But then, again, what is personality? Or why is it that that force which we call personality is so much more forceful in some than it seems to be in others? I do not know. That is part of the mystery of life which cannot be explained.[27]

Lyman Abbott sounded a slightly more hopeful note, indicating that he felt that though this power is somewhat mystical and though it defies complete classification, it can be partially defined and cultivated.

> Is it possible to analyze this ability to impart life, to see what are the elements of which this ability is composed? I think it transcends complete analysis. There is something mystical in what we call sometimes personality, sometimes magnetism. It is in no small measure a gift, gained, acquired, or bestowed we know not how. But it is possible for one to cultivate the gift that is in him; and to do this he must at least endeavor to see

---

[25] Simpson, op. cit., p. 198.
[26] Kelman, op. cit., p. 283.
[27] Greer, op. cit., p. 238.

what is the nature of this gift, what are its constituent elements, and how it can be cultivated.[28]

Although several of the lecturers expressed an inability to define the elements which go to make up the personal power of the preacher, most of them did proceed in subsequent lectures to point out the qualifications which are necessary in the preacher. These qualifications, when taken together, add up to something akin to the personal power concerning which so many spoke. It was concluded, therefore, that the preacher's personality is the sum total of all his qualifications and characteristics. This discussion proceeds upon that assumption. The next chapter presents the views of the various lecturers upon the subject of the preacher's qualifications.

One final consideration remains before the next phase of the general subject is presented. Although several of the Lyman Beecher lecturers did not mention the subject of the preacher or his personality by reason of their preoccupation with some other phases of the subject of preaching, only one, P. T. Forsyth, mentioned the preacher's personal power in a negative way.

You hear it said, with a great air of religious common sense, that it is the man that the modern age demands in the pulpit, and not his doctrine. It is the man that counts, and not his creed. But this is one of those shallow and plausible half-truths which have the success that always follows when the easy, obvious underpart is blandly offered for the arduous whole. No man has any right in the pulpit in virtue of his personality or manhood in itself, but only in virtue of the sacramental value of his personality for his message. We have no business to worship the elements, which means, in this case, to idolise the preacher. . . . To be ready to accept any kind of message from a magnetic man is to lose the Gospel in mere impressionism. It is to sacrifice the moral in religion to the aesthetic. And it is fatal to the authority either of the

[28] Lyman Abbott, *The Christian Ministry* (Boston: Houghton Mifflin and Company, 1905), p. 201.

pulpit or the Gospel. The Church does not live by its
preachers, but by its Word.[29]

SUMMARY

In the great undertaking of lifting men from a lower to a
higher plane of life, the most important factor, outside of the
message itself, is the man who stands in the pulpit. The greatest
persuasive force known among men is that of personality.
The readily apparent differences in effectiveness between different pulpits can largely be explained by the differences in
the men who fill those pulpits.

The great movements of history offer ample evidence that
nothing has great influence upon men that does not have a
great person behind it. The greatest force that the world has
seen, Christianity, had behind it the greatest person that the
world has seen, Christ. It is apparent that the early disciples
of Christ moved great masses of men not alone because of the
message which they preached, but also because of the persuasive force of their lives.

Since the impact of person upon person is so nearly the key
to the persuasive process, it is to be expected that the institu-
tion of preaching should not become outmoded. The printed
sermon has not made the preached sermon less popular. The
invisible radio preacher has not caused the visible preacher
to be less in demand. Congregations desire to see and hear and
know the person who breaks to them the bread of life.

It is widely felt that the personal power of the preacher defies analysis. The closest approach to a satisfactory analysis
of his power results from a study of his many characteristics,
for his personality is the sum of all his individual qualities.
The selection, number, and relative intensity of his many
characteristics determine his influence upon others.

29 P. T. Forsyth, *Positive Preaching and the Modern Mind* (New York:
Hodder & Stoughton, [1907]), p. 60.

Chapter III

QUALIFICATIONS

What are the qualities which a man must possess in order to be an effective preacher? The moment qualifications are listed someone is ready to mention any one of a number of the great preachers of history who was deficient in one or more of the elements named. The fact that a particularly great man may have succeeded in the ministry without a strong physique and general good health is no evidence that good health should be eliminated from the list of desired qualities. It simply means that he succeeded in spite of poor health and that he probably would have accomplished even more had he possessed a strong body. No one dares to say that the preacher who is deficient in one, or even several, of the desired ministerial qualifications will be a failure, for his strong points may compensate for his weaknesses. What can be said is this: Other things being equal, the man who possesses *all* of the qualifications named in succeeding pages will achieve the highest measure of success in preaching.

While most of the Lyman Beecher lecturers unfolded each of the qualifications which they mentioned in rather full fashion, there were several who set forth in a single sentence or paragraph a list of the most important qualifications for preachers. These lists of qualifications are presented first, and are followed in succeeding pages by a fuller discussion of those major elements which were mentioned again and again by the various lecturers.

Inasmuch as Beecher was the first in point of time to set forth his list, his is the first introduced here:

I say, first, the preacher ought to be a man who is *fruitful in moral ideas,* has a genius for them, as distinguished from every other kind. . . .

A second quality fitting a man for the Christian ministry, is the *power of moving men.* . . .

A third qualification is what I may call *living by faith,* the sense of the infinite and the invisible; the sense of something else besides what we see with the physical eyes; the sense of God, of eternity, and of heaven. . . .

Another thing: you should have good health; and a fair portion of common sense, which is the only quality that I think never is increased by education; that is born in a man,—or, if it is not, that is the end. . . .

There is one thing more. I do not think that any man has a right to become a Christian minister, who is not willing and thankful to be the least of all God's servants and to labor in the humblest sphere.[1]

Henry Sloane Coffin gave the following list of qualifications, which are quoted in part: "First, *vision.* . . . Second, *moral intuition.* . . . Third, *sympathy.* . . . Fourth, *daring.* . . . And that brings us to the chief characteristic which must be his—*faith.*" [2] William M. Taylor gave his list in one sentence:

It requires a lively imagination; a calm, unbiased judgment; a correct scholarship, and a true homiletic instinct, to lay every thing under tribute for purposes of instruction and edification.[3]

John Broadus, whose book has had more widespread use as a text than any other book of a similar nature, suggested the following as the qualities most necessary to success in preaching:

The preacher needs the capacity for clear thinking, with strong feelings, and a vigorous imagination; also capacity for expression, and the power of forcible utter-

---

1 Beecher, *op. cit.,* I, 44–46.

2 Henry Sloane Coffin, *In a Day of Social Rebuilding* (New Haven: Yale University Press, 1918), pp. 160–70.

3 William M. Taylor, *The Ministry of the Word* (London: T. Nelson and Sons, [1876]), p. 160.

ance. Many other gifts help his usefulness, these are well-nigh indispensable to any high degree of efficiency.[4]

In his discussion of the disposition of the preacher, Howard Crosby listed first the following undesirable attitudes of mind:

> A minister should never be *irritable* or *irascible*. . . . The irascible disposition is near akin to the . . . *petulant disposition*, which is ready to take offense at the slightest thwarting of the will, and which fancies insult where none is intended, which renders a man difficult to approach, and in a minister deprives him of half his efficiency by reason of this barrier to easy intercourse. . . . The *morose disposition* comes next in order, as one to be carefully shunned by the preacher of glad tidings. . . . The preacher should, moreover, be free from an *impulsive disposition*. . . . The preacher should not show a *careless disposition*. . . . The preacher should never exhibit a *money-loving disposition*. . . .
> . . . The preacher should be free from a *headstrong disposition*. . . . The Christian preacher should not have an *eremitic disposition*. He is eminently, though not of the world, a man *for* the world. He is to mingle freely and fully with men of all classes and descriptions. His message is for all.[5]

Turning from the qualities which the preacher should not possess, Crosby listed some of the ideal qualities:

> As opposed to these eight styles of disposition which a preacher should never exhibit, we say positively that he should be calm, gentle, cheerful, regular, careful, disinterested, reasonable, and social—a man whom all will respect and most will love, whose words of counsel will not be discounted by a life out of harmony with the teachings, and who will not be simply endured as an official teacher, but will be ever welcomed as a trusted friend.[6]

[4] John Broadus, *A Treatise on the Preparation and Delivery of Sermons* (revised edition; New York: Richard R. Smith, Inc., 1930), p. 8. Used by permission of Harper & Brothers Publishers.

[5] Howard Crosby, *The Christian Preacher* (New York: Anson D. F. Randolph & Company, 1879), pp. 88–94.

[6] *Ibid.*, p. 96.

Quite a different approach was taken by James Stalker, who quoted a list of ten qualifications set forth by Luther:

Here is Luther's list of the qualifications of a minister: you will observe that most of them are gifts of nature: 1. He should be able to teach plainly and in order. 2. He should have a good head. 3. Good power of language. 4. A good voice. 5. A good memory. 6. He should know when to stop. 7. He should be sure of what he means to say. 8. And be ready to stake body and soul, goods and reputation, on its truth. 9. He should study diligently. 10. And suffer himself to be vexed and criticized by everyone.[7]

Several times in the course of his lectures, Crosby pointed out that the preacher ". . . shall be no ordinary man, but one raised above others . . . ,"[8] his point being that the minister of God must be one who possesses the finest of abilities in every way. No second-rate men may be preachers. Beecher emphasized this same truth earlier in the course of lectures:

When God calls very loud at the time you are born, standing at the door of life, and says, "Quarter of a man, come forth!" that man is not for the ministry. "Half a man, come forth!" no; that will not do for a preacher. "Whole man, come!" that is *you*. The man must be a man, and a full man, that is going to be a true Christian minister, and especially in those things which are furthest removed from selfishness and the nearest in alliance with true divine love.[9]

CHARACTER

There was no subject mentioned more often in the Lyman Beecher Lectures than that of the preacher's character. Twenty-nine different lecturers mentioned its importance, thus giving it a place of primacy in the list of qualifications for

[7] James Stalker, *The Preacher and His Models* (London: Hodder & Stoughton, 1891), pp. 162–63.
[8] Crosby, *op. cit.*, p. 12.
[9] Beecher, *op. cit.*, I, 40.

effective preaching. Both by specific statement and by continuous repetition, the preacher's character was made the foundation upon which all else rises or falls.

An analysis of the statements made by the different speakers lead to the discovery that the preacher's character was discussed from three slightly different standpoints: first, from the standpoint of his piety, or spiritual grasp of that which he preaches; second, from the standpoint of general righteousness of life, which serves to undergird and make effective his pulpit utterances; and, third, from the standpoint of demonstrating or exemplifying the type of life which he would have others attain. These are set forth in the order mentioned.

Stalker spoke a great deal concerning the piety of the preacher:

> I should like to be allowed to say to you, gentlemen, with all the earnestness of which I am capable, that the prime qualification of a minister is that he be himself a religious man—that, before he begins to make God known, he should first himself know God.[10]

A little later he added:

> It is not because our arguments for religion are not strong enough that we fail to convince, but because the argument is wanting which never fails to tell; and this is religion itself. People everywhere can appreciate this, and nothing can supply the lack of it. The hearers may not know why their minister, with all his gifts, does not make a religious impression on them; but it is because he is not himself a spiritual power.[11]

Brooks too had a word to say on this subject:

> I must not dwell upon the first of all the necessary qualities, and yet there is not a moment's doubt that it does stand first of all. It is a personal piety, a deep possession in one's own soul of the faith and hope and resolution

[10] Stalker, *op. cit.*, p. 50.
[11] *Ibid.*, p. 55.

which he is to offer to his fellow-men for their new life. Nothing but fire kindles fire.[12]

Beginning with a negative approach, Broadus arrived at the same conclusion as the others:

> Men sometimes do good by preaching who turn out to have been destitute of piety. It is one of the many wonderful ways in which God brings good out of evil. But such cases are exceptional, and as a rule, the prime requisite to efficiency in preaching is earnest piety.[13]

The voice of Pepper, the layman, was also heard emphasizing the need for spirituality:

> When I talk with other men in the pews about the kind of man they need in the pulpit a very large percentage of them will cry out for what they describe as a "spiritually minded man." They want an intelligent man, of course, and a man with gumption enough to administer congregational affairs. But there is an increasing emphasis upon the spiritual note.[14]

McDowell proceeded to show how piety cannot be demonstrated by those who do not have it, and that only genuinely spiritual men can give evidence of possessing real spiritual power:

> You cannot give what you have not got. You cannot create consecration unless you have consecration. You cannot cause men to do their best unless you live at your best. Learning will not do it. Eloquence will not do it. Even brilliant deeds will not do it. Life giving is in the hands of life possessors. We have seen such men. We know such men, in large groups and small ones. They bring vitality, they create it. They bring consecration, they create it. They bring the inspiration of perfect devotion, glad and rapturous. They create it because they have it.[15]

12 Brooks, *op. cit.*, p. 38.
13 Broadus, *op. cit.*, p. 7.
14 Pepper, *op. cit.*, p. 190.
15 McDowell, *op. cit.*, p. 291.

Van Dyke pointed the way to the acquisition of piety:

It is only by dwelling with Him and receiving His character, His personality so profoundly, so vitally that it shall be with us as if, in His own words, we had partaken of His flesh and His blood, as if His sacred humanity had been interwoven with the very fibres of our heart and pulsed with secret power in all our veins,—it is thus only that we can be enabled to see His teaching as it is, and set it forth with luminous conviction to the souls of men.

. . . A Christless man can never preach Christ.[16]

Edwin DuBose Mouzon said of the preacher's own experiences, ". . . If preachers are to speak with authority they must speak out of knowledge experimentally established."[17] Freeman spoke of the subject, emphasizing the necessity of a deep consciousness of God:

There is a mysterious and undefinable quality that inheres in the man who possesses in a large degree the God-consciousness. He may lack many gifts and graces that are called for in other professions; he may, like Lincoln, be homely of face and ungainly of bearing; he may have little that would give him place or distinction in pulpit, rostrum or drawing-room, but once we come into his presence and listen to his message we feel the force of his personality, the indescribable spell of his genius and the irresistible power of his utterance.[18]

Parkhurst voiced in rather vigorous language the need for God-filled preachers:

There is a quantity of unpardonable nonsense perpetrated upon the question why the masses do not throng the churches. It is not the fault of the masses. People will fill the churches as fast as God fills the ministers.[19]

16 Van Dyke, op. cit., pp. 201–2.
17 Edwin DuBose Mouzon, Preaching with Authority (Garden City, New York: Doubleday, Doran & Company, Inc., 1929), p. 220.
18 Freeman, op. cit., pp. 42–43.
19 Parkhurst, op. cit., p. 194.

The effect of the preacher's character upon the reception of his truth is the second phase of character to be discussed. It was apparent from the study that the audience's impression of the man is as important as any other single characteristic. In the views of some of the lecturers, this was more important than all other charcteristics. Stalker put the matter rather strongly:

> We are so constituted that what we hear depends very much for its effect on how we are disposed towards him who speaks. The regular hearers of a minister gradually form in their minds, almost unawares, an image of what he is, into which they put everything which they themselves remember about him and everything which they have heard of his record; and, when he rises on Sunday in the pulpit, it is not the man visible there at the moment that they listen to, but this image, which stands behind him and determines the precise weight and effect of every sentence which he utters.[20]

The importance of the man who delivers the sermon in comparison with the sermon by itself was a point of emphasis in one of Robert F. Horton's later lectures:

> I conceive . . . the real preacher of the Word as one who is before all other things occupied in keeping clean the vessel which is to deliver and distribute the things of God, "purging himself from all defilement of the flesh and of the spirit, perfecting holiness in the fear of God." His chief concern is not to prepare sermons, but to prepare himself to deliver sermons.[21]

McKee emphasized the same thought. "What shall we *be?* That is the real question. Not the words first, but the *Man* then the words." [22] Beecher was the first lecturer to emphasize this point of view. "Your work, therefore, as a Christian minister," he said, ". . . requires that you should, first of all,

[20] Stalker, *op. cit.*, p. 167.

[21] Robert F. Horton, *Verbum Dei* (New York: Macmillan and Co., 1893), pp. 265–66.

[22] Buttrick and others, *op. cit.*, p. 124.

see to the elevation of character of the man that preaches." [23]
The qualification was placed first in the list enumerated by
Van Dyke:

> First of all . . . it is necessary to lead a clean, upright,
> steadfast, useful life, purged from all insincerity, and
> lifted above all selfishness. . . . Never has there been a
> time when character and conduct counted for more than
> they do to-day.[24]

Jefferson declared that the preacher's power is a result of the
preacher's character:

> In preaching it is the character of the preacher which
> is the preacher's power. Preaching is not a trick which can
> be mastered some bright morning, or a secret which can
> be transmitted from one man to another for a considera-
> tion. . . . All these things—voice, gesture, rhetoric, il-
> lustrations, quotations, ideas, learning—have a certain
> value, but they are at best superficialities, and all of them,
> unless backed up by something better, soon grow thin
> and tame. After a little time artificial elocution becomes
> unbearable, rhetorical display unendurable, excessive il-
> lustration insufferable, the exploitation of novel or ab-
> stract ideas intolerable. Nothing wears but manhood. To
> remain ten or twenty years in the same parish, a preacher
> must be very simple and very true. Goodness never grows
> stale. Love never becomes monotonous.[25]

Kelman called the preacher's duty to possess a good character
his strongest responsibility:

> Without our power to prevent it, nay even, it may be,
> in spite of ourselves, our own personality is going out
> upon our congregations along with the truths we are pro-
> claiming. The responsibility for our own personal char-
> acter is therefore the greatest of all our responsibilities.[26]

E. G. Robinson warned that preaching must be supported by
character:

[23] Beecher, *op. cit.*, I, 37.
[24] Van Dyke, *op. cit.*, pp. 43–44.
[25] Jefferson, *op. cit.*, pp. 282–86.
[26] Kelman, *op. cit.*, pp. 260–61.

Here then may we not catch a glimpse of the true place of preaching? Surely it is out of its true place when relied on as a substitute for the convincing and persuasive power of character. Indeed preaching unsupported by character in the preacher is a mockery of truth and an offence to God and man.[27]

Warning that even the slightest doubt of the preacher on the part of his congregation will render his sermons ineffective, Simpson pointed out the importance of a good man in the pulpit:

If, then, the personality of the preacher be so necessary and so potent a factor, what manner of person should a minister be, in all holy conversation and godliness! . . . If he causes in the minds of the people even so much as a suspicion that he is a wicked man, his power is at once impaired. Men may admire his mental vigor, his faultless rhetoric, his irresistible logic, and his overwhelming oratory; but their hearts will not be captivated by his utterances.[28]

Crosby reemphasized that the man is more important than the style or technique in preaching:

. . . a fresh and warm sermon spoken from a good man's heart, though it be inferior in style and argument, is far more adapted to the edification of an audience than the most finished and perfect discourse of another who may be a master in sermonizing.[29]

Sounding a note of caution, Crosby continued:

When the world recognizes its own vices in the pulpit, it can receive no heavenly message from that quarter. Evil habits in the minister, even if they do not amount to crimes, have the same general effect. They lead the believer to distrust and the unbeliever to blaspheme.[30]

[27] E. G. Robinson, *Lectures on Preaching* (New York: Henry Holt and Company, 1883), p. 11.
[28] Simpson, *op. cit.*, p. 168.
[29] Crosby, *op. cit.*, p. 48.
[30] *Ibid.*, p. 105.

Another lecturer who pointed out the power that comes from the preacher's good life was John Hall:

> There is power from unselfish service—from living habitually before men's eyes a blameless, beneficent life. The man is felt to be greater than what he says. It is a part of which he is the whole; and his personality is behind his speech. All the weight of him is with his words, as the force of a blow is measured in a gymnasium by, not that of the arm only, but also of the body that is behind the arm.[31]

Jowett pointed out that deeds must back up the sermon:

> The word of grace is to be confirmed by gracious deeds. The Gospel is to be corroborated by the witness of daring exploits. The herald is to be a knight, revealing the power of his message in his own chivalry. That is to say, there is laid upon the preacher the supreme privilege of obligation and sacrifice. He is to be filled with the "love and pity" which are the very energies of redemption. The good news without the good deed will leave us impotent. But the spirit of sacrificial love will make us invincible.[32]

One final quotation will suffice to set forth the widespread feeling that a preacher's character must be such as to inspire confidence rather than suspicion. Behrends said that:

> Few things are of greater practical importance, than securing, and keeping, the confidence of your hearers in your personal integrity, and in your enthusiastic devotion to your work.[33]

In the third phase of the discussion of the character of the preacher, the emphasis was placed upon the power of the preacher's example to influence men. In addition to giving his sermons power in the minds of the congregation, his example is a concrete model which the people can emulate. Stalker

[31] John Hall, *God's Word Through Preaching* (New York: Dodd & Mead, Publishers, 1875), pp. 239–40.
[32] Jowett, *op. cit.*, p. 35.
[33] Behrends, *op. cit.*, p. 229.

drew attention to this function of the preacher when he said that:

> . . . the great purpose for which a minister is settled in a parish is not to cultivate scholarship, or to visit the people during the week, or even to preach to them on Sunday, but it is to live among them as a good man, whose mere presence is a demonstration which cannot be gainsaid that there is a life possible on earth which is fed from no earthly source, and that the things spoken of in church on Sabbath are realities.[34]

Francis Greenwood Peabody cited the example of Christ as evidence that the character of the speaker is the entering wedge in making disciples:

> Character was the gate of conviction. . . .
> If, then, it be the truth of history that the first disciples were led on from moral attachment to spiritual insight, from reverence for the character of Jesus to confession of the faith of Jesus, it may be reasonably believed that the same path of spiritual development may be followed to the same end by the mind of the present age.[35]

Pointing back to the success of Christ, McDowell also emphasized the power of Christ's life:

> The ministry of Jesus was a revealing ministry because he knew God, because he was like God in character and purpose, and because he faithfully presented this God whom he knew, whom he was like, to the people about him—to the dull people, the narrow people, the argumentative people, and all the rest. And if our ministry is to be a revealing ministry, it must be by these same methods. The minister must know him, the minister must be like him, the minister must show him as he is.[36]

Much later in the same series of lectures, McDowell made these additional comments on the same subject:

---

[34] Stalker, *op. cit.*, p. 56.
[35] Francis Greenwood Peabody, *Jesus Christ and the Christian Character* (New York: Hodder & Stoughton, 1910), pp. 36–38.
[36] McDowell, *op. cit.*, p. 37.

But what the divine life can do in the realm of human personality, this we have seen once, and the vision makes us long to see it again. We have seen once what happens when a personality perfectly gives itself up to be invested and invaded by God, when his personality finds another that makes perfect response to it. It is vastly more than the contagion of goodness or the thrill of a noble example.[37]

Horton laid stress upon the universality of the power of the Christian character:

. . . it is not every one that can understand a sermon, it is not every sermon that can be understood; but every one can understand a Christly character, and every Christly character carries conviction to the observer.[38]

Expressing the same thought briefly and succinctly, Walter Russell Bowie said of the preacher, ". . . he must not merely preach a sermon; he must in humility, but with relentless self-requirement, *be* a sermon." [39] Crosby called further attention to the fact that the preacher must be a spiritual man because of the force of his example:

We have tried to indicate in this sketch that a preacher of Christ's Gospel should be before all things else a spiritual man, an example before his people and the world of a man walking with God.[40]

Robinson pointed out that the example of the man behind the gospel is the source of its power and effectiveness when he said, "A gospel unsupported by the example of those who profess to have received and obeyed it will be powerless, and the preaching of it in vain." [41] The same lecturer gave the subject under consideration a fuller treatment in one of his succeeding lectures:

[37] *Ibid.*, p. 281.
[38] Horton, *op. cit.*, p. 252.
[39] Walter Russell Bowie, *The Renewing Gospel* (New York: Charles Scribner's Sons, 1935), pp. 26–27.
[40] Crosby, *op. cit.*, p. 142.
[41] Robinson, *op. cit.*, p. 7.

The demand is now every day growing more emphatic that he who will preach the gospel shall give evidence of an established and consistent character. And the demand is most reasonable. The preacher of salvation to others ought to present in himself some faint semblance of the salvation proposed. The conviction is every day gaining ground, is already deep-seated in many minds, that the best, the enduring, results of preaching are not to be looked for in those sudden gusts of emotion awakened by the preacher's skill, but in those abiding impressions produced by weight of character and not by wit of words. Nor does this conviction forget that the saving efficacy of all preaching is through the renewing agency of the creative Spirit. It believes that the Spirit works through words, but that he works most of all through the characters of those in whom he dwells.[42]

In mentioning the influence of the preacher's daily life, Abbott said that:

. . . the benediction of his presence will mean immeasurably more than the formal benediction which he pronounces at the close of the church service, and his preaching will derive its power from this identification of his official message with his daily life, and the witness of his daily life to the truth and reality of his message.[43]

Simpson marked the need for a concrete manifestation of the truth which is expressed in abstract form in the sermon. That manifestation must, of course, be the preacher:

Your one work must be to hold up Christ before the people, and so present him as you see him and realize his power, that the people shall see him through your life as well as through your representation. People judge not so much of truth in its abstract as in its embodied form.[44]

For a specific example of the weakness engendered by the preacher's inability to demonstrate in his own life the truth

42 *Ibid.*, p. 124.
43 Abbott, *op. cit.*, p. 204.
44 Simpson, *op. cit.*, p. 72.

which he preaches from the pulpit, a passage from one of the lectures of Edwin McNeill Poteat was most appropriate:

> I heard a man protest indignantly the other day at a Lenten sermon by a preacher who lives in luxurious bachelor apartments. "Endure hardness as a good soldier of Christ" was his text, and the commentator was fairly itching to give the dominie a taste of hardness to test his endurance.[45]

Whatever else the preacher may lack and still influence men, he cannot be deficient in character. His congregation must believe that he is the man that he asks others to become.

SINCERITY

A second element widely commended to the young men at Yale was sincerity. Many of the lecturers mentioned the persuasive power of the preacher's sincerity. He must believe what he preaches, and must create a confidence among the members of his audience that he does believe it. Mouzon indicated the high degree of emphasis which he felt sincerity merits:

> First, there must be sincerity. The preacher is a communicator. His convictions pass in some strange way over into the minds of his hearers. If he doubts his own message, others will find it through moral sympathy and understanding. If he is a man of strong faith, his faith will flow down into others. The first requisite, then, is absolute honesty on the part of the preacher.[46]

Weighing the subject of sincerity in relation to the convincing of an audience, William DeWitt Hyde also gave it an important place:

> Special pleading or elaborate argument in the pulpit seldom convinces anybody: but the confident assertion of

[45] Buttrick and others, *op. cit.*, p. 42.
[46] Mouzon, *op. cit.*, p. 244.

a man who is transparently sincere with himself, carries
weight with all who see and feel his sincerity.[47]

Hyde also emphasized the impossibility of the preacher's pro-
fessing, without detection, that which he does not believe:

> The preacher must rid himself of beliefs which he
> holds at second hand; and profess to believe only the
> things which he sees with clearness and holds in sincerity.
> Any make-believe in his own thinking will betray itself
> in a tone of unconscious insincerity when he attempts to
> influence others.[48]

On the subject of sincerity, Beecher said, ". . . if you are
speaking the truth, it is essential that those who hear you
believe you are sincere before you can work with them." [49]
In speaking of moving the members of an audience, Behrends
showed the influence of the speaker's convictions:

> When at their best, they wait to be moved, and they
> can be powerfully and permanently moved only by words
> that convey strong personal conviction, and provoke an
> instant affirmative response. . . . You must speak with
> authority; not the authority of self-conceit, nor that of
> paraded learning, nor that of ecclesiastical decisions, but
> the authority which accompanies personal certitude.
> This is the only personal element which has any legit-
> imate place in the theory of preaching, and without it
> preaching is emptied of its persuasive power.[50]

Later in the same lecture, Behrends added:

> I think you will agree with me that the various recom-
> mendations given in treatises on homiletics, bearing on
> the personal element in preaching, may be reduced to
> this one: the clearness and certitude of self-knowledge.
> There must be no haziness. There must be no doubt.[51]

[47] William DeWitt Hyde, *The Gospel of Good Will* (New York: The Macmillan Company, 1916), pp. 122–23.
[48] *Ibid.*, p. 122.
[49] Beecher, *op. cit.*, I, 101.
[50] Behrends, *op. cit.*, pp. 58–59.
[51] *Ibid.*, p. 71.

Pepper pointed out the readiness with which an audience can detect insincerity:

> It is extraordinary how quickly the man in the pew can distinguish between that which has its source in the recesses of the preacher's being and that which comes only from the lips. A proposition announced by a man convinced of its truth and power may carry the preacher's conviction to many a heart, when the same words will be utterly ineffectual if spoken by one to whom they mean little or nothing. It is just because the man counts for so much that his elocution and fluency count for so little.[52]

In an earlier lecture in the same series, Pepper had made several very strong statements about the vital nature of integrity and sincerity in the preacher:

> My own experience supplemented by extended inquiry satisfies me that it is impossible to exaggerate the weight which the man in the pew attaches to the integrity of the preacher.
> . . . Speaking generally, let the hearer even suspect that all is not well with the man who is exhorting him, and the message, however true, will have lost its penetrating power.[53]

Taylor brought his comments on this subject to a climax in a brief series of telling questions:

> If we be ourselves uninterested, how can we expect to interest others? if we be ourselves insincere, how can we hope to bring others to the faith? if we be ourselves cold, passionless, and dull, how can we expect to rouse others to enthusiasm? [54]

Robinson made the emphatic statement that ". . . the pulpit now needs, as never before, the power of whole-hearted convictions. It knows no weakness equal to that of uncertainty and half-belief." [55]

[52] Pepper, *op. cit.*, pp. 62–63.
[53] *Ibid.*, pp. 23–24.
[54] Taylor, *The Ministry of the Word*, p. 26.
[55] Robinson, *op. cit.*, p. 119.

Several of the lecturers called attention to the practice among some preachers of simulating certain feelings and emotions—of playing the actor. Robinson was among the lecturers who condemned the practice:

> . . . can you think of anything more pitiable, anything to make good men and angels sooner weep, than that one, who has power to handle truth effectively, whose tears and choking utterance apparently reveal profound emotion, who seems almost to bring heaven down to earth in his sermons, should yet be one whose heart is hollow and empty, and who plays on the sensibilities of his hearers as a skilful musician plays on the strings of his instrument. The demand is every day becoming more imperative that the Christian teacher who will claim a right to be heard shall first furnish in himself some practical illustration of the virtues he would inculcate in others. The man must be more than his words; or his words will be wind, and himself be despised as a fraud.[56]

Henson changed the analogy but presented the same idea:

> The conception of a merely forensic advocacy of the Gospel, such as the barrister brings to the service of his client, is wholly intolerable. No contradiction can be imagined more repulsive and degrading than that which is presented by the spectacle of an unbelieving preacher. The mere suspicion of personal insincerity is enough to destroy the preacher's influence, and to sterilize his ministry.[57]

Broadus changed the analogy again, but presented the same thought as did the others:

> For a speaker, then, and above all for a preacher, it is a matter of the highest importance that he should resist the tendency to become in part an actor, should strive most earnestly to say nothing but what he now really thinks and now truly feels.[58]

[56] *Ibid.*, p. 129.
[57] Henson, *op. cit.*, p. 62.
[58] Broadus, *op. cit.*, p. 479.

Speaking several years before Broadus, Crosby had made the same comparison between insincere preaching and histrionics:

> The preacher, therefore, has two errors to guard against in respect of manner in the pulpit: one involving the moral element of insincerity. . . . With regard to the former, we need only remark that, whatever the manner, it is to be condemned. It is an imitation of the stage, and the stage and pulpit have nothing whatever in common, notwithstanding the popular idea that they are run in the same mould. The stage has as its object to amuse, and it has as its uniform method exaggeration; but the pulpit has as its object to instruct, and it has as its method the simplicity that becomes the delivery of truth.[59]

Abbott shifted the line of thought somewhat, urging the preacher never to allow himself to preach anything, no matter how badly it needs to be said, if his heart is not behind it:

> The bane of the pulpit is professionalism,—not hypocrisy, not deliberate false pretense, but the saying of a thing because it ought to be said, not because the heart prompts the speaker to say it.[60]

Brooks also admonished the preacher to be profoundly honest:

> Never dare to say in the pulpit or in private, through ardent excitement or conformity to what you know you are expected to say, one word which at the moment when you say it, you do not believe. It would cut down the range of what you say, perhaps, but it would endow every word that was left with the force of ten.[61]

Along the same line of thought, Freeman added his word:

> The message of value must be the expression of our own deep and unfailing conviction. It cannot be the expression of what someone else has felt or experienced; it must be our own.[62]

[59] Crosby, *op. cit.*, p. 100.
[60] Abbott, *op. cit.*, p. 206.
[61] Brooks, *op. cit.*, p. 107.
[62] Freeman, *op. cit.*, p. 145.

Willard L. Sperry included in one of his lectures an incident which shows how great may be the influence of even the slightest evidence of artifice or the smallest note of insincerity:

My mother once described to me hearing in New York the same sermon preached in three different churches by one of the reputedly great preachers of the last century. His name is known to you all, but since the rule *de mortuis nil nisi bonum* is binding, I withhold the name. At a given point in the sermon, as first heard, he hesitated for a word, and said, "What is the word I want?" The congregation leaned forward with eager sympathy to shout the word he could not find, and settled back with a sigh of relief when he got it for himself. He did precisely the same thing at the same moment in the same sermon on a second occasion, and again on a third, with like effect in each of the latter cases. With like effect save upon one woman, who realized that the transaction was not honest, and who therefore lost moral confidence in a man for whom she had previously had the greatest respect. . . . Preaching can survive countless honest errors; it cannot stand insincerity.[63]

Simpson gave a description of his feelings about his own early efforts to preach. His description indicated a feeling so sincere, so earnest, that it will serve to demonstrate the element of sincerity as needed by every preacher:

I did not try to make sermons. I felt I must, at the peril of my soul, persuade men to come to Christ; I must labor to the utmost of my ability to get sinners converted, and believers advanced in holiness. For this I thought and studied, wept and fasted and prayed. My selection of words, my plan of discourse, was only and all the time to persuade men to be reconciled to God. I never spoke without the deepest feeling, and unless I saw a strong divine influence on the congregation I felt sad, and

[63] Willard L. Sperry, *We Prophesy in Part* (New York: Harper & Brothers Publishers, 1938), pp. 125-26.

sought retirement to humble myself before God in prayer.[64]

It can be understood how this Bishop of the Methodist Church developed such a powerful influence in spite of poor health in his early years.

Enthusiasm or earnestness is a quality closely akin to sincerity. Sincerity of conviction is the foundation upon which enthusiasm may legitimately be built. A number of the Lyman Beecher lecturers were not content to say that the effective preacher must be sincere, but went on to say that he must indicate the genuineness of his convictions by a high degree of enthusiasm. Too many preachers have been sincere without having that contagious enthusiasm so necessary to the moving of their audiences. Taylor made this intensity of feeling one of the major points of his series of lectures:

> It cannot be too constantly remembered by you, that your usefulness to others must depend, next to the influence of God's Spirit, upon the intensity of your own convictions. There is nothing so contagious as conviction. The perception that you are well assured of the truth of that which you affirm, will help your hearers into the same certainty; and often in the times when their faith is sorely tried and is almost ready to fail, their observation of your confidence will lift them into trust. Their reliance on you will lead them to believe in what you say.[65]

He then proceeded in the same lecture to point out the means of securing this earnestness of which he had spoken:

> Here, then, are the twin sources of that earnestness of which so much is said, namely, intellectual conviction of the truth of those things which we proclaim; and loving realization of the fact that our hearers need to have

[64] Simpson, op. cit., pp. 162–63.
[65] Taylor, The Ministry of the Word, pp. 133–34.

these things said to them in order to be saved from the evils of time and the perdition of eternity. Give us these in all the occupants of all our pulpits, and the world will be constrained to listen to them. There is no royal road to earnestness; neither can it be successfully counterfeited by any histrionic art. We can gain it only through personal conviction and pervasive love; but, when we do gain it, we do not so much possess it as it possesses us, and carries us out of ourselves to achievements which are as astonishing to ourselves as they are irresistible to those whom we address.[66]

Parkhurst spoke of this same force as follows:

Once in the region of genuine conviction,—conviction interpreted on its dynamic side,—we are at the heart of a sphere of spiritual energies, energies which do the world's work, energies that work revolutions, and that perpetually lift the times out of old slavery into larger liberty.[67]

Beecher, in one of the earliest of the lectures, showed that enthusiasm has a persuasiveness in and of itself:

In almost all communities enthusiasm stands before everything else in moving popular assemblies. A preacher who is enthusiastic in everything he does, in all that he believes, and in all the movements of his ministry, will generally carry the people with him. He may do this without enthusiasm, but it will be a slow process, and the work will be much more laborious. If you have the power of speech and the skill of presenting the truth, and are enthusiastic, the people will become enthusiastic. People will take your views, because your enthusiasm has inoculated them.[68]

Brooks spoke of a quality which all effective preachers must have, one which could hardly be indicated in a single word. From his description of it, however, it seemed to be the quality under present consideration:

[66] *Ibid.*, p. 138.
[67] Parkhurst, *op. cit.*, p. 20.
[68] Beecher, *op. cit.*, I, 121–22.

I speak of only one thing more. I do not know how to give it a name, but I do think that in every man who preaches there should be something of that quality which we recognize in a high degree in some man of whom we say, when we see him in the pulpit, that he is a "born preacher." Call it enthusiasm; call it eloquence; call it magnetism; call it the gift for preaching. It is the quality that kindles at the sight of men, that feels a keen joy at the meeting of truth and the human mind, and recognizes how God made them for each other. It is the power by which a man loses himself and becomes but the sympathetic atmosphere between the truth on one side of him and the man on the other side of him.[69]

More than three decades later, Charles Reynolds Brown picked up the thread where Brooks dropped it and carried it on in this manner:

The man who can stand before a waiting congregation of expectant people and not feel in a measure almost overpowering the tug and pull of their need upon his own moral reserves, summoning him into the highest action of which he is capable, is altogether too wooden to be in the ministry for a single hour. . . . If any man would preach he must have that spiritual susceptibility which at the very sight of a waiting congregation, causes him to kindle and burn like a steel wire ignited in pure oxygen.[70]

Charles Silvester Horne put it this way: "But *the one supreme qualification for the ministry is a soul of flame.*" [71] Stalker also spoke of the need of enthusiasm in preaching:

As enthusiasm for Christ is the soul of preaching as far as the preacher is concerned, so in a spiritual congregation there will always be found a jealous desire for this element in what they hear.
. . . This is the motive of the ministry which goes deepest and wears longest.[72]

[69] Brooks, *op. cit.*, pp. 41–42.
[70] Charles Reynolds Brown, *The Art of Preaching*, p. 11.
[71] Charles Silvester Horne, *The Romance of Preaching* (New York: Fleming H. Revell Company, 1914), p. 124.
[72] Stalker, *op. cit.*, pp. 199–200.

Using a quotation from Augustine, Simpson indicated his own high regard for earnestness:

> The value of earnestness cannot be too strongly stated. St. Augustine says: "It is more by the Christian fervor of his sermons than by any endowment of his intellect that the minister must hope to inform the understanding, catch the affections, and bend the will of his hearers." In various ages men have appeared who by their earnestness have roused whole multitudes, and even nations, to activity. This earnestness is not to be evinced merely in motion, but in each and every step of the preparation and delivery of the sermon. . . .[73]

Pepper also considered enthusiasm a significant element, for he said, "If the preacher is blessed with enthusiasm, it quickly communicates itself to the people in the pews. Vigor and virility are sure passports to close attention." [74] In another lecture, he warned, "But compassion is impotent without conviction. The preacher must be convinced that he has somewhat to offer which, if received, will mean light and leading to his hearers." [75] Watson chose another word to describe the quality concerning which he spoke, yet it was apparent that he was referring to enthusiasm or earnestness. He said, "The last and greatest canon of speaking is *Intensity,* and it will be freely granted that the want of present-day preaching is spiritual passion." [76] Broadus, likewise, used a different word in speaking of the same quality:

> It is thus plain, according to the view we have taken of eloquence, that the characteristic property of an eloquent style is energy. Perspicuity it needs in common with the philosophical or didactic style; elegance it may possess in common with the poetic style; but energy, that is, animation, force, or passion, is its characteristic.
> The chief requisite to an energetic style is an energetic

---

73 Simpson, *op. cit.,* p. 188.
74 Pepper, *op. cit.,* pp. 14–15.
75 *Ibid.,* p. 62.
76 Watson, *op. cit.,* p. 61.

nature. There must be vigorous thinking, earnest if not passionate feeling, and the determined purpose to accomplish some object, or the man's style will have no true, exalted energy. It is in this sense emphatically true that an orator is born, not made. Without these qualities one may give valuable instruction; without them one might preach what silly admirers call "beautiful" sermons; but if a man has not force of character, a passionate soul, he will never be really eloquent.[77]

Freeman employed an interesting variation of expression on the point under consideration, when he indicated that youthful zeal and enthusiasm may often be more effective than more mature learning with its tempering of enthusiasm:

Obviously, maturity brings with it richer and deeper experiences that serve to make our messages more compelling and varied; but while this is true, it is interesting to note that some of the sermons preached by the greatest of prophets were delivered in the early days of their service. It was then, with a freshness of conviction and an enthusiasm for what they held, that they gave forth their most compelling messages. That our wider reading and broader experience do affect our utterances, is indisputably true; nevertheless, the flaming zeal that comes with the deep convictions of our earlier ministry mightily influences those to whom we bear our messages.[78]

SUMMARY

When one comprehends the difficulty of the task which faces the preacher, he cannot fail to see that special abilities are needed. If the preacher is to be successful in his proclamation of the word of God he must be a man of first-rate ability —a "whole man," to repeat the words of Beecher. Both heredity and training must contribute generously to qualify the man of God for his work.

The foremost qualification of the preacher is character,

[77] Broadus, *op. cit.*, pp. 380–81.
[78] Freeman, *op. cit.*, pp. 147–48.

and the preacher's character may be viewed from three slightly different viewpoints. First, before he can reveal God to men he must know God himself. If his words about God are not to be empty and meaningless, he must know God intimately through many hours of communion with him. Personal piety must precede preaching. Second, his life must be lived on so high a plane that his sermons will not be marred in the minds of the congregation by thoughts of inconsistency between his preaching and his practice. Immoral ministers cannot preach morality. The preacher's life must undergird his utterances. Third, the man of God must show, in his life, the path that men should follow. The worthy guide leads the way and blazes the trail.

Closely akin to character is sincerity. The actor may say that which he does not feel or believe, but the preacher is given no such license. Every sentence that pours forth from his lips must have the heart and mind behind it. The pulpit is not designed for the working of clever experiments, or for the testing of the latest propaganda technique. An earnest soul brings God's truth to bear upon the lives of men. Every word must be sincere.

Finally, it is not enough that the minister be sincere in his own heart. He must give ample evidence of that sincerity to the assembled congregation. By his enthusiasm for the truth his hearers may know the depth of his feeling. Earnestness is the preacher's evidence of his sincerity.

CHAPTER IV

ADDITIONAL QUALIFICATIONS

In addition to piety, the preacher must have mentality. No matter how pious he may be, a man of mediocre mental ability will be limited in his achievements for the Lord. Both the importance of the work and the difficulty of the work demand that the best minds available be pressed into service. Mentality is not an end in itself, but merely a means to an end. The real end is a full and complete knowledge of God and his truth, a thorough knowledge of men, and a firm grasp of the best means of bringing God's truth to bear upon men so as to reshape their lives. Notice mentality first; then the breadth of knowledge desirable for the preacher.

MENTALITY

Fewer than twelve of the Lyman Beecher lecturers spoke specifically of the preacher's need for a good intellect. Only two spoke of the matter with any thoroughness. The remainder merely mentioned it briefly in passing to some other phase of the preacher's qualifications. For example, Burton said, in a passage already quoted, that a man must have gifts in order to be a minister, and suggested that intellect must be one of those gifts.[1] Broadus said that the preacher must have "the capacity for clear thinking." [2] Stalker was mentioned earlier as quoting one of Luther's qualifications for the preacher—namely, "He should have a good head." [3] Beecher, as quoted earlier, must have included this element when he said that a

[1] Burton, *op. cit.*, pp. 36–37.
[2] Broadus, *op. cit.*, p. 8.
[3] Stalker, *op. cit.*, p. 163.

preacher must be not one-fourth or one-half of a man, but a whole man.[4] Horne was another who spoke of the preacher's work as one that demands intellect, but again it was only in passing to something else: "It is work that demands the best brains we possess; and no training can be too thorough, and no reading too wide for the minister. . . ." [5]

The two lecturers who spoke of this qualification at some length were Parkhurst and Crosby. Parkhurst's contribution was:

> . . . we shall give primary attention to the matter of disciplined mentality, as the fundamental prerequisite to ministerial success. . . .
> . . . however complete the moralization and the sanctification of the individual, their practical value and efficiency will depend upon the amount of the personal stuff to which they are respectively applied. . . . The quality of the piety of a man of mediocre intelligence may be on a par with that of Luther, Calvin, Chalmers, Storrs, but its practical worth as an efficiency will be calculated only in terms of the results to which the piety contributes.[6]

In still fuller fashion, Crosby said of mental prerequisites:

> While it is undoubtedly true that the grace of God addresses itself with equal power to every class of mind, and it is the glory of the Gospel that it is adapted to the appreciation of the illiterate as well as to that of the learned, it is equally true that the setting forth of God's revealed truth in its connections and fullness, and the thorough and profound exposition of the Holy Word can be made only by the higher classes of mind, capacious and powerful to deal with the sublimest ideas, and furnished with rich stores of the divine knowledge.[7]

4 Beecher, op. cit., I, 40.
5 Horne, op. cit., p. 229.
6 Parkhurst, op. cit., p. 3.
7 Crosby, op. cit., p. 31.

In the same lecture Crosby said further on this subject:

> In describing the character of mind that a preacher should have, we might be contented with the general remark that a strong, well-rounded development of intelligence was necessary, that he should be above the ordinary level of men in his grasp of truth and powers of analysis, that he should be ready to meet the wants and the oppositions of the many with whom he must come into contact, and so should prove himself a leader of the people.[8]

Why this important element of the preacher's qualifications was so lightly touched upon is difficult to explain. It may be that the speakers took it for granted; it may be that they were preoccupied with other topics; it may be that they saw no practical value in the discussion of a qualification which could not be improved by the preacher's own efforts, since the degree of one's intelligence is generally conceded to be determined before birth. Whatever the reason, they did not discuss it as extensively as its importance would seem to warrant. A good mind is necessary equipment for a field of endeavor in which study and the acquisition of knowledge are such prominent factors.

KNOWLEDGE

The importance of study and the acquisition of knowledge was given almost as strong an emphasis by the Yale lecturers as was the importance of character. There was unanimity of feeling that the successful preacher will be one who has trained himself to spend many hours in careful reading. The lecturers not only emphasized the importance of study, but suggested the areas of knowledge which the preacher should master. The Scriptures were considered the chief textbook of all preachers, but almost every other branch of learning was suggested as a supplement to this central body of knowledge. Among the passages concerning the importance

[8] *Ibid.,* pp. 32–33.

of study, the importance of the study of the Scriptures, and the importance of the study of all other established bodies of knowledge, the most challenging are presented in the following pages.

Concerning the value of study, Brooks said, "In many respects an ignorant clergy, however pious it may be, is worse than none at all. The more the empty head glows and burns, the more hollow and thin and dry it grows." [9] J.R.P. Sclater said briefly, but forcefully:

> Preaching consists not only in speaking, but in speaking *sense;* and that depends on knowledge and "the full mind," which in their turn depend on reading. Wherefore, take time to read.[10]

Almost the same thought was set forth in one of Bowie's lectures:

> The man who studies for the ministry will need whatever expert guidance he can get on *how* to preach. But, nevertheless, the more urgent matter both for him and for his listeners is *what* to preach.[11]

In opposition to the idea held in some quarters that the preacher will become less spiritual through the acquisition of secular knowledge, Horne said:

> . . . for the present let me lay it down that there is nothing in Holy Writ to warrant the assumption that a man is likely to be more spiritual if he is an ignoramus; or that prophetic power in the pulpit especially attaches to the preacher whose heart is full and whose head is empty.[12]

Expressing the need for the fullest and broadest knowledge was Parkhurst:

[9] Brooks, *op. cit.,* p. 45.

[10] J. R. P. Sclater, *The Public Worship of God* (New York: George H. Doran Company, 1927), p. 97.

[11] Bowie, *op. cit.,* p. 39.

[12] Horne, *op. cit.,* p. 58.

There is no vigor of mind that can be operated along any line of thought, that cannot be made to tell in the service of the pulpit. There is no sort of knowledge, whether of things celestial or terrestrial, of things divine or human, that cannot be utilized to the effectiveness of pulpit discourse. No sensible person ever commences preaching without wishing that underneath his effort were a wider and more solid basis of preparation.[13]

Burton expressed his feeling of a need for continuous preparation and study with the word work:

The only way to make substantial sermons is to work. Of course you have genius, but you must work. You are to be a settled minister I suppose; . . . but I can give you my word for it now, that if you stay any, anywhere, you must work.[14]

Paul Scherer referred to his own practice as an evidence of the necessity of study before preaching:

If I have to carry around with me for the rest of my life a plodding mind that wants anywhere from eighteen or twenty hours to thirty before it is willing to have me get up in the pulpit, at least I do not have to be afraid that what I am pleased to call my intellectual machinery will grow rusty and break down from disuse, or that some day I shall have to pay across the counter in still more vapid mouthings and platitudinous banalities the price of all laziness, however able it may be.[15]

Removing all limits on the preacher's knowledge, Beecher said:

If you are going to be a master in your business, you must know about all these things yourself. Having eyes, you must see; having ears, you must hear; and having a heart, you must understand. A minister ought to be the best informed man on the face of the earth. He ought to

[13] Parkhurst, *op. cit.*, p. 6.
[14] Burton, *op. cit.*, p. 124.
[15] Paul Scherer, *For We Have This Treasure* (New York: Harper & Brothers, Publishers, 1944), pp. 143–44.

see everything, inquire about everything, and be interested in everything.[16]

From his own observation, McDowell attributed much preaching failure to cessation of study.

Then carelessness, cessation from study, no mental and spiritual growth, taking success for granted, reliance upon methods and stock phrases, and a sad collapse of power. No form of activity needs truth, rich, abundant, living truth, as evangelism does. Nowhere does intellectual laziness meet surer, swifter punishment. Many mission churches fail utterly in their attempts to reach intelligent workingmen because of the indolent reiteration of threadbare phrases and a failure to respect an audience.[17]

In full agreement with McDowell, Scherer added:

Heaven help the man of us who discovers that he is a ready speaker and presumes to rely on it! The years will undo him and let him down. His undisciplined mind will little by little fall back on "sound and fury," signifying nothing. The sermons he keeps shaking out of his sleeve will soon begin to bring the lining with them, as a dear friend of mine once phrased it (and he was himself no little given to such legerdemain!) It makes no difference how readily preaching comes to you, how quick your wit, how facile your flow of language; you may be "the spiritual speak-easy of America." I beg you never allow yourself to be betrayed into indolence by any such thing.[18]

Scherer decried the lack of reading and study among ministers as reported in a recent survey:

In no case is there much excuse for the facts recorded recently in *The New York Times* as the result of a survey made by the librarian of Cooper Union. It was reported with some satisfaction:

The reading habits of clergymen are slovenly, with-

16 Beecher, *op. cit.*, I, 171.
17 McDowell, *op. cit.*, pp. 184–85.
18 Scherer, *op. cit.*, p. 143.

out plan or discipline, and fall short of the standard one would expect of a group with such high educational background and so rich an opportunity for intellectual leadership.

Nearly all the one hundred twenty-two ministers answering the questionnaire complained of the lack of opportunity and the burden of parish duties. Much has since been said in their defense by sympathetic editors. But little is to be had from offering excuses to life. Life never stamps them "valid." Mastery of our time may not always be possible. When everything is said and done, you and I are men under authority and cannot command our days; yet to lose a battle need not be to lose a whole campaign. One morning ruthlessly torn out of your hands and away from its original purpose by some necessity that does not ask your leave may still be made up, hour for hour, if you really mean this ledger of yours to balance.[19]

Jowett drew a comparison between the preparation of the preacher and that of a practitioner of the law:

And if a barrister is to practically conquer his jury before he meets them, by the victorious strength and sway of his preparations, shall it be otherwise with a preacher, before he seeks the verdict of his congregation? With us, too, "cases are won in chambers." Men are not deeply influenced by extemporized thought. They are not carried along by a current of fluency which is ignorant where it is going. Mere talkativeness will not put people into bonds. Happy-go-lucky sermons will lay no necessity upon the reason nor put any strong constraint upon the heart. Preaching that costs nothing accomplishes nothing. If the study is a lounge the pulpit will be an impertinence.

It is, therefore, imperative that the preacher go into his study to do hard work.[20]

R. W. Dale drew attention to the importance of the preacher's having regular hours of study. "Your strength," he said, "must be given to grave and continuous studies. You will fence

[19] *Ibid.*, p. 149.
[20] Jowett, *op. cit.*, p. 114.

round the prime hours of the day and keep them for hard
work, or else you will be lost." [21]

The discussion now turns from the importance of study to
the need for the specific study of the Bible. Hall is heard
first:

> Gentlemen, if you would speak to the conscience and
> heart of your fellow-men, if you would subsidize all their
> old memories, and enlist all their sacred associations on
> the side of your cause and your Master, have thorough
> and easy possession of your English Bible. [22]

Horton was another who called attention to the need for a
thorough mastery of the Bible.

> Every true preacher must therefore be an earnest Bible
> student. He must spare no pains, and neglect no method,
> to master and grasp the Book. He must know what it is;
> he must know what it is not. He must learn what it con-
> tains; he must learn what it necessarily does not contain. [23]

Sclater called the Bible the preacher's textbook, and suggested
several methods of studying it to secure the greatest good from
it:

> One book, at least, we must study. The Bible is our
> textbook, and familiarity with it is a *sine qua non*. There
> are three ways of reading it, and we should omit none
> of them. We may study it as scholars; we may meditate
> on it devotionally; and we may read it as literature. My
> plea is that we should not neglect the last of these. [24]

Giving advice to the Yale Divinity students who were soon to
leave the university for active work, Greer suggested: "You
must still be students, and diligent students; and there are
three directions which your studies must take. You must be
students first of the Bible." [25] In a fuller and more specific

---

[21] R. W. Dale, *Nine Lectures on Preaching* (London: Hodder and Stoughton,
1890), p. 102.

[22] Hall, *op. cit.*, p. 100.

[23] Horton, *op. cit.*, p. 115.

[24] Sclater, *op. cit.*, p. 99.

[25] Greer, *op. cit.*, pp. 144–45.

way Taylor indicated the reason for concentrated study of the Bible.

> . . . I would give special and peculiar emphasis to *familiar acquaintance with the Scriptures,* as one of the most important prerequisites to pulpit power. You are to be ministers of the Word; and it is by the knowledge of the Scriptures that you are to be thoroughly furnished for your work. The Bible is your text-book, and that not in the sense of being a hunting-ground for texts, but in that of constituting the ground-work of your discourses. You are looking forward to be "pastors and teachers," and the very thing which you are to teach is the Word of God. You are to lead your people up to an intelligent apprehension of its meaning, and a cordial reception of its statements, and it will be impossible for you to do that if you are not yourselves masters of its contents.[26]

The same need for a thorough knowledge of the Scriptures was expressed by Stalker:

> . . . one of the primary qualifications of the ministry is an intimate familiarity with the Scriptures. . . . A large portion of our work is the searching of the Scriptures, and a preacher of the highest order will always be a man mighty in the Scriptures.[27]

Abbott gave still another reason for the preacher's studying the Scriptures.

> He must study the Bible; because in no other literature will he find such an interpretation of the higher spiritual experiences of men, such an exposition of the divine remedies for the sins and sorrow which afflict mankind.[28]

Simpson indicated what the preacher can expect to receive from his careful study of the Bible:

> The Bible should be so studied that it shall be at the command of the preacher at all times. Whatever else he

[26] Taylor, *The Ministry of the Word,* p. 29.
[27] Stalker, *op. cit.,* p. 108.
[28] Abbott, *op. cit.,* p. 227.

may know, or not know, he must, to be successful, have
a ready knowledge of scriptural language. In it he will
find the foundation for his best arguments, as well as his
finest illustrations. Its poetry is beautiful, its imagery is
sublime. Its great value is, that it is truth stated by the
Lord himself in such form and manner as will best reach
the human conscience. The preacher who quotes much
of the Bible has, not only in the estimation of his hearers
the authority of "Thus saith the Lord," but there is also
a divine unseen power so joined to those words that they
cannot be uttered without fruit.[29]

"The most instructive and inspiring preacher," said Mouzon,
"is the one who knows his Bible best." [30]

As was indicated earlier, the various lecturers were not
content to recommend the study of the Bible alone, but hastened to urge a supplementary study of all branches of learning. A statement in one of Greer's lectures will serve as a transition to this point of view.

> But there is still another direction which your studies
> should take. The preacher should be a man of broad and
> generous culture, and should study, not only the Bible,
> but books outside of the Bible.[31]

Crosby, who was one of the most prolific speakers on this
subject, made essentially the same statement:

> But while the acuteness of perception of the preacher
> is to be exercised chiefly upon the written revelation
> of God, it is not to end there. Every subject of impor-
> tance to the Christian life is undoubtedly presented in
> the Bible, but these subjects have analogues in the social
> and political life of men, by which they may be illus-
> trated. A preacher should have his eye traversing the
> course of history and the great facts of human society,
> so as to illustrate and confirm his expositions of the
> Word.[32]

[29] Simpson, *op. cit.*, p. 102.
[30] Mouzon, *op. cit.*, pp. 225–26.
[31] Greer, *op. cit.*, p. 150.
[32] Crosby, *op. cit.*, p. 41.

Horton declared that a preacher cannot preach Bible truths to his own generation without first studying the trends of the times.

> But it is impossible to overstate the certainty that apart from earnest study of the facts around us, the signs of the times, the movements of thought, the trend of development, it is impossible for any man to read aright the Word of the Lord as it comes to his own generation.[33]

Horne said of the preacher's reading, ". . . no training can be too thorough, and no reading too wide for the minister whose aim it is to be to bring the irreligious and the indifferent on to the side of Christ and the Kingdom." [34] As a strong reason why the preacher must read widely, Hall cited the weakening effect which the preacher's deficiency in common education has upon his audience:

> A minister ought to be a well-educated man, in those branches of human learning that are not professional, or rather, that are common to all the professions. The reasons are obvious. A man may be spiritual and theologically well-instructed, whose orthography varies from the popular standard, whose grammar is uncertain, and whose reading in profane history goes little farther back than the Declaration of Independence. But the mass of mankind will doubt the capacity of a teacher in religious things, who is conspicuously deficient in common education.[35]

Taylor also mentioned the reaction of the audience to the preacher's deficiency in some field of common knowledge:

> If the minister is to be a leader of men, he must keep ahead of them, or at least abreast with them in ordinary intelligence, for, if they detect him blundering in matters of history, philosophy, or literature, or if they discover that he is comparatively ignorant in these departments, they will have little respect for his opinions and

[33] Horton, *op. cit.*, pp. 177–78.
[34] Horne, *op. cit.*, p. 229.
[35] Hall, *op. cit.*, pp. 82–83.

small confidence in his judgment, even when he is speaking to them of things that lie within his proper province.[36]

Crosby was another who held this point of view.

The preacher will have little influence in inculcating religious truth, if he is known as a blunderer in the elements of science. Such men can only minister successfully in holy things to those who are as ignorant as themselves. . . . The religious teacher who is ignorant of the great principles of science or the facts of general knowledge in history, geography, and literature, will suffer this same collapse of authority. He can no more be a leader, and men will listen to him, not to receive his instructions, but to criticise his errors.[37]

The same idea was expressed by Robinson.

But natural science is only one of the many fields of knowledge over which men are now roaming, and of which the religious teacher is not expected to be wholly ignorant. History, philosophy, and literature, all open wide their gates and whosoever will may enter. They offer richest materials illustrative of man's need, as well as of the power and glory, of the religion of Jesus. From them, have been abstracted weapons with which the enemies of Christianity have sought to destroy it; and from them must the teacher of religion procure the only weapons with which the enemies can be repelled. Nor can he afford to omit this part of his equipment. A suspicion of his ignorance in matters on which he may, and ought to be, informed will rob him of one element of his power.[38]

In Crosby's lecture on this subject, he suggested a program of study which will secure to the preacher the breadth of knowledge needed.

The general knowledge, for which we contend, is to be obtained first and principaliy by a regular college educa-

36 Taylor, *The Ministry of the Word*, p. 53.
37 Crosby, *op. cit.*, pp. 64–65.
38 Robinson, *op. cit.*, p. 115.

tion with the old curriculum of classics, mathematics, science, and philosophy; and, secondly, by a systematic course of judicious reading on the part of the preacher, by which he keeps fully abreast of the age. The daily newspaper is a necessary part of this training, not simply as furnishing the facts of the day, but also as showing the influence and impression of those facts.[39]

Still another body of reading was suggested by Van Dyke: ". . . I believe that a course in modern novels and poetry might well be made a part of every scheme of preparation for the ministry." [40] Broadening the list, Pepper added:

The time spent on books, the drama, music, contemporary history at home and abroad, is not time taken from work. Comprehension of these things is part of the preacher's equipment.[41]

Still another voice to call for a general acquaintance with these same subjects was that of William Pierson Merrill:

The minister who would be free can never avoid the obligation to read and acquire material. He must read widely and insatiably. He should especially seek out books of human interest. Theological writings will be indispensable; but detective stories will have a value also. I suppose it is important that a minister should keep up with the progress of theology and church history and the other specialties of his profession. But I know it is vital, that he read much of good literature, of biography, fiction, poetry, history, all that in which the soul of man finds free expression, even though it has little or nothing of a distinctively religious flavor about it. He must not only study the Bible critically, that he may know its contents; he must read it appreciatively and uncritically, that he may catch its unrivaled style, and be caught in the swing of its mighty emotions.[42]

[39] Crosby, *op. cit.*, pp. 68–69.
[40] Van Dyke, *op. cit.*, p. 5.
[41] Pepper, *op. cit.*, p. 86.
[42] William Pierson Merrill, *The Freedom of the Preacher* (New York: The Macmillan Company, 1922), pp. 33–34.

A word of caution about this course of reading was given in one of Stalker's lectures.

> In a former lecture I have recommended a wide acquaintance with the masterpieces of literature; but some able men at college substitute this for the studies of their profession; and this is a fatal mistake. Literature ought to be a supplement to these, not a substitute for them.[43]

Bowie marked the preacher's special need of a knowledge of history, saying that "The man who wishes to be a true and understanding preacher may well read history and deepen his sense of identity with all the long movement of the past. . . ." [44] In the midst of a discussion of style, Brooks mentioned the value of history and philosophy.

> . . . I cannot help once more urging upon you the need of hard and manly study; not simply the study of language and style itself, but study in its broader sense, the study of truth, of history, of philosophy. . . .[45]

Dale spoke rather fully upon the varied types of reading necessary to the successful preacher.

> To avoid this "crookedness and deformity," and to maintain free intellectual relations with cultivated men who are not professional theologians, as well as to satisfy your own intellectual tastes, which, I trust, you will always think it a duty to keep healthy and active, there are other kinds of reading which you will not permit yourselves to neglect. History—and especially the history of your own country; the lives of men who have exerted a great and critical influence on the fortunes of great nations, who have originated remarkable religious movements, or who are famous in literature and art; the leading and authoritative books on political economy; books which illustrate the laws of social and national life; books which present the ascertained results of the investigations of modern science: all these will enrich your

---

[43] Stalker, *op. cit.*, p. 252.
[44] Bowie, *op. cit.*, p. 13.
[45] Brooks, *op. cit.*, pp. 146–47.

thought, will prevent you from becoming mere sermon-makers and theological pedants.[46]

Later in the same series of lectures, Dale pointed out the need of keeping in step with the reading of the congregation:

If we know nothing of the books that our congregations are reading, they will soon learn to think of us as intellectual foreigners—strangers to their ways and thoughts, ignorant of a large part, and in some respects the most interesting part, of their lives.[47]

Kelman added, "Every book you read will contribute to your message, and become part of the inspiration of the Spirit." [48] Still other fields of study were suggested by Sockman and Dale. Sockman said of the psychological aspect of the preacher's work:

A few years ago Dr. Richard Cabot of Harvard proposed that there should be two branches of theological training; first, systematic theology with all the evidence necessary to build up the student's fundamental knowledge of God and of man's relation to Him; and secondly, clinical theology, with all the technique essential to alleviating minds in distress.[49]

Suggesting the value of reading lectures on preaching and treatises on the art of rhetoric, Dale said:

Some men speak contemptuously of lectures on preaching and treatises on the science or art of rhetoric. For myself, I have read scores of books of this kind, and I have never read one without finding in it some useful suggestion. I advise you to read every book on preaching that you can buy or borrow, whether it is old or new, Catholic or Protestant, English, French, or German.[50]

Another suggestion, though closely related to this one, was also given in the same lecture by Dale: "But useful as you

46 Dale, op. cit., p. 100.
47 Ibid., p. 102.
48 Kelman, op. cit., p. 261.
49 Sockman, op. cit., pp. 137-38.
50 Dale, op. cit., pp. 93-94.

will find the study of the theory of preaching, you will probably find that the study of the sermons of successful preachers
is equally useful." [51]

Jefferson had in one of his lectures some practical suggestions concerning a proper plan of reading.

> Many a minister has been wrecked by reading without
> purpose and method. He had no plan of his own, and so
> he was at the mercy of every one who volunteered a sug-
> gestion. He can also plan his studies in theology, history,
> biography, and poetry, four branches indispensable to a
> man who wishes to be a master-teacher of men. Certain
> subjects will be assigned to each of the years, and certain
> volumes will be set apart for each of the months, and no
> sort of conspiracy on the part of men or devils will be
> allowed to break down the minister's determination to
> pursue the prearranged course to its end. Desultory read-
> ing and spasmodic study have slain their thousands. A
> man who forms a clean-cut plan and clings to it heroically
> through the oppositions of the years, is a man who ad-
> vances in wisdom and stature, and in favor with God and
> men.[52]

Scherer also offered several very practical suggestions.

> And never as you read, night or morning, be without
> paper and pen. A pen, because penciled notes soon blur
> and become so unattractive and illegible as to be prac-
> tically worthless. The clear and quick recording of illus-
> trations; the copying out of quotations; the jotting down
> of some fleeting, suggestive line of thought: such material
> carefully gathered, preserved, perhaps even entered in a
> permanent book, not too laboriously indexed, is simply
> invaluable. It took me altogether too long to learn that:
> I have lost a hundred sermons. I still lose them. I wish I
> could persuade you to begin with it and save time. You
> will have to find your own system. But stick to it. Stick to
> it when it irks you. Stick to it when the going gets thick.
> Stick to it when the stuff grows thin. Stick to it. The

[51] *Ibid.*, p. 94.
[52] Jefferson, *op. cit.*, p. 264.

effort itself, if nothing else comes of it, will prove an aid to memory. And maybe some day you will not be a slave to *The Preacher's Manual* for your themes and anecdotes, or to the last issue of *The Christian Century Pulpit!* [53]

SUMMARY

Of the two men who worked side by side in the harvest field in the long ago, the one who had the sharper blade cut the most grain. So of the two young men who sit side by side in the library; the one who has the brighter mind will achieve the greater mastery of the truth. Keenness of intellect makes the achievement of higher goals possible. Just as brilliant minds make better lawyers and doctors, so the same brilliance of mind makes for better ministers. Preaching, too, deserves the best natural equipment that the human race can afford.

Even the most brilliant mind will never find that it has mastered the numerous areas of information which are of use in the practice of preaching. First of all, the study of the Scriptures is a life-long task within itself, which must be begun in early life and continued through the years; but even so it can never be completed. This study is first in importance as well as first in the amount of time required.

Beyond the realm of Scripture the preacher's studies take him into the fields of history, literature, art, science—in short into all the established areas of learning. A carefully prepared program of study is a must for every minister, if he would be true to the challenge which he has accepted. No matter what the press of circumstances, he cannot long neglect his reading without finding himself in the unenviable position of the merchant who neglected to replace his stock as his sales continued.

[53] Scherer, *op. cit.,* pp. 150–51.

CHAPTER V

ADDITIONAL QUALIFICATIONS

Beyond the character of the preacher and beyond his wide knowledge lie still other qualifications which must be his if his character and knowledge are to have their maximum effect. To say that these qualifications are as important as personal piety or the grasp of truth would be unwise, but to say that they are unimportant would be equally unwise. Although they are less important than the first named qualifications, they are essential to success in the ministry. In this list are to be found courage, reality, imagination, originality, and health.

COURAGE

Standing somewhat alone among the qualities named by the Yale lecturers as essential to the preacher, or at least not closely related to the other elements, was the element of courage. Those speakers who mentioned the need of courage gave it a very strong emphasis, however. Brooks was one of the earliest to mention this need:

> There is another source of power which I can hardly think of as a separate quality, but rather as the sum and result of all the qualities which I have been naming. I mean Courage. It is the indispensable requisite of any true ministry. The timid minister is as bad as the timid surgeon. Courage is good everywhere, but it is necessary here. If you are afraid of men and a slave to their opinion, go and do something else. Go and make shoes to fit them. Go even and paint pictures which you know are bad but which suit their bad taste. But do not keep on all your life preaching sermons which shall say not what God sent

you to declare, but what they hire you to say. Be coura-
geous.[1]

Abbott was emphatic in declaring that in America the only
successful preachers have been men of great courage:

> Candor is the professional virtue of the minister. He
> cannot be truly successful without it. He must have con-
> victions and the courage of his convictions. Those cynics
> are mistaken who imagine that the preacher is popular
> who panders to popular prejudice. The answer to their
> cynicism is to be found in the history of the American
> pulpit. From Jonathan Edwards to the present day, and
> in all the denominations alike, the great preachers have
> been heroic preachers.[2]

Taylor broadened the scope and said that since the times of
the apostles the signally successful preachers have been coura-
geous men:

> A second quality of effectiveness in the preacher is
> courage. It is said of the apostles that "they spake the
> Word of God with boldness;" and all who since their days
> have been signally successful in the winning of souls have
> been distinguished by the same characteristic.[3]

The same speaker went further. Showing that the preacher
who is deficient in courage eventually brings about his own
downfall thereby, he said that:

> . . . the timid trimmer who is always trying to keep
> from offence, becomes at length an object of contempt;
> while he who faithfully reproves, rebukes, and exhorts
> with all long-suffering and doctrine, becomes a power in
> the community, and draws to himself the confidence and
> affection of his people.[4]

1 Brooks, *op. cit.*, p. 59.
2 Abbott, *op. cit.*, p. 219.
3 Taylor, *The Ministry of the Word*, pp. 138–39.
4 *Ibid.*, pp. 141–42.

Going back into the history of the Hebrew prophets, Stalker
indicated that he thought that this element of courage was
one of the leading factors in their power.

> This was what lent the prophets the wonderful courage
> which characterized them. They forgot themselves in
> their message. The fire of God in their bones would not
> permit them to hesitate. Whether it was a frowning king
> or an infuriated mob the prophet had to brave, he set
> his face like a flint. Comfort, reputation, life itself might
> be at stake; but he had to speak out all that God had told
> him, whether men might hear or whether they might
> forbear.[5]

In one of the most recent series of the Lyman Beecher Lectures, Sockman drew attention to the easy or cowardly way
which many lesser preachers had taken.

> When certain social issues, like war, are found to be too
> sensitive for pulpit handling, the preacher can always
> fall back on vehement denunciations of vicious plays or
> salacious books, since there are usually not many play-
> wrights or authors in his pews. Organized vice and or-
> ganized crime are also pretty useful targets. And even
> organized labor is a convenient target for preachers who
> wish to curry favor with comfortable congregations.
> Long-range shooting at absentee sinners is a temptation
> of those too timid for straight-from-the-shoulder combat.[6]

G. Bromley Oxnam was in full agreement:

> The preacher in revolutionary days must speak of
> imperialism and injustice, of exploitation, of world order
> and equality and creative service—and the land may
> not be able to bear all his words. He must speak of sin
> where sin is—the place may be high or low.[7]

Charles D. Williams was another lecturer who emphasized
the importance of courage on the part of the preacher:

[5] Stalker, *op. cit.*, p. 98.
[6] Sockman, *op. cit.*, p. 38.
[7] G. Bromley Oxnam, *Preaching in a Revolutionary Age* (New York:
Abingdon-Cokesbury Press, 1944), p. 118.

A ministry of power,—that is the first need of a day
of almost universal fear and cowardly subservience
thereto, a ministry endowed with the courage and fearlessness that come only from faith, the conviction that
one has a burden of the Lord, a word of God, a "Thus
saith the Lord," laid upon his lips like the live coal off the
altar, a Divine message that burns in his bones like fire
and will not let him stay till it be uttered, and that God
Himself is behind His Word and will not let it fail. That
is the prophet's fundamental motive and dynamic.[8]

Freeman mentioned the pulpit as the one place in modern
society where courage is most necessary.

I know of no profession that lays a larger claim upon
the heroic element than does the Christian ministry. I
know no place where fearlessness is more urgently demanded than in this ancient office. There are causes all
about us that challenge the best that we have to give.[9]

REALITY

Nine of the Lyman Beecher lecturers spoke of the danger of
preachers' becoming unreal in their preaching. The preacher's
life and experiences are often so different from those of his
congregation that his preaching does not fit into their realm
of experience. It is unreal to them. Bowie gave a good explanation of this danger in saying that:

There is danger always that men who have been
trained in the seclusion of theological seminaries and
have breathed, perhaps, an atmosphere which is largely
academic may find their thought moving thereafter in a
world which is limited, and to that extent unreal. They
may be dealing with shadows, shadows cast by history
and tradition which are magnificent, but shadows none
the less; and they may fail to come to grips with the substance of the real concerns with which most people

[8] Charles D. Williams, *The Prophetic Ministry for Today* (New York: The
Macmillan Company, 1921), p. 179.
[9] Freeman, *op. cit.,* p. 47.

wrestle. Their need is to see contemporary human beings as they are.[10]

Oxnam furnished a concrete illustration of this lack of reality
in the pulpit:

> When I was a student in Boston, I, like all other stu-
> dents, found my way at last to the Old North Church of
> Paul Revere fame. The preacher of the morning was
> Bishop Lawrence, the sermon itself powerful and con-
> vincing. He chose as his text Luke 21:31: "So likewise
> ye, when ye see these things come to pass, know ye that
> the kingdom of God is nigh at hand." The altar window
> of the Old North Church is not of stained glass. The
> worshiper can look through to the tenements that sur-
> round the church, which is located in the North End, the
> center of the Italian population of the city. While the
> Bishop preached, an old woman was at work on a fire-
> escape platform. She was bent over a tub, no doubt doing
> the family washing on Sunday, when free from the regu-
> lar weekday job. As I thought of her, her age, the children
> she had no doubt borne, the tenements, the limited life,
> I could not but reverse the text of the Bishop and say,
> "So likewise ye, when ye see things come to pass, know
> ye that the kingdom of God is *not* nigh at hand." . . .
> it is also true that the preacher who never tests out in
> concrete situations the ethical principles he proclaims
> will find his message so unrelated to the world in which
> he lives that the changes demanded by his changeless
> gospel are not effected and men turn to gospels whose
> faith is effective.[11]

Greer developed the same thought, in speaking of preaching:

> It [preaching of to-day] does not touch as it ought the
> contemporary life, and grapple with its problems,
> its duties, its difficulties, its dangers. There is, in con-
> sequence, a sense of unreality about it, a foreignness, a
> far-away-ness; and to men who are of necessity preoc-

10 Bowie, *op. cit.*, pp. 50–51.
11 Oxnam, *op. cit.*, pp. 71–72.

cupied with the exigencies of contemporary life, it is not helpful preaching.[12]

Looking at the same subject from the positive side, Buttrick spoke of the power of reality in preaching:

> Now let it be said that all these means and methods might almost be cast to the winds so long as preaching is real; and that if preaching is not real every method becomes a broken reed or an offence. If a sermon does not carry an unmistakable accent of reality, then, even though every rule is honored, that sermon will be vanity and vexation.[13]

Quoting a passage from the pen of Emerson, Jowett also spoke of the negative side of the subject, indicating the dire results of unreality:

> "I once heard a preacher," says Emerson in a familiar passage, "who sorely tempted me to say I would go to church no more. . . . He had lived in vain. He had no one word intimating that he had laughed or wept, was married or in love, had been commended, or cheated, or chagrined. If he had ever lived and acted, we were none the wiser for it. The capital secret of his profession, namely, to convert life into truth, he had not learned." [14]

Pepper spoke of the preacher's need for seeing things in their true light:

> . . . in no other sphere of education is there a greater need for emphasis upon honest thinking and upon the determination to see things as they are. Precision and thoroughness are intellectual qualities which the preacher should find indispensable.[15]

Charles Reynolds Brown said of reality, "If you propose to preach, you will have to be the real thing. No shams, no make-believes, no perfunctory machines need apply." [16] Kelman

[12] Greer, *op. cit.*, p. 46.
[13] Buttrick, *op. cit.*, p. 164.
[14] Jowett, *op. cit.*, p. 103.
[15] Pepper, *op. cit.*, p. 188.
[16] Charles Reynolds Brown, *The Art of Preaching*, p. 226.

made a statement in one of his lectures that will serve as a
conclusion to the discussion of the need for reality in preaching:

> All this comes back in the end to the supreme demand
> for reality in preaching. It is demanded of us above all
> else that we be real men dealing in a real way with
> real things.[17]

IMAGINATION

Still another element mentioned in many of the Yale lectures was the preacher's need of imagination. In the first
year that the lectures were delivered, Beecher named imagination as a very vital element, but even more important,
he gave the term a definition which marks a distinction between its use in connection with preaching and its more general use:

> And the first element on which your preaching will
> largely depend for power and success, you will perhaps
> be surprised to learn, is *Imagination,* which I regard as the
> most important of all the elements that go to make the
> preacher. But you must not understand me to mean the
> imagination as the creator of fiction, and still less as the
> factor of embellishment. The imagination in its relations
> to art and beauty is one thing; and in its relations to
> moral truth it is another thing, of the most substantial
> character. Imagination of this kind is the true germ of
> faith; it is the power of conceiving as definite the things
> which are invisible to the senses,—of giving them distinct
> shape. And this, not merely in your own thoughts, but
> with the power of presenting the things which experience
> cannot primarily teach to other people's minds, so that
> they shall be just as obvious as though seen with the
> bodily eye.[18]

A little later in the same lecture, Beecher gave this summary
of his view of the use of imagination:

17 Kelman, *op. cit.,* p. 14.
18 Beecher, *op. cit.,* I, 109–10.

The imagination, then, is that power of the mind by which it conceives of invisible things, and is able to present them as though they were visible to others. . . . It is the quality which of necessity must belong to the ministry.[19]

In the lectures delivered by Broadus seventeen years later, there were two statements which were almost identical with the two just quoted from Beecher:

The popular conception of imagination still is, that it assists the orator only in the way of producing high-wrought imagery, in letting off such fire-works of fancy as sophomores affect, and half-educated people admire. But modern psychology tends more and more to assign imagination a high position and a wide and varied domain. It is coming to be recognized as giving indispensable aid in scientific research and philosophical abstraction, in the formation of geometrical and ethical, as well as of artistic ideals, in the varied tasks of practical invention, and even in the comprehension and conduct of practical life.[20]

A few moments later, he added:

The orator uses imagination in the production of images. Often the idea he wishes to present can itself be converted into an image. . . .

.   .   .   .

It is thus mainly through imagination that we touch the feelings, and thereby bring truth powerfully to bear upon the will, which is the end and the very essence of eloquence.[21]

Buttrick also spoke of the need of putting concepts into pictures through the use of imagination.

Many a promising sermon is stultified because it is woven of concepts rather than of pictures. . . . We find

19 *Ibid.*, p. 117.
20 Broadus, *op. cit.*, p. 420.
21 *Ibid.*, p. 424.

that the sermons of the great preachers almost always betoken a visual imagination. . . . He [the preacher] must cultivate the imagination. He must project the Bible incidents onto the screen of his mind. The greatest thing a preacher "ever does in this world is to see something and tell what he saw in a plain way." [22]

Broadus was one of the first to mention what is generally known as historical imagination:

Another use of imagination, though not wholly distinct from the last, is in realizing and depicting what the Scriptures reveal. We have already noticed how much of the Bible consists of narrative, and how important it is that the preacher should be able vividly to describe its scenes and events. "Historical imagination," in reproducing the past, is one of the favorite ideas of our day.[23]

Burton called historical imagination "an indispensable first thing in the theologian." [24] Jowett was another who mentioned this element:

And here I want most strongly to urge you to cultivate the power of historical imagination: I mean the power to reconstitute the dead realms of the past and to repeople them with moving life. We shall never grip an old-world message until we can re-create the old-world life.[25]

The same speaker had still more to say on the subject a few moments later in the same lecture:

I am urging the cultivation of the historical imagination because I am persuaded that the want of it so often gives unreality to our preaching. If we do not realize the past we cannot get its vital message for the present. The past which is unfolded in the pages of Scripture is to many of us very wooden: and the men and the women are wooden: we do not feel their breathing: we do not hear them cry: we do not hear them laugh: we do not

22 Buttrick, *op. cit.*, pp. 155–56.
23 Broadus, *op. cit.*, p. 425.
24 Burton, *op. cit.*, p. 82.
25 Jowett, *op. cit.*, p. 122.

mix with their humanness and find that they are just like folk in the next street. And so the message is not alive. It does not pulse with actuality. It is too often a dead word belonging to a dead world, and it has no gripping relevancy to the throbbing lives of our own day.[26]

Charles Reynolds Brown declared himself to be of the same mind in regard to the importance of imagination:

By that wholesome use of the imagination which enables him to see the Unseen and to hear the Unuttered, the preacher can give such genuine and living substance to those "hoped-for things" as to cause them to exercise their pull and lift upon the hearts and wills of all those to whom he speaks. He makes the absent present. He takes that which is historic and causes it to live and move and transact spiritual business there in those lives before him. He takes those things which are as yet only ideally possible and causes people to behold them as actually capable of being wrought out in terms of solid achievement.[27]

Dale was another who recognized the power that imagination enables the preacher to wield over his audience. He said that:

. . . imagination is a most legitimate instrument of persuasion. It is an indispensable instrument. The minds of men are sometimes so sluggish that we cannot get them to listen to us unless our case is stated with a warmth and a vigour which the imagination alone can supply. There are many, again, who are not accessible to abstract argument, but who recognise truth at once when it assumes that concrete form with which imagination may invest it; they cannot follow the successive steps of your demonstration, but they admit the truth of your proposition the moment you show them your diagram. Then, again, there are some truths—and these among the greatest—which rest, not upon abstract reasoning, but upon facts. Imagination must make the facts vivid and real.[28]

26 *Ibid.*, pp. 124–25.
27 Charles Reynolds Brown, *The Art of Preaching*, pp. 143–44.
28 Dale, *op. cit.*, p. 48.

Dale also used the term, historical imagination:

> What is commonly described as an historical imagina-
> tion, is indispensable to us if we are to form a right judg-
> ment on the historical contents of Holy Scripture.[29]

Without using the term just mentioned, Kelman referred to
the same concept:

> Above all other men the preacher must possess and cul-
> tivate it. Even for his sermon-building it is an absolute
> necessity. Without it he cannot even read a passage of
> Scripture decently or tell a story to the children. If he
> would make his text interesting at the outset of his dis-
> course, he must apply imagination to it and to its con-
> text, reconstructing them as they actually were in their
> day.[30]

Imagination, according to Freeman, is the means of reach-
ing many people:

> Imagination, yes, imagination, God's great gift to us,
> His chosen servants, recognized, developed, used, it gives
> us a power, an influence of unmeasured potentiality;
> ignored, uncultivated, unemployed, it renders us ineffec-
> tive, cold, dreary and unprofitable. Cultivate it, pray for
> it, struggle for it, it is the golden master-key to open many
> doors, the open-sesame to many human hearts.[31]

Bowie, in his very first lecture, said, "Every Christian preacher
will be a better man and a better messenger if he cultivates
an historic imagination." [32]

Greer spoke a word of warning in regard to the use of this
talent:

> I remark again that you must use your imagination
> . . . — a dangerous weapon and a sharp one, which cuts
> both ways, towards error as well as truth, but which,

29 *Ibid.*, p. 50.
30 Kelman, *op. cit.*, pp. 224–25.
31 Freeman, *op. cit.*, p. 204.
32 Bowie, *op. cit.*, p. 9.

nevertheless, you must use in trying to find in the Bible the living word of God.[33]

ORIGINALITY

The subject of originality as it pertains to the preacher was also mentioned extensively in the Lyman Beecher Lectures. Burton was one of the earliest to mention it, and in his lectures he set forth a division of the subject which is helpful in classifying the statements of other Yale lecturers:

> An original preacher then, has those three marks. First, his thoughts are his own; next, he is fertile in thoughts; and next, he is different from other men. Those three elements, I say, enter into the general idea of Originality.[34]

His division is used in the following pages as the basis for the classification of statements made by the other speakers.

Forsyth spoke of the necessity of the preacher's thoughts being his own:

> He must be original in the sense that his truth is his own, but not in the sense that it has been no one else's. You must distinguish between novelty and freshness. The preacher is not to be original in the sense of being absolutely *new*, but in the sense of being *fresh*, of appropriating for his own personality, or his own age, what is the standing possession of the Church, and its perennial trust from Christ.[35]

Referring to the apostle Paul, Parkhurst explained some of that great preacher's power in terms of the fact that his truth was his own:

> There was nothing second-hand about his deliverances, so that the vitality of them has struck into the hearts of people and dominated religious thought for almost a

[33] Greer, *op. cit.*, pp. 148–49.
[34] Burton, *op. cit.*, p. 64.
[35] Forsyth, *op. cit.*, p. 89.

score of centuries. People have eyes for what is direct and ears for what is original.[36]

Burton's second component of originality was fertility of thought. Jefferson decried many preachers' lack of ideas, saying that:

> Many preachers become after a time intolerable, because of their monotony. They lack variety both in the character of their subjects and in the manner of their treatment.[37]

Broadus spoke of the power of invention, referring to this same need.

> If a man has no power of invention, he has mistaken his business when he proposes to be a preacher. But if he has some natural ability in this direction it is capable of indefinite cultivation. Clearly it is every preacher's imperative duty to train this faculty to do its best. Next to character and piety it is the most important element of his outfit.[38]

The third of the three elements which Burton mentioned had reference to the preacher's individuality. This element was mentioned in the lectures far more often than the two elements just discussed. Greer spoke of it in this fashion:

> Every man in this world is different from every other man; and every preacher is, or ought to be, different from every other preacher, and cannot be a true and effective preacher unless in some respects he is. Copy, therefore, no one. Take no one for your model. In that way failure lies.[39]

In one sentence, Brooks said of this requirement, ". . . if your ministry is to be good for anything, it must be your ministry, and not a feeble echo of any other man's. . . ." [40]

[36] Parkhurst, *op. cit.*, p. 192.
[37] Jefferson, *op. cit.*, p. 96.
[38] Broadus, *op. cit.*, p. 119.
[39] Greer, *op. cit.*, p. 97.
[40] Brooks, *op. cit.*, p. 106.

Freeman spoke at some length to emphasize the need for the preacher to be himself.

> We know of no profession that calls for more of naturalness than the one in which we are engaged. We know of no place where a man should be more truly himself than in the exercise of his office in the sanctuary. Nothing is more repellent and indeed reprehensible in the conduct of corporate worship, or in the preaching of the eternal gospel, than a borrowed or assumed habit or method, entirely foreign to the man who uses it. A fine word for every one of us in this connection is the one that Polonius gave his son Laertes, namely, "to thine own self be true."

. . . .

> I think it will be readily admitted that the true function and high purpose of education is to develop in a man his true personality.[41]

Bowie was emphatic in his agreement with this principle of individuality.

> He is an individual. Let every man who ascends the stairs of every great or humble pulpit, and let every man who is looking forward to becoming some day a preacher, remember the full implications of that. If there is any reality in the man at all, he is different from all other men. He is no sedulous ape to some one else. He is himself, and his business is to bring such a message about man and life and God as he, in his own honest experience, is discovering.[42]

Taylor was another who held that the preacher must be himself.

> Again, it most not be forgotten that no one man can merge his individuality into that of another. If one is to do anything effectively in the pulpit, or elsewhere, he must be *himself*. It is the glory of the Gospel of Christ that it lifts into itself, and transmutes into elements of

41 Freeman, *op. cit.*, pp. 94-95.
42 Bowie, *op. cit.*, pp. 3-4.

power, the very personal idiosyncracies of its preachers. No one of the apostles was cast precisely in the mold of another. John, and Peter, and Paul had their distinctive features, each of which was made instrumental in bringing out some new phase of the truth which they all alike proclaimed. And as it was with them, so it is still. [43]

Simpson added his emphasis to the danger of imitation.

We do well to follow glorious examples of holy living and of earnest devotion to the ministry; but imitation of manner, whether personal or professional, is decidedly injurious. . . . Avoid, then, all the desire for imitation. Be yourselves. Consecrate yourselves, not imitations of others, to the service of Christ.[44]

In speaking of imitation, Brooks pointed out two dangers:

The dangers of imitation are two—one positive, the other negative. There is evil in what you get from him whom you imitate and there is a loss of your own peculiar power. The positive evil comes from the fact that that which is worst in any man is always the most copiable. And the spirit of the copyist is blind. He cannot discern the real seat of the power that he admires. He fixes on some little thing and repeats that perpetually, as if so he could get the essential greatness of his hero.[45]

Kelman spoke of an entirely different facet of the subject of originality. His was a word of caution against trusting too much and too soon in the power of originality, especially as it relates to the technique of preaching.

The technique of preaching is given to no man by instinct, and the preacher who will in the end most daringly depart from such rules as there are, must serve a diligent apprenticeship in the drudgery of learning and obeying them.[46]

[43] Taylor, *The Ministry of the Word,* pp. 4–5.
[44] Simpson, *op. cit.,* pp. 69–70.
[45] Brooks, *op. cit.,* pp. 166–67.
[46] Kelman, *op. cit.,* pp. 142–43.

HEALTH

More than twelve of the Lyman Beecher lecturers suggested the importance of the physical condition of the preacher. All were of the same opinion—namely, that good health is a definite asset, too often overlooked and neglected by the average preacher, and that poor health undermines whatever other strengths the preacher may have.

Freeman mentioned the difficulty of keeping physically fit.

> Physical fitness or physical health is stated by Huxley to be the first requisite to success. The habits of the ministerial profession are not as conducive to physical robustness as are those of other occupations and professions. Possibly here again this is due to the fact that we set for ourselves no definite norm or standard of daily practice. It is certainly evident that lethargy of the body produces lethargy of the mind. Too frequently we find it easier to spend an afternoon in a comfortable chair with a pipe and a book, than out in the open in pastoral visiting, or in some form of healthful recreation. Any form of indolence tends to mental inertia. If our bodies are the temples of the spirit, then they demand unfailing care. Habits of study we must have; periods for mental and physical refreshment are indispensable.[47]

Beecher's definition of health seemed appropriate here:

> Let me tell you that when I speak of health, I do not mean merely not being sick. I divide people into, first, the sick folk; secondly, the not-sick folk; thirdly, the almost-healthy folk; and fourthly—and they are the elect —the folk that are healthy. What I mean by "health" is such a feeling or tone in every part of a man's body or system that he has the natural language of health.[48]

Brooks mentioned good health as essential to the preacher.

> If I go on and mention a certain physical condition as essential to the preacher, I do so on very serious grounds.

[47] Freeman, *op. cit.,* p. 54.
[48] Beecher, *op. cit.,* I, 183.

I am impressed with what seems to me the frivolous and insufficient way in which the health of the preacher is often treated. . . . Therefore the ideal preacher brings the perfectly healthy body with the perfectly sound soul.[49]

Still another to mention the preacher's responsibility for his own health was Scherer:

There is this matter of health, for instance, and the way so many of us think we have it; then we impose on it. . . . You will have to find out for yourself, preferably on the advice of a capable physician, what that responsibility involves for you. It may mean diet, as it did for me; it may mean stated periods in the open air; it may mean any one of a score of disciplines. My word to you is that you regard and treat this aspect of your ministry as fundamental. *The training of the body* may be *of small service,* as Paul says, when you compare it with training *for the religious life* (I Timothy 4:8); but squanderers of health are quite as culpable as any other squanderers and profligates. They will answer for it. The plain fact is that you cannot serve God as you might with an instrument that you have abused; whether from ignorance or with full knowledge, whether by harmful habits or by careless inattention makes no difference. And Life and God will some day render their account and want to know why.[50]

"A man of physical vigor," said Pepper, "has a great natural advantage in the pulpit, just as he has at the bar of the court." [51] Crosby mentioned a special reason why the preacher must possess a good physical constitution:

Another observation is founded on the fact that the duties of the constituted preacher are arduous and constant. It is that he must have a good physical organization. He must be able to bear frequent and copious draughts upon his nervous energy, for his preaching involves not only the labor of preparation, but sympathy, solicitude, and searching emphasis in delivery, as well as the personal

49 Brooks, *op. cit.*, pp. 40–41.
50 Scherer, *op. cit.*, pp. 33–34.
51 Pepper, *op. cit.*, p. 13.

ministry that forms the groundwork of his public appeals and instruction. He is to be touched daily by the sorrows of his people, and feel for their spiritual wants a parent's care; while, in the retirement of the study, he is to spare no pains to furnish his mind for the important didactic function which is peculiarly his. Such a work, bringing into constant exercise the inmost elements and faculties of his being, requires a physical frame sufficient to endure this enormous strain.[52]

Watson connected the spirituality of a congregation with the physical soundness of its preacher.

And first he must see to his *health,* for the spiritual prosperity of a congregation depends very largely on the minister being not only sound in doctrine but also sound in body. . . .

. . . Suppose two men be both saints, you need not expect equally good stuff from each in the way of thought if one be sound in body and the other unsound.[53]

The hindering effect of one who is not strong in a physical way was also mentioned by Beecher:

But, once more, it is impossible for a man who is an invalid to sustain a cheerful and hopeful ministry among his people. An invalid looks with a sad eye upon human life. He may be sympathetic, but it is almost always with the shadows that are in the world. He will give out moaning and drowsy hymns. He will make prayers that are almost all piteous. It may not be a minister's fault if he be afflicted and ill, and administers his duties in mourning and sadness, but it is a vast misfortune for his people.[54]

While discussing the subject of delivery, Merrill spoke of the importance of the preacher's physical condition:

But the chief concern in the delivery of the message is the condition of the man at the time of speaking. The preacher should give careful and constant attention to

---

[52] Crosby, *op. cit.,* pp. 20–21.
[53] Watson, *op. cit.,* pp. 275–277.
[54] Beecher, *op. cit.,* I, 189.

the problem of being at his best when in the pulpit. . . . It is hard or impossible to overestimate the importance of the physical and spiritual condition of the preacher at the time of the delivery of his message. Happy is the man who comes to the pulpit with a clear head, a clean heart, an unflurried mind, a confident faith, a sense of thorough well-being and vigor, and straight from personal contacts of an inspiring and not of a depressing sort.[55]

Charles Reynolds Brown followed the same trend of thought in one of his lectures.

Your own physical condition will enter decisively into the quality of your delivery. It is altogether wise for a preacher who is responsible for two sermons on Sunday to refrain from all hard work on Saturday afternoon and evening. . . .

The minister can well afford to play with his children on Saturday evening, or to play games with his wife, or to indulge himself in light and pleasant reading which imposes no particular strain upon his intellectual faculties. He had best sleep soundly for eight or nine hours on Saturday night. He might well sleep vicariously on behalf of the congregation he is to meet the next day. If he sleeps well on Saturday night the people are much less likely to sleep while he is preaching to them on Sunday morning.

The minister who is to preach a second sermon at an evening service may well go to bed on Sunday afternoon.[56]

Broadus also had some practical suggestions for the care of the body.

Let the physical condition be as vigorous as possible. In order to do this seek good health in general; take abundant sleep the night before speaking; at the meal before speaking eat moderately, of food easily digested, and if you are to speak immediately, eat very little; and do not, if it can possibly be avoided, exhaust your vitality during the day by exciting conversation. A healthy condition

[55] Merrill, *op. cit.*, pp. 36–37.
[56] Charles Reynolds Brown, *The Art of Preaching*, p. 160.

of the *nervous* system is surpassingly important; not a morbid excitability, such as is produced by studying very late the night before, but a healthy condition, so that feeling may quickly respond to thought, so that there may be sympathetic emotion, and at the same time complete self-control.[57]

Twelve years before Broadus, Brooks had said of the preacher's vigor:

And last of all, be vital, be alive, not dead. Do everything that can keep your vitality at its fullest. Even the physical vitality do not dare to disregard. One of the most striking preachers of our country seems to me to have a large part of his power simply in his physique, in the impression of vitality, in the magnetism almost like a material thing, that passes between him and the people who sit before him.[58]

Speaking in a general way, Hall was another who recognized the value of a strong body.

Physical considerations are not despicable, as many a feeble-bodied preacher knows. You cannot determine the strength of your chests, or the vigor of your constitutions; but you can conserve what you have received, by proper food, little enough of it, pure air, and sufficient exercise. [59]

Watson not only affirmed the need for physical care, but also set forth in detail the program of exercise that the minister should follow.

And the working minister should have his own rules of health—to have his study re-charged with oxygen every hour, to sleep with his bedroom window open, to walk four miles a day, to play an outdoor game once a week, to have six weeks' holiday a year and once in seven years three months—all that his thought and teaching may be

[57] Broadus, *op. cit.,* p. 482.
[58] Brooks, *op. cit.,* p. 107.
[59] Hall, *op. cit.,* p. 82.

oxygenated and the fresh air of Christianity fill the souls of his people.[60]

Behrends was not so detailed in his comments, though he did recommend a study of the body's needs:

> It is your business to understand your body, as much as it is your business to understand your soul. It is as much your duty to watch over and care for your body, as it is to save your soul.[61]

In terms less strong Simpson said, "To accomplish the most for humanity you must carefully guard your health and strength." [62] Freeman, likewise, put the matter more conservatively, saying that he was "confident that we would have more persuasive preaching if we had more men of robust bodies." [63]

SUMMARY

Because of the very nature of his calling, the preacher must be a man who has the moral stamina to stand against the gale. He speaks not primarily to please men, but rather to persuade men. God's message to mankind is not always pleasant, but welcome or not the preacher must declare it with full force. Just as the timid physician or cowardly general would be unworthy of his calling, so would be the preacher who lacks courage.

There is a very real danger that the man of God may become so enamored of books and of the great age-old theological concepts that he may forget the daily struggle in the lives of the men and women who hear him. The needs of the people are real, not theoretical; hence, preaching must have in it a maximum of reality and a minimum of theory. In his quest for reality the preacher must make use of imagination, which, as

60 Watson, *op. cit.*, p. 281.
61 Behrends, *op. cit.*, p. 61.
62 Simpson, *op. cit.*, p. 75.
63 Freeman, *op. cit.*, p. 59.

the word itself suggests, is the formation of mental images. His preaching must be pictorial and vivid. The power to make the ancient scenes of the Scriptures live again, peopled with real men and women who struggle with the realities of life, is indispensable.

Still another of the qualifications desired in the pulpit is originality. The preacher's influence upon others is heightened by his presentation of his own ideas in his own peculiar way. No congregation follows long the man who must depend upon the pronouncements of other men for his sermon ideas. His power diminishes as he repeats the words of another, or as he copies the manner of another.

Because of the strenuous demands which are continuously made of the minister, he should be a man of robust health. Vigor of body will be translated into vigorous mental activity and forceful presentation of the message.

These, then, were the qualifications most often mentioned by the Yale lecturers for the preacher who would aspire to success. Brief paragraphs from McDowell and Brooks seem appropriate as a conclusion to this section of the study. McDowell was speaking of a list of the qualifications of a preacher when he said:

> They are all necessary to characterize the kind of ministry we are thinking of. Do not choose between them, nor set them over against one another. If all these qualities be in you and abound, they will make you to be neither barren nor unfruitful.[64]

Along the same line of thought the words from Brooks were:

> There is nothing more striking about the ministry than the way in which very opposite men do equally effective work. You look at some great preacher, and you say, "There is the type. He who is like that can preach," and just as your snug conclusion is all made, some other voice rings out from a neighboring pulpit, and the same power

[64] McDowell, *op. cit.*, p. 238.

of God reaches the hearts of men in a totally new way, and your neat conclusion cracks and breaks. Spurgeon preaches at his Surrey Tabernacle, and Liddon preaches at St. Paul's, and both are great preachers, and yet no two men could be more entirely unlike. It must be so. If the preacher is after all only the representative man, the representative Christian doing in special ways and with a special ordination that which all men ought to be doing for Christ and fellow-man, then there ought to be as many kinds of preachers as there are kinds of Christians; and there are as many kinds of Christians as there are kinds of men.

It is evident, then, that only in the largest way can the necessary qualities of the preacher be enumerated. With this provision such an enumeration may be attempted.[65]

[65] Brooks, *op. cit.*, pp. 37-38.

CHAPTER VI

ATTITUDES

As important as are the preacher's qualifications, they are not more important than his attitudes. Although somewhat intangible and rather difficult to measure, the minister's attitudes have a significant bearing upon the success or failure of his work. There are at least three areas in which he must have clearly defined attitudes. First, there is the preacher's attitude toward himself; next, there is his attitude toward the congregation; and finally, there is his attitude toward the work of preaching. These three were discussed rather fully in the Yale lectures, and are here traced in the above-mentioned order.

ATTITUDE TOWARD SELF

Almost half of the speakers in this series devoted a part of their lectures to the discussion of this important matter. For the sake of clarity, this material is here divided into two parts, the first concerning itself with the subject of self-consciousness. Upon this phase of the preacher's attitude toward himself, Brooks said:

> I put next to this fundamental necessity of character as an element of the preacher's power the freedom from self-consciousness. . . . No man ever yet thought whether he was preaching well without weakening his sermon. I think there are few higher or more delightful moments in a preacher's life than that which comes sometimes when, standing before a congregation and haunted by questionings about the merit of your preaching, which you hate but cannot drive away, at last, suddenly or gradually, you find yourself taken into the power of your

truth, absorbed in one sole desire to send it into the men whom you are preaching to; and then every sail is set, and your sermon goes bravely out to sea, leaving yourself high and dry upon the beach, where it has been holding your sermon stranded.[1]

Kelman called self-consciousness the preacher's greatest enemy.

The fear of men, and the inordinate desire for their praise, are but different aspects of that self-consciousness which is the preacher's greatest enemy. First and last we ourselves are too much in evidence, and we must learn to keep ourselves more out of the picture. We are sensitive not only to the praise and blame of others, but to the visible results of our preaching, and that is the subtlest of all forms of egotism. We grow downcast under the sense of failure and over-anxious for visible success. But the greater part of our success and failure we can never see. We know that quite well, and still we remain oversensitive. So we must learn to force ourselves back from self and from men's opinions of us, and to fix our gaze steadily on the vision that was given us for our message. At least we have heard and seen and we must school ourselves to be content with that.[2]

Expressing his concern over the danger of self-consciousness, Abbott said, "Self-consciousness is perilous to success in any profession; nowhere is it so perilous to success as in the ministerial profession." [3] Considering this subject, Merrill said:

Freedom from self; that is the preacher's first, and last, and deepest need. Given that, he is free indeed. The dark shade that hovers over his best work is his own shadow. He never finds himself until he has lost himself.[4]

Merrill also pointed out the self-unconsciousness of many of the outstanding preachers.

1 Brooks, *op. cit.*, pp. 51–52.
2 Kelman, *op. cit.*, p. 280.
3 Abbott, *op. cit.*, pp. 205–6.
4 Merrill, *op. cit.*, pp. 132–33.

That which strikes one about the greatest preachers is their self-unconsciousness. But we are mightily mistaken when we suppose that this is in every case a native gift, or an easily acquired attitude. It may be the supreme and most hardly won achievement of their souls.[5]

Jefferson had a few sentences on this same subject which are admirably suited to serve as a transition at this point.

Adulation and disparagement are both deadly. Conceit and despondency are twin enemies of pulpit power. Both of them are the children of self-consciousness. A minister is undone whose eyes are fixed on himself. Only by looking away from himself is it possible for him to be saved.[6]

Attention is now directed to a discussion of the first of these two children of self-consciousness, conceit. Stalker pointed out that the realization of special gifts often leads in the direction of vanity.

The first consciousness of the possession of unusual powers is not unfrequently accompanied by an access of vanity and self-conceit. The young soul glories in the sense, probably vastly exaggerated, of its own preeminence and anticipates, on an unlimited scale, the triumphs of the future. But there is another way in which this discovery may act. The consciousness of unusual powers may be accompanied with a sense of unusual responsibility, the soul inquiring anxiously about the intention of the Giver of all gifts in conferring them.[7]

According to McDowell, not even the most talented can overcome the disadvantage resulting from pride and conceit.

You may well be the ablest person in your group. You will need all the ability you have; but if you use it proudly, with contempt or scorn for those less able, then you fall far short of the ability that makes a leader.[8]

[5] *Ibid.*, p. 134.
[6] Jefferson, *op. cit.*, p. 275.
[7] Stalker, *op. cit.*, p. 163.
[8] McDowell, *op. cit.*, p. 264.

Pepper also spoke of the disadvantage that may come to a minister through his recognition of his own abilities.

> If any young man has extraordinary gifts as a preacher it is to be hoped that he will be the last of all to discover the fact. It is far better that every man should assume himself of mediocre ability and should seek by personal contact with his people both to prepare the way for his sermon and also to reinforce it after it is preached.[9]

Simpson was still another who spoke of the danger of conceit.

> The young minister will need to guard against self-conceit. He may have been successful in preaching, and fancy he has already overcome all difficulties, and will take his place as one of the orators of the land. He has scarcely descended from the pulpit when some one is silly enough to tell him, and he is foolish enough to believe, that he has preached a fine sermon. He compares himself with some able and aged minister, and fancies that he is already more popular; and he lays aside his sermon with the conviction that it is as nearly perfect as a human performance can be, and that he has little more need for study or care, because his fame is already secure.[10]

On this point, Crosby said, "The habit of *self-laudation* is a hindrance to a successful ministry. The minister is to forget self in his message. He is to hide self behind his Master."[11] Frank W. Gunsaulus added, "Probably egotism never flings so dismal a shadow, as in the case of the minister."[12] Still another to indicate the special danger which self-esteem holds was Scherer.

> I can think of no more insidious or deadly foe than self-esteem, the habit so many people have of being "starched even before they are washed." Yet I would

[9] Pepper, *op. cit.*, p. 71.
[10] Simpson, *op. cit.*, p. 87.
[11] Crosby, *op. cit.*, pp. 114–15.
[12] Frank W. Gunsaulus, *The Minister and the Spiritual Life* (New York: Fleming H. Revell Company, 1911), p. 196.

hazard the guess that this is peculiarly the sin par excellence of the clergy. It is a dark presence in the cellar of every man's life; we more than others should recognize its devious ways and keep ourselves as best we may from stroking it.[13]

These men pointed out the danger of pride in one's abilities or personal virtues. Following is a group of quotations from men who called attention to the danger of becoming proud of the profession of the ministry. Robinson explained the danger:

And here is suggested another evil that detracts from the influence of preachers. The public regard them, they sometimes appear to regard themselves, as a special caste, standing quite apart from the rest of mankind. Some of them seem to take special delight in making themselves conspicuously distinct from all other men. Tone, dress, manner, language, all are specifically clerical. They deal with ghostly subjects, are leading to a ghostly future, and all they do and say is after a ghostly fashion. They seem desirous to have it understood that they are not made up of flesh and blood and bones and passions and hopes and fears and aspirations and yearnings like other men. The result is a feeling of unreality in whatever is religious.[14]

Simpson also saw this danger and said against it:

We must beware of thinking ourselves better than others because we have different work to do, or of in any way separating ourselves from the society around us. We are God's embassadors, and yet servants. Christ identified himself with the common people.[15]

Freeman was another who warned of the danger of the preacher's having this attitude. His words were these:

Insistence upon certain prerogatives or rights on the part of him who is called to minister to a people, has again and again produced a situation that effected lamentable

13 Scherer, *op. cit.*, pp. 58–59.
14 Robinson, *op. cit.*, p. 97.
15 Simpson, *op. cit.*, p. 75.

results. We have known men of marked ability whose ministry signally failed, because of this tendency to undue self-exaltation.[16]

In a fine discussion of this subject, Hall suggested the proper attitude for the preacher to hold regarding his ministry.

> There is a legitimate influence founded on official standing. Of course, if we had no other right to be respectfully heard; or if we paraded our license to preach with puerile and ridiculous vanity; or if we assumed, on the strength of it, airs which even as men and as gentlemen, we should not affect; or if, in virtue of being licensed and ordained, we walked on stilts, spoke loftily, and otherwise displayed weakness and vanity, we should have slender claim to respectful hearing. It will be easy to instance such folly, to caricature it, and to swing round to the conclusion that there is no such thing as official standing.
>
> But we assume ministers to have the average measure of taste, common sense, and modesty (if they lack these they should not be ministers); to be no more elated by their license than a physician by his diploma, or an officer by his commission; and no more reliant on the license for success than the doctor on his parchment or the officer on his uniform. To such a man there is a certain amount of influence derived from his official standing. That influence he carries to the pulpit.[17]

The second of the children of self-consciousness is discouragement. Simpson named one situation which young ministers often face, and suggested the proper attitude toward it.

> While the young minister should be guarded against self-conceit, he is also to be cautioned against discouragements. Eminence is not gained at once. The orators of to-day, like orators of old, struggle with difficulties. The preacher who seems to speak with ease and power has gained his position by long-continued effort. The work

16 Freeman, *op. cit.*, p. 29.
17 Hall, *op. cit.*, pp. 233–34.

he does to-day is not of to-day. . . . I presume there are
but few young men who have not a sense of discouragement when they listen to the efforts of superior thinkers
and orators. They should, however, remember, first, that
quite possibly they may equal these orators at some future
period, and their example should be a *stimulus;* secondly,
that God gives but few such men to his Church, and that
there is plenty of room for earnest workers, even if not
so highly talented.[18]

Of the over-critical attitude that some conscientious preachers
have toward themselves, Beecher said:

I think the best rule for a man in society—and it is
good for the pulpit too—is to have right aims, do the best
things by the best means you can find, and then let yourself alone. Do not be a spy on yourself. A man who goes
down the street thinking of himself all the time, with
critical analysis, whether he is doing this, that, or the
other thing,—turning himself over as if he were a goose
on a spit before a fire, and basting himself with good
resolutions,—is simply belittling himself. This course is
bad also in the closet.

There is a large knowledge of one's self that every man
should have. But a constant study of one's own morbid
anatomy is very discouraging and harmful.[19]

In one of the lectures of his second series, Beecher spoke a few
words that might well have followed those just quoted.

Dismiss it forever; and do not, all the time, act as if
you thought you could be perfect, and it was only from
want of vigilance or anxiety that you had not been perfect. Let a man simply have this testimony in himself: "I
am ready to do anything; I am willing to put all the
strength I have into my work. Here I am, what there is of
me; I throw it all into the work." Thus let him have some
use for his God; trust him; believe in him. What is the
use of having redemption through Jesus Christ, recon-
ciliation and love, and all promise and hope, and then
going bowed down as if you were a galley slave? Be your-

[18] Simpson, *op. cit.,* pp. 93–94.
[19] Beecher, *op. cit.,* I, 119.

self, before your congregation, what you want them to be; and, while you preach the love of Christ for human souls, show them that *you* have it, by your confidence and cheer.[20]

One year later, in his third series of lectures, Beecher said again of discouragement:

Now, every effort that you make to do something that requires tact and skill and the various subtle combinations of mind which are called forth in preaching, if it throws you back in discouragement, and causes you to feel that it is of no use, it will harm you; but it should not, for no man ever undertook a subject honestly and faithfully, and failed in it, that he was not better prepared to succeed the next time.[21]

Indicating another advantage of discouragement, Freeman said, "No man who is discontented with what he has done, consistently discontented, ever grows stale and uninteresting." [22]

Still another result of self-consciousness is the desire for applause. In every age the preacher has desired to be well thought of by his congregation. This fact has presented the temptation to modify the truth preached so as to heighten that approval. It has often developed into a craving for applause on the part of the preacher. Inasmuch as this problem arises out of an attitude which the preacher holds toward himself, it is legitimate to include a discussion of the problem at this point. Robinson's treatment of the subject was as follows:

The desire to be well thought of is natural; and Christianity does not condemn it. Within certain limits, the desire is both useful and wholesome. It becomes dangerous the moment it grows into craving for applause. Like any other perverted principle, its perversion corrupts and turns into deadly evil the very good it is capable of. But

20 *Ibid.*, II, 286.
21 *Ibid.*, III, 167.
22 Freeman, *op. cit.*, p. 196.

a reputation worth coveting never comes to him who directly seeks it. If it comes at all, it comes only as a reward to honest and self-forgetful work. He who thinks only of making a reputation for himself, may attract attention; but it will be attention to the pasteboard front of a wreched hovel.[23]

Kelman said that "the first advice to give to anyone who aspires to the holy ministry must be, Do not try to be a popular preacher, try only to be an honest man." [24] Warning against the danger of popularity, Horton said:

And before I go any further, let me utter my protest against the danger of popularity. Popular preacher! it is a term that fills one with misgiving. What has the preacher to do with popularity! Is it not enough that the disciple should be as his Lord? Was his Lord a popular preacher? [25]

In a very short but effective sentence, Simpson added, "Do not try to please so much as to do good." [26] Sockman used John the Baptist as an example:

John the Baptist was no sycophant, no private chaplain to the privileged. His sturdy independence stood four square to the passing winds. He was not a weathervane, but a guide-post.[27]

Sockman further warned against an over-zealous desire to have the approval of the crowd:

The pulpit is in more danger of selling its freedom through catering to the public than of losing its liberty through governmental pressure, real as this latter peril is. The selling of the soul is such a subtle process in any sphere, and especially so in the realm of spiritual leadership. A man may spurn the idea of selling his soul outright and yet succumb to the temptation of mortgaging it.

[23] Robinson, *op. cit.*, pp. 125–26.
[24] Kelman, *op. cit.*, p. 141.
[25] Horton, *op. cit.*, pp. 245–46.
[26] Simpson, *op. cit.*, p. 151.
[27] Sockman, *op. cit.*, p. 33.

The minister is ordained to preach the word of God as sincerely as he can know it. . . . In trying to put our message across to the people, it is so easy to allow our concern for its reception to dull the edge of its thrust.[28]

Brooks made some practical suggestions which point the way to the overcoming of the dangers which result from a desire for approval.

The true balance, if we could only reach and keep it, evidently is in neither courting nor despising the popular applause, to feel it as every healthy man feels the approval of his fellow-men, and yet never to be beguiled by it from that which is the only true object of our work, God's truth and men's salvation. And remember this, that the only way to be saved from the poison of men's flattery is to be genuinely devoted to those same men's good. [29]

Developing the thought still further, Dale said:

. . . if we have any sense of the tremendous issues of the conflict in which we are engaged between righteousness and sin, the love of God and the miseries of the human race, it will seem to us the greatest impiety to yield to the impulses of personal ambition, and we shall care for nothing except the glory of Christ and the salvation of mankind.[30]

In general, Taylor had the same admonition to offer.

And while you are thus careful to be yourselves, DO NOT PREACH YOURSELVES. Preach Christ. Beware of hiding Him behind yourselves; rather hide yourselves behind Him; and while your audience hear the voice, let them "see no man but Jesus only." Do not make the sermon an end: use it only as a means; and let your end be, not the gathering of a multitude, nor the making of a name for yourselves, but the saving of them that hear you, and then you will not lack success.[31]

---

28 *Ibid.*, pp. 34–35.
29 Brooks, *op. cit.*, p. 213.
30 Dale, *op. cit.*, p. 62.
31 William M. Taylor, *The Scottish Pulpit* (New York: Harper & Brothers, 1887), p. 278.

The second division made is that of humility. Merrill considered this attitude essential, for he said that:

> Fundamental to the character of every true spokesman of God, every leader of the spiritual advance of humanity, is a great and deep humility which would keep him silent and lost in the crowd but for the overwhelming compulsion of a message which must be spoken. Every prophet bears that hall-mark of humility.[32]

Tucker was another of the lecturers who spoke of humility as fundamental.

> The preacher has the right to know that humility is the one sure possession which gives him entrance into the high places of his high calling. . . .
> The safety of the preacher, the safeguard from himself, lies in the growth of humility. All God's chosen ones have had it. It is the sure and fine quality which underlies their natures.[33]

When suggesting the attitude the talented preacher should take toward his special gifts, Williams said:

> If we have any gifts that shine and attract, let us remember they are not plaques and pictures to hang on our walls and then call in the world to admire. They are our tools of service. Let us thank the Lord for them, keep them sharp and shining as befits efficient tools, and use them to the utmost of our ability for the converting of sinners and the comfort and edification of the saints and the upbuilding of the Kingdom of God on earth and then forget them absolutely in their use.[34]

To the young minister Brooks made two suggestions along the line of humility. They were:

> First, count and rejoice to count yourself the servant of the people to whom you minister. Not in any worn-out figure but in very truth, call yourself and be their servant.

32 Merrill, *op. cit.*, p. 18.
33 Tucker, *op. cit.*, pp. 87–88.
34 Williams, *op. cit.*, p. 22.

Second, never allow yourself to feel equal to your work. If you ever find that spirit growing on you, be afraid, and instantly attack your hardest piece of work, try to convert your toughest infidel, try to preach on your most exacting theme, to show yourself how unequal to it all you are.[35]

The same feeling of inadequacy was recommended by Pepper. He said of the preacher, "I do not say that he must be confident of his ability to deliver the message with effect. Rather he must distrust himself and lean on God." [36] McKee said, on the subject of humility:

And so the preacher of today like Isaiah in the Temple will ask for his own cleansing, acknowledge his dependence upon God and then find to his sheer amazement that God can use even him. But it is a chastened and humbled "him." A glib and facile tongue is no longer a part of him.[37]

Stalker gave this evidence of an humble spirit:

. . . I always seem to myself to be only beginning to learn my trade; and the furthest I ever get in the way of confidence is to believe that I shall preach well next time.[38]

A similar spirit of humility was evidenced by Buttrick.

A small statuette of Thorwaldsen's *Christ* stands on a bookcase top in our living room. . . . On most Sundays, when sermons have been preached, there is no shining in those eyes. The only good sermon a man ever preaches is on his way home from church—or on his knees. Often, the sermon becomes badly entangled with the preacher. But sometimes the eyes seem to smile, as if he were saying, "I do believe that one day, a million years from now, you may learn. Feed my sheep." [39]

[35] Brooks, *op. cit.*, pp. 106–7.
[36] Pepper, *op. cit.*, p. 60.
[37] Buttrick and others, *op. cit.*, p. 91.
[38] Stalker, *op. cit.*, p. 3.
[39] Buttrick and others, *op. cit.*, p. 25.

Even more directly, John Brown demonstrated a spirit of humility in introducing his series of lectures.

> In entering upon the series of Lectures I begin to-day let me do so with a preliminary word of personal sort. When a preacher consents to lecture on Preaching he is very apt to be haunted by a fear lest that consent should be interpreted to mean that he presents himself as an example of the ideal he is about to hold up to others. Lest my consent to speak to you should be so construed let me hasten at once to shelter myself behind the modest words with which even so great a Church Father as Augustine felt it needful to conclude the fourth book of his treatise on Christian Doctrine. This work, intended as a manual for preachers, thus concludes: "I give thanks to God that with what little ability I possess I have in these four books striven to depict not the sort of man I am myself (for my defects are very many), but the sort of man he ought to be who desires to labor in sound, that is, in Christian doctrine, not for his own instruction only, but for that of others also." [40]

ATTITUDE TOWARD AUDIENCE

The second of the three attitudes recommended by the Yale lecturers for the preacher concerns his audience. Thirty-one of the speakers mentioned the preacher's need for a proper attitude toward the congregation. For the analysis of the attitudes recommended, a division is made as follows: the preacher must have a genuine love for the men he addresses; to this feeling of love he must add a feeling of understanding and sympathy; and, finally, he must possess a wholesome respect for his audience. These divisions are here presented in the order named.

The love that the preacher must feel for the men whom he addresses was mentioned by Raymond Calkins.

> First of all, there must be the love. No one has a right to be a Christian minister whose supreme interest does

[40] John Brown, *Puritan Preaching in England* (New York: Charles Scribner's Sons, 1900), pp. 3-4.

not center in human beings. He may possess all other
qualifications, but if he likes books or study, investiga-
tion or research, administration or organization, speaking or lecturing, more than he likes human beings, he
will never make a successful minister of Jesus Christ. He
ought to value books; he must continually and ener-
getically study; he should have abilities as an organizer
and administrator; but above all, beyond all and within
all, he must have an absorbing interest in the lives and
souls of men. This must be his supreme preoccupation.
These are his specialty.[41]

Scherer also spoke of the affection which the preacher should
feel for humanity.

You may begin your career with a doctrinaire interest
in theology or in preaching as one of the fine arts. But
pray God you may find yourself, little by little, drawn
to human lives and human hopes and human fears!
You may begin with the aloofness of the scholar. But pray
God you may continue with a tenderness, a warmth of
affection for all the weary souls of earth, that will go far
to keep you human and to make you great.[42]

The same general need was shown by Tucker through the relating of an incident which had passed in conversation between two outstanding preachers.

Dr. Pentecost has told this of himself. He was preaching at one time in the presence of Dr. Bonar, enjoying,
as a man will, the luxury of proclaiming the gospel.
Dr. Bonar came to him at the close, touched him on the
shoulder, and said, "You love to preach, don't you?" "Yes,
I do." "Do you love men to whom you preach?" That was
a much deeper question, and it is worth every man's
asking, when he finds himself more in love with the truth,
or with the proclamation of it, than with men to whom,
and for whom, the truth has been revealed.[43]

[41] Raymond Calkins, *The Eloquence of Christian Experience* (New York:
The Macmillan Company, 1927), p. 176.

[42] Scherer, *op. cit.*, p. 23.

[43] Tucker, *op. cit.*, p. 163.

Kelman spoke of the persuasive power which accrues to the preacher whose congregation senses his love for them.

> When men perceive one among them, who manifestly loves them and whom they love, to be a prophet, they see the lines of right and wrong in clearer light and sharper edge. He, above all other men, has the power to enlist their conscience and their reason upon his side, winning them through their affections.[44]

An illustration of this power was given by Oxnam.

> Phillips Brooks, whose preaching moved the hearts and minds of his generation and whose message was heard across the seas, is remembered and revered not alone because of magnificent hours in Trinity pulpit when the truth was preached, one might say torrentially, but also because of days given gladly to the poor and the rich, the weak and the strong, the untutored and the scholar.[45]

Simpson also spoke of the power which love for men brings to the preacher.

> The strongest element of power is love for humanity. Christ loved men so much that he gave himself to die for them. The true minister must also exhibit an intensity of love.[46]

Another to speak of the preacher's love for men was Horton.

> To be specific, it is vain to preach any sermons at all, unless, as St. Paul says, the preacher has love in his heart —love to God, love to men. If frankly he finds he cannot love, is too cold and callous, or perhaps too soured, embittered, and cynical, let him come down from the pulpit, and go to the Cross, and see if his bitter-thoughted heart can there be sweetened. If not, he had best not enter his pulpit again.[47]

---

[44] Kelman, *op. cit.*, p. 277.
[45] Oxnam, *op. cit.*, p. 148.
[46] Simpson, *op. cit.*, p. 83.
[47] Horton, *op. cit.*, pp. 254–55.

Stalker said that:

> . . . the preacher is not worthy of the Christian name
> who does not know what it is to hunger and thirst for the
> salvation of individuals, and who does not esteem the
> salvation of even one soul well worth the labour of a life-
> time.[48]

According to Buttrick, this love for men is the true measure
of a preacher.

> The preacher may be appraised, as may any other man,
> by this simple but final test: "Does he see faces or things?"
> . . . There are would-be preachers who see only things—
> church buildings, card-indices, year-book figures; and
> there are other preachers, ordained by a tenderness be-
> yond the hand of man, who see faces—faces wistful and
> sin-scarred, lonely and brave.[49]

McDowell gave the following statement in explanation of the
difference between the ministry of his own day and of the day
of his forefathers:

> . . . I have preached all too many sermons full of
> passion for truth as it appeared to me, full of concern
> for the faith, but wholly without any visible passion or
> concern for men and women and their reconciliation to
> the God of Jesus Christ or to one another. I think we
> have ten times as good a theology as our forefathers had,
> ten times as good an understanding of Jesus and his teach-
> ing, ten times as good a theory of social service and human
> welfare, but nothing like their ardor to bring men to
> God, to bring men and God together, to restore lost men
> to God, that made some of our forefathers imperial in
> their ministry.[50]

Brooks explained the difference between the ministries of
modern preachers and the ministry of Christ in the same way.

> That power still continues wherever the same value
> of the human soul is present. If we could see how precious

48 Stalker, *op. cit.*, p. 77.
49 Buttrick, *op. cit.*, p. 120.
50 McDowell, *op. cit.*, p. 158.

the human soul is as Christ saw it, our ministry would approach the effectiveness of Christ's. "I am not convinced by what you say. I am not sure that I cannot answer every one of your arguments," said a man with whom a preacher had been pleading, "but one thing which I confess I cannot understand. It puzzles me, and makes me feel a power in what you say. It is why you should care enough for me to take all this trouble, and to labor with me as if you cared for my soul." It is a power which every man must feel.[51]

Sockman showed the impossibility of simulating this love.

When we convince another that we care for his welfare, we win his interest. To be interested in others is to be interesting to them. And a genuine concern cannot long be simulated. Little children are especially alert to artificial tactics. Grown children may flock for a time to hear the clever speaker who has mastered the techniques of "how to win friends and influence people," but they will not follow such a leader far in any sacrificial service; for in fact such a person lacks the essentials of leadership. A good memory, an engaging manner, an eloquent tongue, may help to gather a congregation; but the church of the living God cannot be built by a "good mixer" unless he has the mortar of true compassion.[52]

Sclater said on the subject of love for men:

People are only delivered, as a rule, by those that love them. In the Christian realm this is always true. Jesus was a Savior, because He was a friend of publicans and sinners. Wherefore, a minister will cultivate his genius for friendship, and thank God for its possession.[53]

Noyes spoke of the necessity of love when the preacher calls men's faults to their attention.

Is the pastor interested in people, not as psychological specimens but as persons? No pastoral relationship is possible without that kind of friendly interest. "Can one

51 Brooks, op. cit., p. 257.
52 Sockman, op. cit., pp. 127–28.
53 Sclater, op. cit., pp. 177–78.

point out to people their mistakes, their sins, their faults
without hurting them?" Leo Tolstoy once wrote in his
diary. "There is a spiritual chloroform, and it has long
been known—always the same—love. . . . The soul is
such a sensitive creature that an operation performed on
it without the chloroform of love is never anything but
injurious." A few months before his death, Alexander
Whyte wrote in pencil a postscript to An Appeal for
Prayer on Behalf of Ireland. It was 1919, when Irish
troubles were at high tide. The postscript might well be
in every pastor's study:

> "Truth often separates:
> Love always unites.
> 'Love me' says Augustine, 'and then say anything
>   to me and about me you like.'
>
> And Richard Baxter's people were wont to say, 'We
> take all things well from one who always and wholly
> loves us.' " [54]

In his third series of lectures, Beecher made this suggestion
to the preacher:

> When we turn from these things to the New Testa-
> ment, and see the way of our Lord, may we not under-
> stand that one mode of preaching to men so as to bring
> them to a sense of their sinfulness is to preach to them,
> I will not say excusatorily, I will not say in a manner
> which will make sin seem less sinful, but so that they shall
> not think of you as standing over them like a sheriff who
> has a writ to serve upon them, or who has a sentence of
> execution which is to take them to the block? You are to
> preach so that men shall feel that the things which you
> say to them are spoken out of kindness and love. [55]

On this subject Jacks said, in his own peculiar way:

> The qualities a preacher needs most are those of Mr.
> Greatheart; those of Mr. Talkative, though useful on

[54] Noyes, op. cit., p. 167.
[55] Beecher, op. cit., III, 226–27.

occasion, are of quite secondary importance, and this no matter what brand of theology they represent.[56]

Jefferson's comment was, "Eloquence is a force, but affection is a force still more potent." [57]

A number of the Lyman Beecher lecturers further developed the subject of the preacher's love for men by showing that that love is characterized by understanding and sympathy. The effect which a preacher's lack of proper sympathy will have on his hearers was pointed out by Beecher.

> I know men of great learning . . . men of the greatest breadth of thought, and really and interiorly men of profound emotion; but their ministry has never been very fruitful; that is, they have never moved either the multitudes, or, very largely, the individuals, of the community where they have been. I have thought I saw the reason of it in this: that their sympathy ran almost exclusively toward God. . . .
>
> .   .   .   .
>
> Then I have seen another class of men who were so constructed and educated that they had an intense sympathy with ideas, with organized thought, religious system, or philosophy; who studied profoundly, who constructed ably, who had much that was instructive in their work. But after all, while everybody felt the strength of their sermons, almost nobody was moved or changed by them. And I have seen ministers with not one quarter of this equipment really lift and inspire a congregation, producing an effect which, with a proper following up, might have been permanently crystallized into life and disposition.
>
> There should be in you a strong sympathy with the intellectual elements of the ministry; but it should never overlie, and certainly should not absorb or impede, the more legitimate sympathy you are to have with men themselves.[58]

[56] Jacks, *op. cit.*, p. 27.
[57] Jefferson, *op. cit.*, p. 70.
[58] Beecher, *op. cit.*, I, 33–34.

Watson saw a need for a balance between the preacher's feeling for man and for God.

> He who feels the breath of the human spirit only is a secularist—there are such, although they know it not, in the Christian pulpit,—and he who feels the breath of the Divine Spirit only is an ascetic. It is best when the soul lies open to both influences, for so the preacher is in touch with God and man, a go-between and mediator.[59]

Still another to point out the preacher's need for a sympathetic feeling for men was Sockman.

> In this two-fold task of preparing the people for the word, and preparing the word for the people, the Lord's roadmaker must be motivated by creative compassion. Henry Ward Beecher once caustically commented on the unlovely attitude of certain preachers who were always on God's side against the people. All too familiar is the preacher who tries, as he says, "to put the fear of God into people," but in a way which makes both God and himself seem hostile to the people. There comes to mind an earnest young student minister who was given charge of a boys' club. He went at the job somewhat as a policeman swings into a street gang. He felt it his duty to save them, but he clearly had no affection for them. Of similar spirit are some of those who are shouting that we must "get America back to God." They say it as grimly as if they were calling in the militia to preserve order.[60]

Coffin gave as his conception of a true minister the following:

> The best metaphor for the pastoral office seems to be that of friendship. A minister's relations with his own congregation and with outsiders whom he may touch, his leadership, his authority, his influence, are most akin to those of a close friend. And he must be a unique kind of friend; let me describe him as a trusted, inspired, trained, and accredited friend at large.[61]

[59] Watson, *op. cit.*, p. 68.
[60] Sockman, *op. cit.*, p. 126.
[61] Coffin, *op. cit.*, p. 136.

In his entire seventh lecture, Coffin [62] emphasized the need
for the minister to know his people and be intimately known
by them. His strong implication was that much of the minister's influence and power grows out of this close relationship.
Pepper said, in expressing his own agreement with this view,
"If the preacher can first become the friend of his people his
sermon will be preached to receptive minds." [63] While elaborating upon this thought, Pepper added in another place:

> This much is certain: that it is only by ministering
> to people in pain and by comforting them in adversity
> that a man can earn the right to counsel or to rebuke
> them when he disapproves of their way of having a good
> time. It is almost always a futile thing for one who holds
> himself aloof from the life of his community to thunder
> denunciations against that which his people rightly or
> wrongly believe to be innocent fun. [64]

The same thought was expressed by Buttrick.

> If their minister has been with them in stress of joy
> and sorrow, in overcoming and failure, they will not
> question too strongly his right to speak the whole truth
> as he sees it in Christ. [65]

The same speaker in another series of the Yale lectures expressed a similar thought.

> No man can preach to the individual who does not go
> where he lives, and who does not say to him in urgent
> fidelity of pastoral care, "Would that my soul were in
> your soul's stead!" [66]

Taylor said on this same subject, "My young brethren, be
much in the homes of sorrow, for through your ministrations
to the afflicted, your pulpit utterances will acquire increasing

[62] Ibid., pp. 134–53.
[63] Pepper, op. cit., p. 70.
[64] Ibid., p. 76.
[65] Buttrick and others, op. cit., p. 20.
[66] Buttrick, op. cit., p. 118.

power." [67] In speaking of the sympathy which the preacher must have, Kelman made somewhat of an analysis of the most desirable type of sympathy.

> In a word, it is sympathy that is required of us. The interpreter must know, as only sympathy can let him know, the souls he has to interpret. There is a sort of sympathy, which may be called dramatic sympathy, that is of great value to the preacher. It is the result of a quickened imagination playing upon a wide knowledge of men's lives. . . .
> . . . There is another sort of sympathy, not dependent either on such wide knowledge or such powerful imagination—the sympathy of the open-hearted. You will reach a truer knowledge of men by loving them and keeping your heart open to them, than by studying their ways for a lifetime. [68]

Crosby said on the subject of sympathy:

> The sense, on the part of the people, of the preacher's sympathy will be a powerful agent of impression and conviction, and will be apt to prevent their occupation of the critic's unbecoming position. [69]

At this point a personal illustration from one of Oxnam's lectures is especially appropriate.

> It was my privilege to study under a remarkable philosopher, a man who wrote no books. He tried to teach students to think. He was an old man, stooped and gray. His eyes were keen, his hair long, his jaw firm, and his lips tender. . . . I loved that old man. He loved us, but he did not wear his heart on the sleeve of his academic gown. Just before leaving for Boston to enter the theological seminary, I summoned up a bit of courage and asked the old man a question in private: "Dr. Hoose, what advice would you give a young man entering the ministry?" He puckered up his lips; his eyes flashed; there was a moment of silence. "Scholarship, no manner-

[67] Taylor, *The Ministry of the Word*, p. 271.
[68] Kelman, *op. cit.*, pp. 244–45.
[69] Crosby, *op. cit.*, p. 49.

isms." He turned and walked away, dragging his weary old feet down the hall. I was disappointed. Just three words, "Scholarship, no mannerisms." The next day I was at the Southern Pacific station. My father and mother, my brothers and sister, were there, and, of course, some friends. We were about to say good-by when through the doorway of that station came the old man. Stooped, yes; gray, yes. The long hair tousled out from the big black hat he always wore. He came up and greeted us. Then he pulled me aside and said almost gruffly: "Oxnam, I want to change the advice I gave you last night. I want to add a word: Scholarship, sympathy, no mannerisms." And there it is, and I give it to the younger men who are to preach in a revolutionary age—scholarship, sympathy, no mannerisms.[70]

Burton's unique expression was, "And then there is such a luxury in preaching, when you preach sympathetically;—such a luxury for you and such a luxury for the people." [71] Albert Edward Day spoke of a real concern for the welfare of the people.

Only a genuine interest in the people who attend our ministry and vivid understanding of their needs artificial and real, and of the conflicts into which those needs precipitate them, and of the deforming, mutilating, paralyzing effects of those conflicts, and of the spiritual therapy which can eliminate those effects, and of the personal strategy which can give the real and fundamental needs some satisfying answer—only this can make our preaching a real ministry to personality—a re-creation of souls.[72]

Greer spoke out boldly against an attitude sometimes found among preachers—a feeling of aloofness toward the people.

I would not willingly say a word which would tend in the least to disparage or depreciate the ministerial office,

[70] Oxnam, *op. cit.,* pp. 133-34.
[71] Burton, *op. cit.,* p. 96.
[72] Albert Edward Day, *Jesus and Human Personality* (New York: The Abingdon Press, 1934), pp. 238-39.

to lower it, to cheapen it, or to detract from the dignity of it. It is, in my judgment, the noblest and highest of all offices, as I have been trying to make you feel; and in every proper and lawful way I would magnify it and proclaim its worth and value, and set its dignity and greatness forth. And yet I cannot but think it is a great mistake to so regard that office as to make it like a fence, and a high fence, and difficult to get over, between the man on one side, and his fellow men on the other. They should not so regard it, and he should not so regard it. Let him go among them rather, and live and be among them, simply as a man among men, as an honorable and high-minded man, living like other honorable and high-minded men, trying thus to win their confidence, and to secure and have their respect, not chiefly because of his office, but chiefly because of himself. And if there is to be a difference between them, let it be a difference in manhood and character, and not in official status. Let it be a difference which attracts and binds them more closely to him, and not a difference which repels and puts them further away.[73]

The third aspect of the preacher's attitude toward his audience to which various lecturers' comments seem logically to belong is his wholesome respect for his audience. The first lecturer to discuss this attitude was Brooks.

The next element of a preacher's power is genuine respect for the people whom he preaches to. I should not like to say how rare I think this power, or how plentiful a source of weakness I think its absence is. There is a great deal of the genuine sympathy of sentiment. There is a great deal of liking for certain people in our congregations who are interesting in themselves and who are interested in what interests us. There is a great deal of the feeling that the clergy need the coöperation of the laity, and so must cultivate their intimacy. But of a real profound respect for the men and women whom we preach to, simply as men and women, of a deep value for the capacity that is in them, a sense that we are theirs and

[73] Greer, op. cit., pp. 160–61.

not they ours, I think that there is far too little. But without this there can be no real strength in the preacher.[74]

Jefferson emphasized the fatal results to be expected when a preacher holds a contemptuous view of his congregation.

If a man has a contemptuous view of his church he is well-nigh certain to be afraid of it. But love casts out fear. If a man loves his church and proves his love by his life, he can say to it anything which is proper for a Christian teacher to say to his pupils, anything which it is fitting for a Christian man to say to his friends. The preachers who get into trouble by talking plainly to their people are as a rule preachers who do not love their churches. If a man stays in his study through the week, wishing he could get a call to a larger church, secretly despising the flock of which he is the appointed shepherd, and then goes into the pulpit on the Lord's day, and thunders against his people's sins, there may be a storm, and there ought to be.[75]

Oxnam gave an illustration of just such a man as Jefferson described.

Unfortunately, the development of the cultured personality has a tendency to separate men of good taste from the man of no taste, to create barriers between the untutored and the man of scientific mind. I met a pastor some time ago who objected strenuously to serving in a certain parish. He stated that the people were laboring people, that they could not understand him. He insisted that his culture was beyond them, that he lived in a realm of philosophy which they could not enter. Perhaps it was unkind, but I did suggest to that brother that Jesus of Nazareth saw no such barrier.[76]

Recommending the preacher's respect for his congregation as a basic factor in persuasion, Abbott said:

With this candor and courage must go another quality which does not always accompany them, respect for one's

[74] Brooks, *op. cit.*, pp. 52–53.
[75] Jefferson, *op. cit.*, pp. 17–18.
[76] Oxnam, *op. cit.*, pp. 141–42.

fellow men. "Thou shalt love thy neighbor as thyself"
involves more than a spirit of mutual good-will, it involves also a spirit of mutual respect. The preacher must
understand, and he must have intellectual respect for,
opinions which he believes to be thoroughly erroneous.
It may be laid down as an axiom that you can never persuade another man to your point of view until you appreciate his point of view. You can never get another to take
your position until you have in imagination taken his
position.[77]

The necessity of respect was also mentioned by Oxnam.

The pastor must respect man as man. He must see men
in terms of their possibilities. He must see them as sons
of God. His reading will help him to understand and to
serve; but close association with a great surgeon, friendship with an inspiring teacher, visits in the home of a
great executive who is also a father, fellowship with a
leader of labor, hours with the boys and girls of the parish, will bring to him, as nothing else can, the goodness
of human beings—their integrity, kindness, and love;
their worth. More men have been brought to Christ by
the preaching of his love than by the denunciation of
their sin. And more men are held fast to their resolves
by the pastor who has faith in the essential goodness of
all men than by the brother who sees his fellows as de-
graded beings to be snatched from the burning.[78]

Tucker gave a basic reason for this respect for men.

The preacher, as we have seen, if he has caught the
secret of his Master, has learned to pay his respects to
humanity in whomsoever it may be represented, and at
any cost. Respect is the prince of influence. It is the respecting element in Christianity, more than the pitying
element, which is the peculiar sign of its power.[79]

Stalker spoke of the importance of belief in men.

No one will ever win men who does not believe in
them. The true minister must be able to see in the mean-

[77] Abbott, op. cit., pp. 219–20.
[78] Oxnam, op. cit., p. 156.
[79] Tucker, op. cit., p. 156.

est man and woman a revelation of the whole of human nature; and in the peasant in the field, and even the infant in the cradle, connections which reach forth high as heaven and far as eternity.[80]

Approximately twelve years after Stalker had spoken of the importance of the preacher's having faith in his audience, Peabody repeated the same thought with slight variations of expression.

The first condition of all effective leadership is faith in those who are to be led. Many a parent forfeits, by the habit of distrust, his right to guide his child; many a leader finds his followers fail him because they are driven, not led. The good shepherd goes before, and need not turn his head to see if the sheep are following. They know his voice, and follow because he is sure they will. His faith in them kindles their loyalty to him.[81]

The only speaker to warn of giving the audience too much respect was Pepper, but even in this warning he seemed to be speaking of the degree of maturity which the audience had reached rather than the worthiness of the audience.

The preacher should avoid the mistake of rating his hearers too high. He will be wise if he accords to them at least as much spiritual perception as they really have.
But for the preacher to make a just appraisement is by no means easy.[82]

ATTITUDE TOWARD THE MINISTRY

An impressive number of the Yale lecturers mentioned the importance of the preacher's attitude toward preaching. Noyes said, briefly but succinctly, "A minister is not likely to be a preacher of the Word of God unless that is his highest ambition." [83] Simpson was another who spoke of this factor.

[80] Stalker, *op. cit.*, pp. 171–72.
[81] Peabody, *op. cit.*, p. 91.
[82] Pepper, *op. cit.*, p. 32.
[83] Noyes, *op. cit.*, p. 26.

The first great requisite to the success of the young minister is, as I think, a proper appreciation of the character of the wonderful work upon which he is entering, especially in its nature, duties, and responsibility.[84]

The most extensive discussion of the preacher's attitude toward his work was given by Oxnam. He first described an unworthy attitude.

There is the man who thinks he is a minister but who is really a high-pressure, boisterous, back-slapping, hand-shaking salesman. He is a politician gone religious. He has no sense of refinement. He does not know that light travels faster than sound. Kenneth Fearing has described him in his attempt to portray a high-pressure salesman:

And wow he died as wow he lived,
  going WHOOP to the office and BLOOIE home to sleep
    and
    BIFF got married and BAM had children and OOF got
    fired.
    ZOWIE did he live, and ZOWIE did he die.

. . . This man is a promoter, not a priest. He suffers from aprosexia. That is a term that indicates a lack of power to concentrate the mind. He reveals flickering attention. In words of the camera expert, he "panorams" too much. There is too much "movie," too much "talkie." He possesses a split-second mind. Of course, we need aggressive leadership; but this need not be divorced from the cultural, the spiritual, from poise and dignity. This man seldom knows what he creates; he is the man who leaves the debt behind.[85]

His second description was of an equally unworthy attitude.

Then there is another picture. We may entitle this "The Professional." He is a job-conscious, highly trained professional, a master of religious ceremony, basically cynical though often a delightful fellow, a gentleman who looks out for his own interests in the job of serving the

84 Simpson, op. cit., p. 11.
85 Oxnam, op. cit., pp. 122–23. The lines from "Dirge," in Poems (New York: Dynamo, 1935), used by permission of the author, Kenneth Fearing.

Lord. Religion is largely a matter of form. This professional expounds Christianity but really accepts the philosophy of George M. Cohan in one of his musical
comedies, "When you're rich, you're the smoke; and
when you're broke, it's a joke." The pen is mightier than
the sword, that is, when it is writing checks.[86]

Finally, he set forth the attitude which must be a part of
every acceptable public servant of God.

But it is not these pictures that I would emphasize.
There is another. It is of such a man as I find in the
large percentage of our churches, great and small. We
may entitle this "The Called Messenger." He is sustained
by a sense of being called, driven by the spirit of Christ,
seeking naught save the privilege of serving, losing his life
and finding it, the devoted slave of the suffering Christ,
bearing in his heart and on his body the scars that speak.
The Called Messengers! These men impress me. They
are like Paul: "I was not disobedient unto the heavenly
vision." . . .

. . . .

It is the preaching of the Called Messenger that the
revolutionary day eagerly awaits and desperately needs.[87]

Freeman mentioned that the people expect the preacher to
have a high regard for the ministry.

Those to whom we preach, who for themselves demand
liberty in all things, even to the point of gross indul-
gence, demand of us, and rightly so, that we shall remember at all times the dignity and sacredness of the
office we carry.[88]

Henson declared that:

So long as the obligation of this sublime response to
the vocation and claim of GOD be paramount in the
preacher's mind, he will be in little danger of falling into
either of the different yet allied errors which mostly

[86] *Ibid.*, p. 123.
[87] *Ibid.*, pp. 124–26.
[88] Freeman, *op. cit.*, p. 53.

threaten him. On the one hand, he will not be able to think meanly of his office; on the other hand, he will not exaggerate the value of his personal contribution to the ministry of preaching.[89]

The need for full confidence in one's work was shown by Behrends.

No man can achieve solid and satisfactory success in any calling, who is not convinced that the services which he renders are of substantial benefit to the public, and that what he gives is a full equivalent for what he receives.[90]

Several of the lecturers spoke of the motives behind the minister's entrance into the vocation of preaching. Emphasizing their key position, McDowell said of these motives:

We study other men's methods, thinking that the method is the chief thing. But the motive is vastly more important in this as in all other parts of the ministry. Wise methods abound, motives are weak or lacking.[91]

Charles Reynolds Brown discussed the failure that would result from the wrong motives behind the preacher's efforts.

If your preaching is a burden to you; if you are doing it because you must do something in order to live; or if your work is done in a mechanical sort of way much as a man might get out fence posts, or cut cord wood; or if you are preaching mainly because you find a certain intellectual satisfaction in standing in a public place, the admired of all beholders, then you will fail. And you ought to fail. You cannot succeed except as your heart is joyfully set upon the deeper, spiritual values bound up with this work of preaching.[92]

Simpson gave the following warning:

If you have ever looked at the ministry as a life of ease, either abandon the thought, or at once abandon the min-

[89] Henson, *op. cit.*, pp. 4–5.
[90] Behrends, *op. cit.*, p. 1.
[91] McDowell, *op. cit.*, p. 188.
[92] Charles Reynolds Brown, *The Art of Preaching*, p. 235.

istry. It is a busy hive, with no room for drones. There is work in the pulpit, and work out of the pulpit; work in the study, and work out of the study; work publicly and work privately.[93]

When speaking of the minister's attitude toward his work, several of the lecturers emphasized the need for full concentration upon the work of the ministry. Stalker said:

We must have men of more power, more concentration on the aims of the ministry, more wisdom, but, above all, more willingness to sacrifice their lives to their vocation. We have too tame and conventional a way of thinking about our career.[94]

Simpson believed that:

For great success, the preacher cannot afford to divide his thoughts and energies. He cannot spend part of his time on matters wholly foreign, and then return to his pulpit with the power which he might have exercised. This intense interest or absorption of soul is the greatest power we can exercise over our thoughts.[95]

Three years earlier, Taylor had delivered a call for all ministers to give themselves wholly to the work of preaching.

Let it never be forgotten, then, that he who would rise to eminence and usefulness in the pulpit, and become "wise in winning souls," must say of the work of the ministry, "This one thing I do." He must focus his whole heart and life upon the pulpit. He must give his days and his nights to the production of those addresses by which he seeks to convince the judgments, and move the hearts, and elevate the lives of his hearers.[96]

Taylor also presented the example of Chalmers, who continued to teach mathematics and chemistry at St. Andrews after he was first settled at Kilmany, Scotland, as a minister.

[93] Simpson, *op. cit.*, pp. 20–21.
[94] Stalker, *op. cit.*, p. 16.
[95] Simpson, *op. cit.*, p. 144.
[96] Taylor, *The Ministry of the Word*, p. 7.

After some time, "he was constrained to devote every moment of his time and every energy of his being to the duties of his office." [97]

One other suggestion was made concerning the preacher's attitude toward his life work. Brooks thought it necessary that he enjoy his work.

> I think, again, that it is essential to the preacher's success that he should thoroughly enjoy his work. I mean in the actual doing of it, and not only in its idea. No man to whom the details of his task are repulsive can do his task well constantly, however full he may be of its spirit.[98]

Parkhurst expressed the same opinion nearly four decades later.

> We never do well that which we do not enjoy doing, that toward which our faculties of thought, feeling and temperament do not converge with unanimity of assent. Success in the best sense of the term and in the higher lines of achievement, is unattainable, if, while certain of our powers throw themselves into effort with glad spontaneity, other of those powers stand by in frowning dissent. A man in order to do perfectly well must be unanimous.[99]

SUMMARY

Within the area of the preacher's attitude toward himself the greatest dangers lie in too great a consciousness of self. This overawareness of self results in one of two extremes. Either the person becomes conceited or he becomes discouraged, and either attitude is disastrous to the success of his work. The preacher's goal is to avoid these two extremes, and to think of himself sanely and soberly; and this he can best do by forgetting self through his preoccupation with his message and his audience.

[97] *Ibid.*, p. 283.
[98] Brooks, *op. cit.*, pp. 53-54.
[99] Parkhurst, *op. cit.*, pp. 13-14.

In order to persuade men, the man who stands in the pulpit must have a genuine love for them, a love characterized by understanding and sympathy. In addition, he must have a wholesome respect for those to whom he preaches. When these attitudes are known to the congregation his sermons will take on new persuasive power.

Not only must the preacher have a proper attitude toward himself and toward the people whom he serves, but he must also be thoroughly convinced that the work of preaching is the earth's noblest calling. For him, it must be the only calling. The most effective work will be done by the minister who holds his profession in high honor, who is driven by pure motives, who gives his full time to the work, and who thoroughly enjoys the work.

PART II

THE SERMON

CHAPTER VII

STYLE

In his great task of persuading men to move from a lower to a higher plane, the preacher has as his chief instrument the sermon. It is given an honored place in the lives of millions of people as, week after week, they devote a half-hour or more of their time to the hearing of a sermon. The enormity of the preacher's responsibility is apparent when it is realized that each time he addresses his Sunday audience of a thousand people his half-hour sermon takes five hundred hours of their combined time.[1] The conscientious preacher spends a lifetime in perfecting the art of preparing and delivering sermons.

The chapters of this section are devoted to a study of the various elements of the sermon. First comes a consideration of style because so many of the qualities named by the Lyman Beecher lecturers as essential to the sermon can be most logically discussed under this heading. Before a detailed consideration of the various elements of style, a general discussion of the subject is in order.

IMPORTANCE OF STYLE

Quite a number of the speakers mentioned the importance of the preacher's style. Typical of these remarks were the statements made by Tucker, Merrill, and Broadus. Tucker named style as one of three leading elements of preaching:

The pulpit, as much as any agency of public speech, places insistence upon style. The truth in itself, how-

[1] Charles Reynolds Brown, *The Art of Preaching*, p. 8.

ever true it may be, will not insure the preacher a hearing. It is in preaching as in all good speech, the truth, plus the man, plus the style.[2]

Merrill also gave style an important place.

A good English style is as essential to the preacher as a good delivery wagon is to the grocer. There are too many men in the pulpit who know a good deal, and think well enough, but have never gained the mastery of effective and simple language, through much companionship with the best writers, through deliberate and painstaking cultivation of a homely forceful use of words. A preacher without skill in words is like a knight with no knowledge of sword play.[3]

After pointing out the assistance which matter receives from style, Broadus mentioned the rarity of excellent style.

The best style attracts least attention to itself, and none but the critical observer is apt to appreciate its excellence, most men giving credit solely to the matter, and having no idea how much the manner has contributed to attract and impress them. The thought is certainly the main thing; but the style also is important. . . .

It follows from all this that every writer and speaker should pay great attention to the improvement of his style. High excellence in style is necessarily rare; for a discourse, a paragraph, even a sentence, is really a work of art, fashioned by constructive imagination—and artist-gifts of every kind are rare. But any man who will try, long enough and hard enough, can learn to say what he means, to say forcibly what he deeply feels, and to clothe his thoughts in a garb at least of homely neatness.[4]

These paragraphs indicate the general approval of good style in preaching. Still another to point out the importance of style was Scherer, who also gave a serviceable definition of it.

Now one of the foremost results of all the discipline which I have been trying so hard to describe and recom-

2 Tucker, *op. cit.*, p. 103.
3 Merrill, *op. cit.*, p. 34.
4 Broadus, *op. cit.*, pp. 344–45.

mend is the achievement of a certain "style." There is a word for you that is often misunderstood. "Style" is not a mysterious something that you acquire only after years of laborious and painstaking effort; style is merely the way you have of expressing yourself. Your style may be good; it may be bad: but you have it already. You can change it for a better, or you can let it get altogether out of hand, if you like, and flop over into something that is worse. But you already have it. Improving it, strengthening it, beautifying it, pointing it, is no end of good sport. Forcing ideas to associate or come apart, bullying stubborn words to assume a certain pattern, all the fun, as someone has said, of being a dictator without any of the risks! [5]

Broadus, as well as other lecturers, was not content to call attention to the importance of style, but hastened on to give an analysis and a discussion of its elements.

The qualities or properties of Style have been variously classified and named by different writers on Rhetoric and Homiletics. It is perhaps well to distinguish between the *grammatical* and *rhetorical* qualities, the former including principally correctness and purity of *language,* while the latter refer more particularly to the *impression* or *effect* of discourse, whether written or spoken. Of these rhetorical qualities the best classification is that adopted from Campbell by Whately and others, namely, Perspicuity, Energy, and Elegance. Some prefer to say clearness, force, and beauty. . . .[6]

Following the same trend of thought, Charles Reynolds Brown analyzed style in almost identical fashion. He used a quotation from Augustine in setting forth his analysis:

You will recall the familiar word of Augustine, "Veritas pateat, veritas placeat, veritas moveat." "Make the truth plain! make the truth pleasing! make the truth moving." [7]

5 Scherer, *op. cit.,* p. 186.
6 Broadus, *op. cit.,* p. 361.
7 Charles Reynolds Brown, *The Art of Preaching,* pp. 4-5.

Much later in his course of lectures the same speaker enumerated some of the qualities of an effective style in saying that, "The best style for public address is one which makes your thought presentable, interesting, effective, without ever attracting the attention of the people to itself." [8] The second lecture delivered by Watson [9] was a detailed enumeration of the elements of style. His list included seven canons: unity, lucidity, beauty, humanity, charity, delivery, and intensity. In a succeeding lecture the same speaker named still other qualities of a good style: "Above all must the speaker of today be clear, terse, forcible; in a word, real, without cant or superfluity—a good leader-writer on religion." [10]

McDowell and Behrends admonished the students of the Yale Divinity School to adopt a style acceptable to the common people, a style which grows out of a knowledge of the language of the people. McDowell made reference to Christ as one who had adopted a style suited to the common man.

> I beg you, therefore, to cure yourselves early of that conceit which despises the right sort of popular preaching. If you have not the kind of speech that common people love to hear, do not be proud of it or think yourself a superior person because you lack it. Remember whose company you are not in when the common people do not hear you gladly. And His company we principally covet.[11]

Behrends called for the preacher's style to be akin to the language of the people.

> Style is the dress of thought. It must conform to popular usage. It must not be antique and antiquated, but modern and practical. Instruction in rhetoric and logic is not confined to a few classical models; it must

[8] *Ibid.*, p. 177.
[9] Watson, *op. cit.*, pp. 37–62.
[10] *Ibid.*, p. 83.
[11] McDowell, *op. cit.*, pp. 92–93.

be sought, with equal diligence, in the language which the great majority uses.[12]

From these references it might be concluded that there was unanimity of emphasis among the Yale lecturers on style. Such was not the case. Beecher was one who expressed a different point of view.

No matter how unbalanced, how irregular and rude, that is a great sermon which has power to do great things with the hearts of men. No matter how methodical, philosophic, exquisite in illustration, or faultless in style, that is a poor and weak sermon that has no power to deliver men from evil and to exalt them in goodness.[13]

Greer was another to give style a less vital place in the work of preaching.

Your rhetoric may not always be the best, nor your language always the choicest, and yet sometimes it will be; and it is quite likely that you will hesitate at times, and be at a loss for a word, and become a little involved. But if it does not matter much to you, it will not matter much to the people, and if you are not confused by it they will not be confused; and your message, though broken in form a little, nor always to your satisfaction when you come to review it from a literary point of view, will have, in spite of its ruggedness, and sometimes because of its ruggedness, an impressiveness and a power which it would not otherwise have.[14]

Although these men undoubtedly would not have said that style is unimportant, they did say that the preacher can sometimes accomplish his task of persuading men without the degree of beauty, polish, or elegance normally considered to be essential. This phase of the discussion will be carried further under the term "elegance" in succeeding pages.

12 Behrends, *op. cit.*, p. 222.
13 Beecher, *op. cit.*, I, 227–28.
14 Greer, *op. cit.*, pp. 184–85.

ELEMENTS OF STYLE

For the sake of a clear presentation the different elements of style are discussed in separate sections of this and the following chapter. The remainder of this chapter is devoted to a consideration of clearness, concreteness, interestingness, sensationalism, elegance, originality, and unity; while the next chapter is devoted to a consideration of the illustrations, language, and organization of the sermon.

CLEARNESS

Nine of the Yale lecturers mentioned clearness as the first requisite of a good style. Still others made it simply an element in their list of qualities necessary for a good style. Robinson called for style to be like transparent glass:

> The best style is like plate-glass, so transparent that in looking at the objects beyond it, you forget the medium through which you see them. Alas! that so much pulpit rhetoric distorts and discolors and half conceals, if it does not hide, the very truth it professes to be making clear.[15]

Broadus made the figure even stronger:

> The most important property of style is perspicuity. Style is excellent when, like the atmosphere, it shows the thought, but itself is not seen. Yet this comparison, and the term "perspicuity" which was derived from it, are both inadequate, for good style is like stereoscopic glasses, which, transparent themselves, give form and body and distinct outline to that which they exhibit.[16]

Using the same degree of emphasis, though not the same figure of speech, Sclater said, "The main thing is to be simple and clear, remembering that simplicity and clarity are the friends,

[15] Robinson, *op. cit.*, p. 155.
[16] Broadus, *op. cit.*, p. 361.

and not the enemies, of beauty." [17] Jefferson also exalted the
element of clearness in saying that "The natural style is the
clear style. The first duty of a preacher is to make himself
easily understood." [18] Still others to name clearness as the
prime element in style were Beecher,[19] Park,[20] Behrends,[21]
and Charles Reynolds Brown.[22] Seldom was there found so
complete a degree of agreement among the various speakers
concerning the importance of an item as in the case of clearness.

CONCRETENESS

Seven of the Yale lecturers spoke of the need for concrete,
specific elements in the sermon. Crosby, for example, pointed
out the ineffectiveness of abstractions:

> Men are taught best, as children are, by object lessons,
> and if the object may not be actually seen, it can be de-
> scribed. A sermon of mere abstractions may do for the
> trained thinker, but as the vast majority of men are not
> trained thinkers, it is most important to reduce the ab-
> stract as far as possible to the concrete.[23]

Horton made the same point by means of an illustration:

> Let the preacher do his thinking in the abstract, as
> Michael Angelo studied the human frame in a skeleton,
> but let him clothe it for the people in the concrete, and
> see that all his language is that of one who, though he
> spends long hours in heavenly places, yet lives and moves
> among men.[24]

Beecher drew attention to the importance of this element in
moving men when he said that ". . . that which will touch

17 Sclater, *op. cit.*, p. 188.
18 Jefferson, *op. cit.*, p. 95.
19 Beecher, *op. cit.*, I, 228.
20 John Edgar Park, *The Miracle of Preaching* (New York: The Macmillan
Company, 1936), p. 25.
21 Behrends, *op. cit.*, p. 217.
22 Charles Reynolds Brown, *The Art of Preaching*, pp. 178–82.
23 Crosby, *op. cit.*, pp. 65–66.
24 Horton, *op. cit.*, p. 288.

men most sensibly, and arouse them most effectually, and
bring them to a new life most certainly, is that which is
specific." [25] Referring to Christ, Abbott attributed at least
part of his great influence to the concrete expression of his
truth.

> His [Christ's] preaching, therefore, is concrete. His
> illustrations are never mere ornaments, introduced to
> relieve a wearied audience or lighten the strain upon
> their attention; they are concrete expressions of vital
> truth; and the only truths with which he concerns him-
> self are those capable of concrete interpretation. An ab-
> stract truth which exists only in the realm of pure intel-
> lect has apparently for Jesus Christ no interest; it cer-
> tainly has no place in his teaching. The only Christianity
> which Jesus Christ inculcated was applied Christianity.[26]

Reference to Christ was made by Greer in connection with
the same point.

> And he, the preacher, the man, the living man and
> preacher, was living in the creed, and making the creed
> live, and breathe, and move, and talk. And as a living
> thing we heard it, and as a living thing we felt it,—not
> as truth in abstract form, but as truth in form concrete;
> as truth in flesh and blood. And that was his secret and
> power, or the secret of his power. It is always the secret
> of power. And when the pulpit loses that power it will
> have none. . . .[27]

Parkhurst showed the effectiveness of concreteness in the
specific application of the sermon to the immediate audience.

> Still I think that, as a rule, presentations of truth
> that are shaped with a reference that is specific, carries
> with it, on the part of speaker and hearer both, a livelier
> sense of personal touch, for the hearer will best feel the
> truth when he feels the preacher and when he realizes that

25 Beecher, *op. cit.*, III, p. 215.
26 Abbott, *op. cit.*, p. 265.
27 Greer, *op. cit.*, p. 75.

he is himself the one that is being particularly approached and addressed.[28]

INTERESTINGNESS

Only a few of the speakers mentioned the necessity of making sermons interesting, though it must not be assumed that these were the only ones who favored the quality. Watson placed this element at the top of his list in saying that "The one indispensable quality of the former sermon was soundness —of the contemporary sermon that it be interesting." [29] In emphasizing this quality, Kelman gave an interesting explanation of the term.

> The secret of reality in preaching is intelligibility, and the secret of intelligibility is interest. "Interest," "interesting," are to be understood in their etymological sense —*inter est*—that which is common to speaker and hearer, that which they have between them. Allow me to insist upon this first necessity.[30]

The lecturer who spoke most fully of the need for interestingness was Dale. "Monotony is almost always fatal to interest; monotony of voice, monotony of style, monotony of intellectual activity," [31] was his comment upon the subject. A few moments earlier in the same lecture he had suggested certain appeals by which interest may be secured.

> We ought to remember that for an ordinary speaker to excite and maintain the interest of his audience it is indispensable that he should appeal to various susceptibilities of emotion and bring into play various intellectual powers.[32]

Lastly, he visualized the ideal sermon-interest situation for his hearers.

[28] Parkhurst, *op. cit.*, p. 50.
[29] Watson, *op. cit.*, p. 80.
[30] Kelman, *op. cit.*, p. 12.
[31] Dale, *op. cit.*, p. 33.
[32] *Loc. cit.*

. . . I am bound to maintain that it is your business
to make your sermons so interesting, that the people, so
far from having to make an effort to think of what you
are saying to them, shall have to make an effort to think
of anything else.[33]

SENSATIONALISM

Ten of the Lyman Beecher lecturers condemned sensational
preaching. It is interesting to note that while only four of the
speakers were found to indicate the need for interestingness
in the sermon, ten pointed out the danger of too great a
striving for interest and attention. A passage from William
Herbert Perry Faunce showed, among other things, the close-
ness of the relationship between attention and interest on the
one hand and sensationalism on the other.

Any man can secure attention for a few Sundays—but
can he hold it for twenty years? Any man can secure absorbing interest by sensationalism in speech or garb or
action; but the penalty of using strong spices is that the
quantity of spice must be constantly increased to stir the
jaded palate. Mere exhortation soon becomes wearisome
to him that gives and him that takes. Physical fervor will
not long serve as substitute for ideas. Pulmonary eloquence soon exhausts itself and its audience.[34]

Simpson pointed out still another weakness of sensational
preaching.

You should discourage that sensational preaching
which, while it excites the curiosity and fancy, is of no
permanent value. There is a class of preachers who always
advertise their topics, and who very generally endeavor to
draw some persons by the quaintness or eccentricity of
their titles.[35]

---

[33] *Ibid.*, p. 35.
[34] William Herbert Perry Faunce, *The Educational Ideal in the Ministry*
(New York: The Macmillan Company, 1908), p. 169.
[35] Simpson, *op. cit.*, p. 136.

Kelman denounced sensational methods in no uncertain terms:

> Smartness of any kind is out of place in preaching. Smartness is trick-preaching, and brings the level down from that of the chariot racer to that of the circus horse. All stagy cleverness, all intentional accidents and deliberately prepared impromptus, are to be condemned.[36]

In a footnote, he cited sensational sermon titles:

> Smartness in advertised titles of sermons is an abomination against which I would fain warn you. It is cheap to begin with, and brands a man as a vender of cheap wares. And, besides that, there are but few preachers so unfortunate as to be able to keep it up. You begin with advertising as your subject "The Prodigal from the point of view of the Fatted Calf," or "The submarine experiences of Jonah": you end with advertising "A good man," or "A noble race." As if any self-respecting man would cross the street to hear you on the latter subject, or would not flee into another city rather than hear you on the former.[37]

Broadus was another to warn against sensationalism.

> There is, however, a marked difference between freshness and *sensation* in preaching. In trying to be fresh, preachers sometimes succeed only in being sensational. Pertinency and timeliness in the application of Christian truth to the real present life and its grave problems are supremely important, but ministering to the prurient curiosity of the excited crowd, assailing men and measures with cheap and unseemly invective, spending valuable time and strength in discussing mere side issues which have been unduly exaggerated for the time being into momentous concerns,—this is sensationalism. It is true that in this whole matter discrimination is both necessary and difficult. A man is not likely to think himself sensational,—he is only keeping up with the times;

[36] Kelman, *op. cit.*, p. 161.
[37] *Loc. cit.*

the ranter around the corner is the blatant sensationalist!
Each man is thus a law unto himself,—only let him be
most careful that there is some law in the case.[38]

Hall was primarily concerned with tricks in the pulpit.

> There should be *manliness* both in composition and
> delivery. Any trick obviously meant to startle; any at-
> tempt at stage-effect; any small device that might be
> proper enough in an after-dinner speech is felt to be un-
> worthy the pulpit, and is condemned by good taste. Man-
> liness implies straightforward simplicity, appreciation of
> the truths presented, and superiority to theatrical expe-
> dients. Many of the stories retailed in gossiping reports
> regarding eminent men are either colored or exag-
> gerated; but there are well-authenticated accounts of
> great men descending to small shifts of ingenuity which
> you and I had better not imitate, and which even they
> could not have used often with success.[39]

Striving for effect to the point of unreality was condemned by
Tucker.

> A second point at which unreality may come into the
> pulpit is through undue striving after effect. . . . Truth
> must have a hearing. But when we take unfit, exag-
> gerated, unscrupulous methods to get a hearing for the
> truth, we rob it of its reality. Here is the vice of sensa-
> tionalism. Truth in the hands of a sensationalist does not
> impress us with its reality. We discount so much that the
> little which is left is ineffective. . . . And all like striv-
> ings for effect, whether in style of speech or manner of
> delivery, fall under the same charge of unreality.[40]

Faunce spoke of the possibility of dishonoring God through
sensational preaching.

> But a minister who is to be an ethical teacher must at
> least resolve that he will never, in order to be vivid and
> effective, violate the deepest convictions of our moral

[38] Broadus, *op. cit.*, pp. 149–50.
[39] Hall, *op. cit.*, p. 169.
[40] Tucker, *op. cit.*, pp. 64–65.

nature, or dishonor God in the very attempt to bring him nearer to man.[41]

Six of the preachers who addressed the Yale Divinity School spoke of that phase of style which can best be indicated by the term "elegance." Of the six, Broadus was the only one to find it desirable, or even permissible. He said of it:

> Elegance, in speaking, is less important than perspicuity or energy, but it greatly contributes to the objects of even the most serious discourse. Real elegance will of course be widely modified by subject, occasion, and design; and thus modified, it is free from all just objection, and worthy of very earnest pursuit.[42]

Although the other lecturers probably visualized a more extended use of elegance than did Broadus, they left no inferences in their speeches that it might ever receive their approval. Faunce spoke more fully upon the subject than did the others. In his first lecture he said:

> An age in which "economy of attention" is proposed as the basis of good writing has no time or inclination for the sonorous periods, the word-painting, the perorations of other days. A good style, written or spoken, is like a pane of clear glass through which we can see all objects in true proportion and perspective. A bad or "eloquent" style is like a stained-glass window—men look at it but cannot see through it. The directness, sincerity and simplicity of public speech in our time makes the "pulpit orator" as much out of place as the sounding-board and the hour-glass.[43]

A moment later in the same discourse, he added another paragraph concerning the elaborate style.

> The elaborate works on homiletics which once were on every minister's shelves now seem curiously cumbersome

41 Faunce, *op. cit.*, p. 130.
42 Broadus, *op. cit.*, p. 405.
43 Faunce, *op. cit.*, pp. 17–18.

and antiquated. They conceived the sermon as a work of art or architecture, something to be built up piece by piece, consisting always of the same sort of introduction, proposition, development, etc.—something ingenious, artificial, and too often lifeless. Preachers of that school thought far more of the development of a subject than the attainment of an object, and when we hear one of them to-day, he seems ghostly and unreal. The pulpit is not a place for display of rhetorical or logical skill, not an easel for a work of art, not a "throne of eloquence." It is an opportunity to grapple with human lives; it offers "thirty minutes to wake the dead in." [44]

Beecher spoke of the natural style in relation to the literary style in this manner:

> Above all other men, the preacher should avoid what may be called a literary style, as distinguished from a natural one; and by a "literary style," technically so called, I understand one in which abound these two elements,—the artificial structure of sentences, and the use of words and phrases peculiar to literature alone, and not to common life. [45]

The beautiful style was the subject of Jefferson's censure:

> A beautiful style, so beautiful that the rustling of the verbal finery drowns the music of the thought, is also a burden. When all the sentences roll out after the fashion of those of Macaulay or of Burke, men sigh for relief. The best pulpit style is the style that is not seen. Blessed is the preacher who succeeds in beating his style down into invisibility. [46]

In speaking of the sermon, Dale said, "Mere ornament, instead of making our meaning clearer, is likely to conceal it, just as architectural decoration sometimes conceals the true

[44] *Ibid.*, p. 18.
[45] Beecher, *op. cit.*, I, 229.
[46] Jefferson, *op. cit.*, p. 284.

lines of a building." [47] John Brown used Dale as an example in drawing the following conclusion:

> So we come to this: the lesson other preachers may learn from Dr. Dale's self-revelations is that *stateliness* of style, elaborate literary finish, even in the hands of a master, is *not* the most effective style for the pulpit. That which may make a man's work good as literature may mar it for spoken discourse.[48]

ORIGINALITY

Nine speakers called attention to the need for originality in preaching. The various expressions concerning this element fall logically into two distinct groups. First, there were several of the lecturers who called for the preacher's style to be his own, hence, original. Second, there were several who expressed a desire for the preacher to vary his own style from time to time to prevent monotony.

Expressing the first point of view was Kelman.

> Style is concerned with the manner, as contrasted with the matter, the form rather than the essence, of a man's utterance. It is true that style as much as matter—perhaps even more than matter—is given by a man's own personality, of which it is or ought to be the natural expression.[49]

Brooks declared himself in favor of individuality in style when he said, "Every preacher's sermon style, then, ought to be his own; that is the first principle of sermon-making. 'The style is the man,' said Buffon." [50] Broadus was another to speak of individuality in preaching style.

> And then in the choice of topics, the construction of discourse, the illustration and application of truth, a preacher may perpetually devise what shall be in some

[47] Dale, *op. cit.*, p. 44.
[48] John Brown, *op. cit.*, pp. 257–58.
[49] Kelman, *op. cit.*, p. 154.
[50] Brooks, *op. cit.*, p. 147.

respects fresh, and relatively to him, original. And in fact a man has *his own* way of presenting any subject whatever, which derives power from association with his personality; and other things being equal, this is for him *the best way*. "Put honor upon your individuality." [51]

Dale, putting the same principle in negative terms, said, "You will not, if you are wise, try to imitate the style of any of the men whom you admire." [52]

The second phase of the subject of originality concerns the problem of avoiding monotony. Jowett said on this point:

> When all the preliminary labour is finished, and you begin to write your message, let me advise you not to be the bondslave to much-worn phraseology, and to forms of expression which have ceased to be significant. . . . A "new way of putting a thing" awakens zest and interest where the customary expression might leave the hearer listless and indifferent.[53]

Dale spoke of the part that imagination plays in an original, interesting style.

> The difference between vivid and languid speaking depends very largely upon the extent to which the imagination contributes in this way to the expression of thought. The imaginative speaker instinctively rejects words, phrases, symbols, which are incapable of being animated with vital warmth. He rejects them as a tree rejects withered leaves and dead wood. His style is alive in every fibre of it.[54]

Robinson said of the need of variety in preaching style:

> The preacher who ministers stately to the same congregation needs, above all men, the power, if he can possibly acquire it, of varying his style with the varying subjects of his discourses. No matter how admirable the

[51] Broadus, *op. cit.,* p. 131.
[52] Dale, *op. cit.,* p. 169.
[53] Jowett, *op. cit.,* pp. 138–39.
[54] Dale, *op. cit.,* p. 47.

style he may have acquired, it cannot be the fittest for all subjects.[55]

Charles Reynolds Brown was another to mention the need for variation.

> It is well for the young preacher especially to avoid sameness in his sermon plans. He will greatly weaken his power if he undertakes to pour all the refined silver and gold of the Bible into one or two narrow sets of molds. He had better vary the pattern as he mints the unsearchable riches into coins which will serve as a circulating medium in the King's business.[56]

"Every preacher, no matter how talented," said Jefferson, "needs all available weapons for the slaying of that arch enemy of all preachers—Monotony." [57] Calkins dealt in vigorous language with preaching that lacks freshness and originality.

> Such preaching suffers from the want of variety. A minister conceives of the Gospel in certain terms, and he comes to the point where he can present it in those terms and in none other. Small wonder, then, if congregations become restive. . . . Many ministers commit professional suicide at just this point and then imagine themselves to be martyrs. They think they have suffered as a result of their moral fearlessness; as a matter of fact it is as a result of their wrong-headedness. It is not because they were so brave, but because they were so foolish.[58]

Broadus spoke of the yearning a congregation often has for something different to come out of the pulpit.

> The plan ought to be *simple*, not only free from obscurity, but free from all straining after effect, and yet ought, so far as possible, to be *fresh* and striking. So many sermons follow the beaten track, in which we can soon foresee all that is coming, as to make it a weary task even for devout hearers to listen attentively. One feels inclined

[55] Robinson, *op. cit.*, p. 156.
[56] Charles Reynolds Brown, *The Art of Preaching*, p. 76.
[57] Jefferson, *op. cit.*, p. 260.
[58] Calkins, *op. cit.*, p. 156.

to utter a plaintive cry, "Worthy brother, excellent brother, if you could only manage to drive us sometimes over a different road, even if much less smooth, even if you do not know it very well—I am so tired of this!" [59]

UNITY

Two of the Yale lecturers named the quality of unity as desirable in the sermon. Watson called for singleness of thought.

A sermon ought to be a monograph and not an encyclopedia, an agency for pushing one article, not a general store where one can purchase anything from a button to a coffin.[60]

Dale had issued the same advice several years earlier.

We should all preach more effectively if, instead of tasking our intellectual resources to say a great many things in the same sermon, we tried to say a very few things in a great many ways.[61]

SUMMARY

To suggest that the preacher should pay careful attention to the development of a good style is not to say that his manner is more important than his matter. The chief concern is with the message, but the message ought not to be handicapped by a bad style. While it is true that a poor message cannot be made good by a good style, it is equally true that a good message may be rendered ineffective by a poor style. The wise preacher, therefore, gives thoughtful attention to the development of a good style so that it may reinforce the content of the sermon.

When developed, the good style first of all makes the message clear. Its chief function is to create in the minds of the

59 Broadus, *op. cit.*, p. 278.
60 Watson, *op. cit.*, p. 18.
61 Dale, *op. cit.*, p. 150.

hearers the exact ideas which the speaker wishes them to have. In achieving its goal of clarity, the good style is concrete rather than vague or indefinite.

Instead of being dull, the desired style will be interesting, yet in emphasizing interest qualities it does not become sensational. Sensational sermons are undoubtedly interesting, but in striving overmuch for attention these sermons fail to accomplish the higher goals of preaching. Beauty or elegance, likewise, is dangerous for it may distract from the real purpose of the sermon by its own prominence. Originality endeavors to prevent dullness and lack of interest, yet it does not possess the dangers of sensationalism. The preacher needs to be original in the sense that he develops his own style rather than imitating the style of another. He also needs originality in order to achieve a wide variety of treatment within his own range of style. Still another of the desired elements is unity. The sermon should develop one theme well, rather than several themes sketchily. The hunter is wise who aims at a single squirrel rather than at the whole tree.

Chapter VIII

ADDITIONAL ELEMENTS OF STYLE

In addition to the elements of style discussed in the last chapter as desirable for the preacher, three other elements were given extended treatment in the Yale lectures. Inasmuch as these elements are somewhat different from those listed in the last chapter, they are given separate consideration. In the order in which they appear here, they are: the illustrations, the language, and the organization of the sermon.

ILLUSTRATION

Almost a score of the Yale lecturers commented on the importance of illustrations in the sermon. Although there were exceptions, the remarks made by the various speakers usually developed through three phases. First, the use of the illustration was commended. Second, the various uses to which the illustration may be put were named. Finally, strong warnings were sounded against various misuses of the illustration. In so far as is possible, the present discussion follows these three phases in the order named.

"Every sermon should have illustrations," said Simpson. "They are like pictures to the eye which rivet attention, and help to fasten the truth in the memory." [1] Another to commend the use of the illustration was Charles Reynolds Brown.

The illustration is a concrete picture as distinguished from the dry, abstract statement of truth. Now all children love pictures—they must have them. The people

1 Simpson, *op. cit.*, p. 147.

in our congregations for the most part are only grown-up children.[2]

Watson said that:

Illustrations are of the last value to a sermon, because they both give colour to the style and interest to the thought, and the preacher ought to practise the art with diligence.[3]

In giving his approval to the art of illustrating sermons, Crosby enumerated the breadth of the area from which illustrations may be drawn.

Without this general knowledge, he [the preacher] is, moreover, unable to illustrate truth pointedly and entertainingly. The metaphor, simile, and analogy which play so important a part in all public speaking to the general mind, should be drawn from a copious reservoir containing a large variety, and to this end the preacher should have his mind well informed in the various departments of knowledge which are represented in the members of his congregation, as well as in those which are unknown to them, and yet might furnish apt elucidations of important truth. The homely illustrations drawn from the trades and occupations of men, as well as the illustrations from the discoveries of physical science, are equally potent to arrest the attention and to secure the memory. The study of nature is a fruitful source of this power, and every preacher should be a close observer of animate and inanimate life. The greater the variety that is ready at the subject's call, the more interesting will be the presentation of the more recondite truth.[4]

Like Crosby, Scherer gave advice concerning the best methods of securing good illustrations.

Certainly the most effective of all illustrations are the scenes, the incidents, the stories, from Scripture, from fiction, from life, that come most readily to a well-

2 Charles Reynolds Brown, *The Art of Preaching,* p. 124.
3 Watson, *op. cit.,* p. 51.
4 Crosby, *op. cit.,* p. 65.

furnished mind, so readily that they seem themselves to be integral parts in the movement of the whole. They are not often to be had from books of so-called illustrative matter, though no doubt at the beginning we all use such first-aid kits; but in the end, nothing that is set down there is really yours. That is the trouble with it: it is alien, it has not your spirit, it does not speak your language. Let me urge you to gather your own, if you must be a gleaner of them; index them as you go, if you have a bent for such methodical practice; better still, review them, appropriate them, get them somehow into your very system, so that they come running with a kind of inevitableness when your need of them is hardly conscious. That way and no other, by open-eyed awareness and the fixed habit of assimilation, on a day not too far distant, the dividends will begin trickling in. For a while it may be nothing more than a trickle; but things will improve. It is in this realm, too, that the rewards of diligence are most sure.[5]

Horton gave the subject of illustration a prominent place in his series of lectures, recommending its widespread use.

It may seem to some to be giving a disproportionate place to the subject of Illustration, when I select it from the innumerable points of the preacher's craft, and set it among the five [technical points of the preaching art]. But it is in many cases the crucial point for one who is to teach and lead a mixed congregation, and therefore a student cannot turn his attention to it too soon. Abstract modes of thought grow upon us too easily when we spend much time with books, and in the reverie of study. Illustrations become tiresome and impertinent to a trained thinker. The fascination of close and connected reasoning, and of convincing the understanding by logical methods, becomes almost irresistible to a growing mind. To breathe in the higher circles of thought, and to see the small matters of the field or the market-place from a serene altitude, is undoubtedly proper to a philosopher; and if a preacher studies diligently, and exer-

[5] Scherer, *op. cit.*, pp. 185–86.

cises himself in the company of great thinkers, he is apt
to become a philosopher, and insensibly to drift away
from common life, and lose touch with ordinary people.[6]

A moment later in the same lecture, he concluded his point
with the following paragraph:

> If, then, we would interest them in the affairs of the
> heavenly kingdom, we must, like the King Himself,
> speak in parables or allegories. Our discourse must be of
> tangible things and familiar persons while we suggest
> the invisible and the eternal.[7]

The second phase of the discussion of the illustration was
the enumeration of its uses. Charles Reynolds Brown [8] named
four: (1) it makes one's meaning more clear; (2) it helps
people to remember the truths taught; (3) it is capable of
varied and continued application; and (4) it serves to show
how unity of purpose and of method runs through all things.
Taylor [9] listed the following uses of the illustration: (1) it
helps to make the thought clear; (2) it exerts a force of proof
which helps to persuade; (3) it awakens and sustains interest;
and (4) the impressions it helps to produce are longer remembered. Broadus spoke of the influence which the illustration may have upon the emotions.

> They [illustrations] also frequently serve to render a
> subject impressive, by exciting some kindred or prepara-
> tory emotion. . . . Most preachers use illustrations very
> freely for this purpose. The story or description may have
> some value for explanation, proof, or ornament, but their
> chief object in employing it is to arouse the feelings.[10]

Later in the same lecture he enumerated still other uses:

> The importance of illustration in preaching is beyond
> expression. In numerous cases it is our best means of ex-

[6] Horton, *op. cit.*, pp. 284–85.
[7] *Ibid.*, p. 286.
[8] Charles Reynolds Brown, *The Art of Preaching*, pp. 126–29.
[9] Taylor, *The Ministry of the Word*, pp. 186–91.
[10] Broadus, *op. cit.*, pp. 227–28.

plaining religious truth, and often to the popular mind
our only means of proving it. Ornament, too, has its
legitimate place in preaching, and whatever will help us
to move the hard hearts of men is unspeakably valuable.
Besides, for whatever purpose illustration may be specially employed, it often causes the truth to be remembered.[11]

Beecher spoke of the illustration in its relationship to reasoning.

Now an illustration is a window in an argument, and
lets in light. You may reason without an illustration;
but where you are employing a process of pure reasoning
and have arrived at a conclusion, if you can then by an
illustration flash back light upon what you have said,
you will bring into the minds of your audience a realization of your argument that they cannot get in any other
way. I have seen an audience, time and again, follow an
argument, doubtfully, laboriously, almost suspiciously,
and look at one another, as much as to say, "Is he going
right?"—until the place is arrived at, where the speaker
says, "It is like—" and then they listen eagerly for what
it is like; and when some apt illustration is thrown out
before them, there is a sense of relief, as though they
said, "Yes, he is right." [12]

He also spoke of instruction as a major function of the illustration.

Experience has taught that not only are persons pleased
by being instructed through illustration, but that they
are more readily instructed thus, because, substantially,
the mode in which we learn a new thing is by its being
likened to something which we already know. This is
the principle underlying all true illustrations.[13]

Beecher mentioned as one other use to which the illustration
may be put, its utility as a means of enforcing a point by indirection.

11 *Ibid.*, p. 228.
12 Beecher, *op. cit.*, I, 158.
13 *Ibid.*, pp. 154–55.

There are many very important themes which a minister may not desire to preach openly upon, for various reasons, especially if he wish to remain in the parish. But there are times when you can attain your object by an illustration pointed at the topic, without indicating whom you are hitting, but continuing your sermon as though you were utterly unconscious of the effect of your blow.[14]

The third phase of the discussion of the place of the illustration in preaching was the sounding of warnings against misuse. Taylor pointed out certain uses to which illustrations might not legitimately be put.

When illustrations will help to make your argument more simple, they are to be used with discretion; but when they are employed purely for the sake of the stories of which they consist, and to hide the poverty of the thuoght [thought], they are a snare to the preacher and an offence to the hearer.[15]

Horton also placed a limitation upon the use of illustrations.

And lest this counsel should be abused, let me observe that, while to string together anecdotes in which "thrill is everything and relevancy nothing," is the easiest and most shambling mode of popular and idle speech; to get and to use real illustrations—illustrations, that is, which actually illustrate, and are not only brought in to show their own brilliance—is a very laborious task, demanding very careful study and close observation, a methodical collection of incidents and facts, and a long meditation on the eternal relation between Nature, which Goethe called the garment of God, and God who is the Interpreter, as He is the Creator, of Nature. No idle man can use illustrations or tell anecdotes properly—and yet they are the constant resource of the idle.[16]

---

14 *Ibid.*, p. 166.
15 Taylor, *The Ministry of the Word,* pp. 183–84.
16 Horton, *op. cit.,* pp. 288–89.

Jowett called attention to the function which illustrations are designed to perform, and condemned their use unless they perform this function.

> And as for the illustrations we may use in our exposition of a truth I have only one word to say. An illustration that requires explanation is worthless. A lamp should do its own work. I have seen illustrations that were like pretty drawing-room lamps, calling attention to themselves. A real preacher's illustrations are like street lamps, scarcely noticed, but throwing floods of light upon the road. Ornamental lamps will be of little or no use to you: honest street-lamps will serve your purpose at every turning.[17]

Brooks proposed a test for the selection of illustration.

> Let me offer only a few suggestions upon one or two other points, and first with regard to illustrations. The Christian sermon deals with all life, and may draw its illustrations from the widest range. The first necessity of illustration is that it should be true, that is, that it should have real relations to the subject which it illustrates. An illustration is properly used in preaching either to give clearness or to give splendor to the utterance of truth. Both objects, I believe, are legitimate. . . . But both sorts of illustration, as you see, have this characteristic: they exist for the truth. They are not counted of value for themselves. That is the test of illustration which you ought to apply unsparingly. Does it call attention to or call attention away from my truth? If the latter, cut it off without a hesitation.[18]

Scherer, in giving his test for illustrations, sounded the same warning that Brooks had given earlier.

> If your congregation has to leave the main thread of your discourse, travel away to something that was intended to illumine but has succeeded only in distracting, then come back to the thought again—that always hap-

17 Jowett, *op. cit.*, pp. 140–41.
18 Brooks, *op. cit.*, pp. 175–76.

pens when you force the last good story you heard to come in and do yeoman's service on Sunday morning under division II, subhead 1a, whether it fits or not; when your people cannot quite get the point of your illustration, or get it ten minutes before you arrive at it, or like it so well that they sit down inside of it with a chuckle and bring their lunch: in every such event you have stultified your own purpose, utterly, devastatingly. And the darkness is all the more intense for the light that failed.[19]

Sockman indicated the undesirable results which may come from certain misuses of illustrative material.

Life-situation preaching need not be limited to the minister's own experience. The range of reality can be extended through reading, especially the reading of biography. Illustrations from the lives of historical personalities are far more arresting and convincing than analogies, however clever. But let us be very careful about the historicity of our biographical material. And let us not in Emil Ludwig fashion take liberties with the minds of celebrities by reading plausible motives into their actions. Integrity is as truly a Christian virtue as is piety. Many a thoughtful listener has lost confidence in a preacher's reliability because of slovenly inaccuracies in literary or biographical allusions.[20]

The warning issued by Robinson concerned reasoning by analogy.

There is a semblance of reasoning sometimes indulged in by preachers, that ought to be used with a little more caution than it commonly is. I refer to the use of illustrative analogies. An argument from analogy is as sound as any other, where there is an undoubted analogy to reason from. But it is an old device of sophistry to make an apparent analogy—an apt illustration—do the work of a real argument. And sometimes even well-intentioned public speakers, preachers included, are themselves misled by striking resemblances. It may be the habit of an

[19] Scherer, op. cit., p. 185.
[20] Sockman, op. cit., pp. 119-20.

animal, or it may be a process of nature, that is appealed to. Accidental points of resemblance are seized on; a parallel is carefully drawn; the result is an apparently sound argument from analogy; but it is nothing more than an apt illustration. Imaginative preachers often abound in these. Working them up with great skill, they are themselves often as much misled by them as their hearers. And it is not extremely rare that the resemblance appealed to is only apparent. Exact knowledge would show that, as an illustration even, not to say argument, the supposed analogue is wholly illusive.[21]

Behrends, too, spoke of the illustration in connection with reasoning.

Illustrations are impressive and useful, so long as they are used by way of suggestion; but they are mischievous when they are charged with the office of logical construction; and a very large part of the preacher's intellectual task consists in seizing the vital truth, which hides behind all analogies, and which must not be allowed to become imprisoned in any, using them all, dispensing with them all, and creating more fitting ones, as the case may require.[22]

Condemning certain methods of collecting illustrations, Greer said:

. . . an apt illustration in preaching is always helpful. But here let me say, in passing, that it must be an illustration which is the preacher's own; not necessarily one which he has invented and in that sense made his own, but one that he has found in the course of his general reading.[23]

In the same lecture he added:

Illustrations in preaching are good; but they must be illustrations drawn, not from books of stories and encyclopaedias of anecdotes, but from that general fund of

[21] Robinson, *op. cit.*, p. 150.
[22] Behrends, *op. cit.*, p. 204.
[23] Greer, *op. cit.*, p. 151.

knowledge which by his personal study the preacher has made his own. Then they are good and helpful, and may be legitimately used.[24]

Charles Reynolds Brown spoke in full agreement on this point.

I would also cast out all those tempting encyclopedias of illustration. There are volumes on sale which contain vast collections of illustrations and stories applicable to every situation in life. They are all there arranged in alphabetical order and "ready to serve," like the soups and the spaghetti advertised in the street cars, only not nearly so appetizing. But the man who preceded you may have used the same encyclopedia of illustration. The people in the congregation may have already eaten all of those "fifty-seven varieties" of canned goods several times over. Your predecessor in that pulpit may indeed have so far forgotten himself—even ordained flesh sometimes shows itself weak at this point, though the spirit be willing—as to tell some of those thrilling stories as experiences of his own. If you begin to tell them all over again, as personal experiences which have come to you, your people will have thoughts in their hearts.[25]

Jefferson showed how illustrations should be developed in order to be effective in the sermon.

Illustrations are also a nuisance, unless they grow up naturally like flowers along the path which the sermon takes. Expert illustrators grow irksome after the second year.[26]

Buttrick condemned certain types of illustrations.

A sermon without illustrations is like a house without windows. A sermon with trivial or bathetic illustrations is worse: it is like a house with the windows broken, and the holes stuffed with rags and straw.[27]

24 *Ibid.*, p. 152.
25 Charles Reynolds Brown, *The Art of Preaching*, pp. 73–74.
26 Jefferson, *op. cit.*, p. 284.
27 Buttrick, *op. cit.*, p. 159.

While commending the use of illustrations, Kelman also referred to the way in which they are told.

> Another point is the use of illustration and anecdote. I need not remind you of the immense value of this, in sustaining interest, breaking the strain of continuous pursuit of a theme without losing the thread of the discourse, and driving home the point illustrated. But the story needs to be well told, and every preacher should give earnest attention and deliberate study to the art of telling a story. It is a thing which everybody supposes himself to be able to do, and which surprisingly few can really do well. On the other hand, the effect of illustration will depend to a considerable extent upon the sparing use of it. When a sermon degenerates into a string of anecdotes it is lost. As in the case of quotation, so here, no anecdote should ever be told for the sake of the anecdote, but only because it forwards the object of the sermon.[28]

LANGUAGE

Almost as many of the speakers included admonition on the subject of language as had discussed illustrations. Agreement was nearly unanimous in the views expressed on the subject, for most of the speakers called for two things: simple, understandable language, and language which expresses the thought clearly and accurately.

Inasmuch as Beecher spoke first in point of time, his remarks are given first consideration here.

> I have known a great many most admirable preachers who lost almost all real sympathetic hold upon their congregations because they were too literary, too periphrastic, and too scholastic in their diction. They always preferred to use large language, rather than good Saxon English. But let me tell you, there is a subtle charm in the use of plain language that pleases people, they scarcely know why. It gives bell-notes which ring out suggestions to the popular heart. There are words that

28 Kelman, op. cit., pp. 160–61.

men have heard when boys at home, around the hearth
and the table, words that are full of father and of mother,
and full of common and domestic life. Those are the
words that afterward, when brought into your discourse,
will produce a strong influence on your auditors, giving
an element of success; words which will have an effect
that your hearers themselves cannot understand. For,
after all, simple language is loaded down and stained
through with the best testimonies and memories of life.[29]

Charles Reynolds Brown described the types of words which
the preacher should, and should not, use in addressing his
audience.

You are to speak "to every man in the tongue in which
he was born." Now no man was ever "born" in the professional patois of the theological school or the philosophical
club. The Lord who is merciful and gracious would
not allow it—he would not permit any innocent child
to start off with such a cruel handicap. It is a habit and
a bad habit at that. It is an acquired taste and in the
presence of an untrained public a vicious taste. It may
be well enough to speak that language when we are addressing those who thoroughly understand it but not
otherwise. If you would interest and influence everyday
people you must speak to them habitually in the language of everyday life.[30]

Behrends suggested the same type of language for use in the
pulpit.

The current speech may not be as classical and polished as your scholarly tastes might wish it were, but
you must take it as you find it, avoid its coarseness, and
make the best use of it possible. You may not ignore
it, any more than you would ignore the coat, vest, and
pantaloons, which society has adopted as a man's regula-
tion dress.[31]

[29] Beecher, op. cit., I, 131.
[30] Charles Reynolds Brown, The Art of Preaching, p. 116.
[31] Behrends, op. cit., p. 221.

Tucker advised several restrictions upon the use of words:

> . . . the words employed in the sermon [must] be
> the words of well understood and accepted speech. They
> must be current words. Some preachers need to take
> their ideas to the exchangers. They will not always re-
> ceive in return short, homely words. A term of Latin
> derivation may be more common than its corresponding
> Saxon form. Familiarity is the chief test. Still, the pref-
> erence goes with the strong, sinewy, terse word rather
> than with the more elegant or even more scrupulously
> exact word. I commend to you the advice which Charles
> Kingsley puts into the mouth of the wife of the country
> esquire of Harthover House: "So she made Sir John
> write to the 'Times' to command the Chancellor of the
> Exchequer for the time being to put a tax on long words:
> a light tax on words of over three syllables, which are
> necessary evils, like rats, but which like them must be
> kept down judiciously; a heavy tax on words of over four
> syllables, such as heterodoxy, spontaneity, spuriosity, and
> the like; and on words of over five syllables a totally pro-
> hibitory tax, and a similar prohibitory tax on words
> derived from three or more languages at the same
> time." [32]

Calkins was equally emphatic in his disapproval of certain
types of language.

> All great preachers are the simple preachers. . . .
> Academic language is the curse and ruin of preaching.
> You cannot be too simple in your phrasing, whatever
> you are in thought. You will weary people with high-
> sounding rhetoric, copious quotation, and vague phi-
> losophy. But if you try out of your own experience to
> speak in language that is simple, in ways that are solid
> and true, and applied to their experience, people will
> not become wearied at all. And simplicity of manner
> may well accompany simplicity of diction. [33]

[32] Tucker, *op. cit.*, pp. 106–7.
[33] Calkins, *op. cit.*, pp. 142–43.

Twelve years before Calkins, Horne had expressed a similar view.

> I cannot explain to you just why it is, that the true prophet is always a master of simple speech, but it is certain that no man can speak home to the hearts of his fellow-men without it.[34]

On the matter of the preacher's vocabulary, Jefferson used phraseology similar to that of Charles Reynolds Brown, who was quoted above.

> If the preacher desires to create a sympathetic and social temper, he will pay attention to his vocabulary. He will eschew so far as possible all technical and abstract words. Words which are cold and unfamiliar will be promptly banished and only those retained which the heart knows. Words used by specialists and words born in distant lands will give place to the native words which are used in street and school and home. To come close to men the preacher must speak to them in the language in which they were born. It is the words of the mother tongue which find the blood. There is a necromancy in language and a preacher ought to understand and use its magic. Words in themselves are powers and have strange potencies to awaken desires, quicken impulses, create ambitions, give shape to ideals and direction to feelings, and kindle all those subtle flames which burn upon the soul's central altars. Some preachers use a vocabulary cold enough to form icicles. Their sermons sound like pages torn from an almanac, or a text-book, or a volume of statistics. They are not acquainted with the words which poets use nor can they speak the syllables which start and feed a fire. Words have moods as people do, and the preacher must be master of the words which carry in their hearts the dispositions which he desires to communicate to his people. There are reverent, kneeling words, warm, tender and affectionate words, open-handed, open-hearted, hospitable words, laughing, shouting, hallelujah words—words which are so rich in human

34 Horne, *op. cit.*, p. 204.

experience, so saturated with laughter and tears, that
if the preacher breaks them upon his congregation they
fill with perfume, like precious alabaster boxes, all the
place where he is preaching.[35]

In describing the type of words to be used in the pulpit,
Horton was in substantial agreement with those men who
were quoted above.

But the true vernacular in which men are to be approached, especially on high and momentous themes, is
that pure well of English undefiled which even common
minds, when they hear it, recognise as their real mother
tongue, and welcome with gratitude as an ennobling relief from the debased lingo and the nickel slang with
which they are too familiar.[36]

Simpson agreed with the speakers already quoted, in regard to
the matter of simplicity, but he mentioned other elements as
also desirable in the preacher's language.

Use such language as the people can understand;
though, while your language is simple, there is no reason why the gold in your sentences may not be burnished;
nor will your steel be less strong because it is polished.
. . . This plainness of speech must not, however, be
confounded with that which is low or trivial, much less
with what is vulgar.[37]

Jowett commented upon the use of elaborate language.

Is it not true that our language is often too big for
our thought, and our thought is like a spoonful of sad
wine rattling about in a very ornate and distinguished
bottle? Men may admire the bottle, but they find no
inspiration in the wine. Yes, men admire, but they do
not revere; they appreciate, but they do not repent; they
are interested, but they are not exalted. They say, "What
a fine sermon!" not, "What a great God!" They say,

[35] Jefferson, op. cit., pp. 149–51.
[36] Horton, op. cit., p. 279.
[37] Simpson, op. cit., pp. 151–52.

"What a ready speaker!" and not, "Oh, the depth of the
riches both of the wisdom and knowledge of God!" [38]

The second quality of language widely recommended by
the Yale lecturers was precision or accuracy. Taylor spoke
of this quality.

> As another quality of an effective sermon I name pre-
> cision of language. In a passage which I have already
> quoted it is said, "The preacher sought to find out ac-
> ceptable words." He did not take the first which came;
> but he selected those which best expressed his meaning,
> and were most suited to the people whom he was ad-
> dressing. The relation of style to thought is of the closest
> kind; and the aim of the preacher should be to get the
> clearest possible medium for the transmission of his
> thought. . . . So, if the end of language is to transmit
> thought, then everything in it that withdraws attention
> from the thought to itself, or dims the lustre of the
> thought, is a blemish.[39]

John Brown included in one of his lectures a quotation concerning accuracy of expression from the pen of Erasmus.

> In one of his letters Erasmus says to Colet: "You say
> what you mean, and mean what you say. Your words
> have birth in your heart, not on your lips. They follow
> your thoughts instead of your thoughts being shaped by
> them. You have the happy art of expressing with ease
> what others can hardly express with the greatest labor." [40]

Saying that, "We must use words and phrases that *exactly express* our thought," [41] Broadus stated the matter in terms of
necessity. Burton explained why it is necessary to select words
with care.

> But let us not pretend that these dice [words] we play
> with are perfect. If only they were, some questions would
> have been settled thousands of years ago. But how can
> they be settled when the coin of interchange is of inde-

[38] Jowett, *op. cit.*, p. 98.
[39] Taylor, *The Ministry of the Word*, p. 113.
[40] John Brown, *op. cit.*, p. 38.
[41] Broadus, *op. cit.*, p. 367.

terminate value? How much are those dimes and half dollars and dollars, that are flying about in such helter-skelter fashion? Nobody quite knows. Often, when a speaker passes a dollar, as he supposes, the man in the pew sees but ten cents in it. And occasionally the speaker's ten cents is worth a hundred dollars.[42]

In speaking of another aspect of style which is usually discussed as one of its chief elements, Brown was almost alone. Although others may have made slight reference to sentence and paragraph structure, he and Beecher were the only ones to pay very much attention to the matter. As quoted earlier, Beecher condemned "the artificial structure of sentences, and the use of words and phrases peculiar to literature alone. . . ."[43] Charles Reynolds Brown compared the effectiveness of the long circuitous sentence with that of the shorter, more direct sentence.

If it is a full Sabbath day's journey from a man's nominative case to his leading verb, there are a great many tired, reluctant minds in any congregation which will decline to make the trip. The sentence which moves straight from start to finish like an arrow shot from the bowstring to the target, without being too long about it, is always the more effective.[44]

Several lectures later the same speaker developed his point further:

If you would have a good speaking style use short words for the most part! Short sentences for the most part! The long involved sentence which looks like the map of an archipelago with various outlying islands of meaning and of qualifying clause scattered along on either side of the main body of land is fatal to an effective delivery. Short paragraphs, where you round out your treatment of some particular idea with measurable completeness and then pass on to something else! Put it clearly

42 Burton, *op. cit.*, p. 245.
43 Beecher, *op. cit.*, I, 229.
44 Charles Reynolds Brown, *The Art of Preaching*, pp. 101–2.

when you prepare your sermon if you would deliver it with power.[45]

Seventeen of the men who appeared before the Yale Divinity School affirmed a need for organization in the sermon. Not a great deal was said about the different parts of the sermon plan, the introduction, the body of the sermon, and the conclusion. Most of the speakers seemed content to recommend organization. Hall [46] suggested certain textbooks where further information could be found.

In making a list of four elements necessary to the attainment of plainness in the sermon, Tucker gave the following two which pertain to organization: ". . . second, that the sermon have order of thought. . . . And third, that the sermon have simple construction, or movement in its parts." [47] Burton gave several emphatic sentences upon the subject of organization.

> We have our topic; we have assembled our materials; and the next thing is to organize those materials; for let it be said to the credit of human auditors and congregations, they refuse to be blessed to the full by unarranged and disorderly masses of sermon matter, thrown out with whatever fine delivery, or whatever moral earnestness. It must be organized.[48]

Kelman also found occasion to speak of organization in one of his lectures.

> Thus the structure of the sermon may vary in many different ways, but the main point is that the sermon must have structure. It is true that only one or two of the hearers may recognise the presence or absence of struc-

[45] *Ibid.*, pp. 179–80.
[46] Hall, *op. cit.*, pp. 127–28.
[47] Tucker, *op. cit.*, pp. 105–6.
[48] Burton, *op. cit.*, p. 52.

ture for what it is; but they will all recognise the presence or absence of point, and point is the effect of structure.[49]

Another to express concern over the matter of organization was Sclater.

> The most severe criticism I have heard of our pulpit work today was given not long ago by a lady. "It's nearly all a knotless thread," she said. No grip, no catching-point in it. Much of it is clever; some of it—too much perhaps—is entertaining; a little of it is brilliant. But it can be all these and remain a knotless thread—a thing that slips through the mind, pleasantly it may be, like the sound of a very lovely voice, but ineffectively, leaving no trace.[50]

Merrill mentioned the issue of how clearly the audience should see the logical plan of the sermon.

> No less vital is the art of ordered thinking. In the long run men will be most impressed and most helped by sermons which, without making the logical framework stand out, nevertheless do proceed through ordered argument to a clearly indicated conclusion.[51]

In one of Charles Reynolds Brown's lectures there were a few sentences dealing with the question of how apparent the plan of organization should be.

> Have a solid backbone hidden away somewhere in your sermon so that it can stand up man-fashion and do its work. Organize your material around that spinal column, heads, arms, legs, fleshy parts, muscles to grip the people and nerves to respond to the movements of their own feelings, so that it may accomplish the desired end. You cannot afford to be one of those preachers who always give the impression that having lost the trail, they are now going hither and yon on any chance impulse like silly sheep which have erred and strayed from the way.

49 Kelman, op. cit., p. 151.
50 Sclater, op. cit., p. 88.
51 Merrill, op. cit., p. 34.

Have a definite plan but do not have it too much in evidence.[52]

Robinson also gave his opinion concerning the question of how conspicuous the organization of the sermon should be.

And here let it be distinctly understood that the plan of a sermon is never for its own sake. The less conspicuous it can be made, the better. The skeleton of a man is not outside of the flesh, but covered and concealed. It yet is none the less necessary because hidden. A sermon without a framework is but an intellectual mollusk; and mollusks can never do the work of vertebrates. The use and value of a plan is easily discerned. Even its necessity is apparent on a moment's reflection. Without it, those first two qualities of every effective sermon, transparency and unity, are impossible. All thought to be lucid must be orderly; and unity always requires articulation of parts. But it is not of the least possible consequence that the heads or divisions of a discourse should be remembered or even noticed.[53]

Another to give his view on the question under consideration was Broadus.

Distinctly marked divisions are not *necessary,* and need not be made where the plan of the discourse can be easily followed without them; only the preacher must remember, in judging on this point, that the plan is of course familiar to him, and his hearers may not note transitions which are obvious to his eye, unless attention be somehow called to them. But while not necessary, distinctly marked divisions will usually be of service, not only in making the train of thought plain to the hearers, but also of service to the preacher himself, both as compelling to logical correctness and completeness of preparation, and as helping him to remember, in extemporaneous delivery.[54]

[52] Charles Reynolds Brown, *The Art of Preaching*, pp. 107-8.
[53] Robinson, *op. cit.*, pp. 147-48.
[54] Broadus, *op. cit.*, p. 284.

Brooks expressed a point of view different from those quoted above.

> But give your sermon an orderly consistent progress, and do not hesitate to let your hearers see it distinctly, for it will help them first to understand and then to remember what you say.[55]

Like Brooks', Scherer's advice was to let the framework show.

> After you have determined what emphasis your subject and material call for, it is then that you begin to organize your thought under heads. And I am definitely of the opinion that it is well for the structure to show. There is no painting the human figure without some knowledge of human anatomy; and unless the framework is manifest to a degree, what you have is no longer human. It is either surrealism or it is a jellyfish. I have listened to sermons that without aim did "go round," as Browning has it, "in an eddy of purposeless dust, effort unending and vain." And I have preached them, too. The technique is not difficult. Like an Englishman at his bath, you plunge right in and splash around a bit. Having nothing to say which has seemed to you of sufficient importance to compel a clear analysis, you fill in the necessary time with a few remarks. You aim at nothing in particular, and hit it squarely in the middle. The only sane question a hearer can ask when it is over is, What on earth was it all about? And the only sane answer anyone can give is, About everything. On nothing. You are to have a framework—and let it show. . . .[56]

Simpson described two different types of organization, which are designed to fit two different types of minds.

> The structure of the sermon will vary according to the taste and mental habits of the individual. A man of systematic habits, of logical power, and of little imagination, will need his divisions accurately made to serve as steps of the stair-way on which he ascends. Those of a

[55] Brooks, *op. cit.*, p. 178.
[56] Scherer, *op. cit.*, p. 167.

more philosophical cast of mind, especially if blended with imagination, will see their subjects rather in the light of a growth. There will be the seed-thought, the young blade, the stalk, the leaves, the flower, the fruit, without precise divisions technically marked. The form of division is best for severe argumentation; of growth, for illustration.[57]

The part that arrangement plays in the process of persuasion was discussed by Broadus. He said that:

> . . . a good arrangement makes a discourse more *persuasive*. Both in presenting motives and in appeals to feeling, order is of great importance. He who wishes to break a hard rock with his sledge, does not hammer here and there over the surface, but multiplies his blows upon a certain point or along a certain line. They who lift up huge buildings apply their motive power systematically, at carefully chosen points. So when motives are brought to bear upon the will. And the hearer's feelings will be much more powerfully and permanently excited, when appeals are made in some natural order.[58]

Faunce indicated that in his day there was a definite trend away from one type of sermon organization toward an older type.

> For this reason, the former doctrinal sermon, in which logical coherence and demonstration were in the forefront, has now given way to a more human and direct approach in which the speaker closely grapples with his congregation, according to O'Connell's saying, "A great speech is a great thing; but after all the verdict is *the* thing." And this is a return to the earliest methods of the Christian church. The logical method was never employed by the Semitic mind. We are often puzzled because the sayings of our Lord are gnomic, epigrammatic, pictorial, startling us like a flashlight in a dark room, when our Western intellect expects propositions, major and minor premise, and irrefutable conclusion. We are

[57] Simpson, *op. cit.*, p. 140.
[58] Broadus, *op. cit.*, p. 263.

troubled and baffled because Christ seems interested in people rather than discourses, and persists in lighting up the recesses of human hearts instead of helping us in the formation of our creeds and theologies. But he was wiser than we are.[59]

A few additional sentences will serve to set forth this idea more clearly.

We do not care for sermons built up as a carpenter builds a row of houses, all of the same reiterated design. We demand novelty—novelty not by the addition of ornaments and anecdotes, but rather by new aspects of the subject which shall relate it to new parts of our own experience. We feel a repugnance to fourthly and fifthly, not (let us hope) because we dislike coherent thinking, but because the mere announcement of laborious subdivisions is a declaration that the preacher is primarily interested, not in the lives before him, but in the logical analysis of doctrine.[60]

It was Charles Reynolds Brown who warned the young preacher against the borrowing of sermon plans.

Let your plan be your own—strictly, exclusively, preeminently, your own. The sermon plan should be a thing as personal as a toothbrush. You will consult your own interest if you shun, as you would shun the plague, all those books of "sermon plans" wherein skeletons long since lifeless are steadily grinning at the foolish men who have been beguiled into walking in that graveyard in quest of outlines. Those books are known among the ungodly as "First Aids to the Lazy." [61]

The question of introductions was given a limited discussion by the Yale lecturers. Broadus spoke in favor of their use.

It can scarcely be necessary to argue at length to the effect that sermons ought generally to have an introduc-

[59] Faunce, *op. cit.*, pp. 171–72.
[60] *Ibid.*, pp. 170–71.
[61] Charles Reynolds Brown, *The Art of Preaching*, p. 77.

tion. Men have a natural aversion to abruptness, and delight in a somewhat gradual approach.[62]

Watson spoke in favor of a direct entrance into the subject at hand.

> This generation desires to be ushered into the subject of the day without wearisome preliminaries, and nothing will more certainly take the edge off the appetite than a laborious preface.[63]

In agreement with Watson, Abbott held that there is no real need for an introduction.

> As to introductions, generally the less introduction the better. The whole service of prayer and praise and Scripture reading has been introduction; that is, it has been preparing the mind and heart of the congregation for the message of the preacher. He who strikes the heart of his subject in the first sentence is the one most likely to secure an attentive listening at the outset of his discourse.[64]

Simpson recommended the use of a brief introduction.

> The introduction should have a proper relation to the length of the sermon. It stands as the portico of a building, the arched entrance and public pathway to a garden. Generally the introduction should be very brief, and should contain a simple exegesis of the text, the relation in which it stands, or some biblical or other incident which may prepare the mind for the coming train of thought.[65]

Pepper challenged the wisdom of the traditional text-announcement introduction.

> My suggestion is that the sermon should be begun in the way most appropriate to the particular occasion, and that, more often than not, this will require some other

[62] Broadus, *op. cit.*, p. 266.
[63] Watson, *op. cit.*, p. 30.
[64] Abbott, *op. cit.*, p. 215.
[65] Simpson, *op. cit.*, pp. 139–40.

opening than the announcement of a text from Scripture.[66]

Scherer's comment on the subject of introductions touched still a different point, for he suggested the proper time to prepare the introduction.

> Once we have got the main heads of our discourse clearly in mind, their relationships and sequences clearly indicated, the points arranged in the most telling order, without overlapping, driving on toward some great truth or obligation, for always man's only peace lies in his acceptance of a challenge, then it is time to block out the introduction and the conclusion. Not before, lest the introduction fail to introduce, and the conclusion fall short of concluding.[67]

The views of the various lecturers were so divergent concerning the necessity, length, and types of introductions that it can hardly be said that a trend was established.

Very few of the speakers chose to devote part of their limited time to a discussion of the conclusion of the sermon. Perhaps the comment of Broadus is of double significance when he points out that the conclusion is often neglected: "Preachers seldom neglect to prepare some introduction to a sermon, but very often neglect the conclusion; and yet the latter is even more important than the former." [68]

SUMMARY

The part of a discourse which makes the strongest and most lasting impression upon the average audience is that portion in which the preacher's words create very definite mental pictures. The wise preacher knows that he must paint pictures if he would move men; hence he searches for appropriate illustrations to make his lofty spiritual concepts real.

[66] Pepper, *op. cit.*, p. 19.
[67] Scherer, *op. cit.*, pp. 169–70.
[68] Broadus, *op. cit.*, p. 298.

Rather than say, "Some men will accept my gospel more completely and more permanently than others," Jesus, the Master teacher, chose to say:

> Behold, the sower went forth to sow; and as he sowed, some seeds fell by the way side . . . and others fell upon the rocky places. . . . And others fell upon the thorns . . . and others fell upon the good ground. . . .[69]

His discourses abounded in forceful illustrations. The Yale lecturers were enthusiastic in their recommendation of the use of illustrations, pointing out the many uses to which they can be put, but warning against their overuse and their misuse.

Inasmuch as words form the chief medium through which the minister makes known his message, they must be chosen with care. Complicated, vague, indefinite words will not do. The language must be simple, clear, and accurate. If it can also be beautiful that is an added virtue.

Finally, the effective sermon will possess a definite order and plan. No haphazard wanderer can have the maximum effect upon men. The underlying plan, while being very clear to the speaker, will best be only partially revealed to the hearers. The introduction and conclusion, which occupy the most emphatic spots in the sermon, will also be planned with extreme care.

[69] Matthew 13:3–7, from the American Standard Version of the Revised Bible (copyrighted by the International Council of Religious Education) and used by permission.

Chapter IX

DELIVERY

The preacher's responsibility does not end with the completion of the preparation of the sermon. Still to be considered is the crucial matter of its delivery. Good sermons may fail because of ineffective delivery, while it is also true that some mediocre sermons may achieve surprising results because of a fine handling at the time of delivery. Twenty-nine of the Yale lecturers spoke of the delivery of the sermon, including in their discussions comments upon each of the following phases of the subject: importance of delivery, voice, appearance, imitation, style, and methods of delivery. These subdivisions of the subject are set forth in succeeding pages in the order named.

IMPORTANCE OF DELIVERY

One of the most enthusiastic voices was that of Charles Reynolds Brown.

> Here is the final test! Here you win or lose! All that has gone before helps or hinders, as the case may be, but the proof of the pudding is the eating. Here in the delivery of your sermon the nourishment which you have brought for a hungry congregation is either eaten with relish, satisfaction and resultant strength, or it is left on the plate as a bit of cold victuals, useless and repellent. Take heed therefore how you deliver!
> . . . Many sermons are never "delivered" at all. The minister gets his words out; he gets the sermon off his mind and out of his system, but he does not lodge it in

the minds and the hearts of the people to whom it is
addressed.[1]

Although he gave delivery a place of importance, Taylor was
far less enthusiastic than Brown.

I would not go so far as to say that articulate and
earnest delivery is everything in a sermon; for truth is
in words as well as in manner, and far more in the former
than in the latter. Yet it is undeniable that effective utterance will give force even to a feeble sermon; while
careless, hesitating, and indistinct speech, will make the
finest composition fall flat and powerless upon the listeners' ears. In itself the manner may be far less important than the matter; but it is valuable, as giving its
full force to the matter, and ought not to be lightly
esteemed. You will do well, therefore, to cultivate elocution. But here, as in other things, you must be on your
guard against artificiality. What you have to do is not
to imitate another, but to cultivate yourselves.[2]

In speaking of delivery Brooks said that:

. . . no expedient which can make that truth a little
more effective in its presentation to the world is trivial,
or undignified, or unworthy of the patient care and study
of the minister of Christ.[3]

"It can never be necessary to urge the importance of delivery
upon persons who correctly understand its nature, and who
appreciate the objects of public speaking," [4] was Broadus'
single sentence summary of the importance of delivery.
Beecher indicated by a comparison that he felt that training
in delivery is necessary for the young preacher.

But the same considerations that make it wise for you
to pass through a liberal education, make it also wise for

1 Charles Reynolds Brown, *The Art of Preaching*, p. 155.
2 Taylor, *The Ministry of the Word*, p. 72.
3 Brooks, *op. cit.*, p. 179.
4 Broadus, *op. cit.*, p. 477.

you to pass through a liberal drill and training in all
that pertains to oratory.[5]

Still another to speak of the importance of training in this
field was Merrill.

> Of importance also to the real freedom of the preacher
> is careful attention to the art of delivery. There is vastly
> more involved in this than the externals of voice, ges-
> ture, and manner, but these are vital. There are few min-
> isters who would not gain by instruction and practice
> in the art of delivery; and there are many who fail of the
> effect they might have through lack of attention to the
> manner in which they present their message. Every
> preacher should be humble and eager in welcoming
> criticisms.[6]

Stalker briefly compared the view of the man in the pew with
that of the preacher upon the subject of delivery.

> If the Senate of this University were ever to try the
> experiment of asking a layman to deliver this course of
> Lectures on Preaching, I am certain he would lay more
> stress on this than we do, and put a clear and effective—
> if possible, a graceful and eloquent—delivery among the
> chief desiderata of the pulpit. I do not know how it may
> be among you; but, when I was at college, we used rather
> to despise delivery. We were so confident in the power of
> ideas that we thought nothing of the manner of setting
> them forth. Only have good stuff, we thought, and it will
> preach itself. . . . and many of us have since suffered
> for it. We know how many sermons are preached in the
> churches of the country every Sunday; but does anyone
> know how many are listened to?[7]

In his speaking of delivery, Horton sounded a word of warning.

> It may be well to say at once that the noble gift of
> oratory and the fine art of elocution may be pressed into

[5] Beecher, *op. cit.*, I, 129.
[6] Merrill, *op. cit.*, p. 36.
[7] Stalker, *op. cit.*, p. 119.

the service of preaching, but they have to be watched; they are saucy slaves who with their castanets and bangles will always be seeking to gain the upper hand, superseding their master and covering his absence with their noise and sparkle. A good voice is invaluable if God speaks through it. A commanding presence is a great help if God's presence commands it. The rich flow of language may be fertilising as well as charming if the tide of God is in it. But the preacher is not a Reciter or an Orator. His purpose, his power, his practice, are quite independent of these accomplishments.[8]

VOICE

The importance of the preacher's voice was mentioned by a number of the speakers. Charles Reynolds Brown gave it a place of prime importance.

The main tool to be used in the delivery of the sermon is your voice. See to it that you keep your tools in good order as workmen approved unto God who need not be ashamed! The minister is under moral obligation so to train and so to use his throat and other vocal organs as to avoid all sore throat, colds and hoarseness, which always diminish where they do not actually destroy effective delivery.[9]

Simpson spoke of several voice elements to be given careful consideration by the preacher.

The proper management of the voice is of great importance. The preacher should aim to speak with sufficient force to be distinctly heard by the audience. . . . Care should be taken that the pitch should be as nearly as possible the ordinary tone of conversation, as this produces less weariness, and allows a greater range of compass both above and below. This variety is essential to prevent injury to the vocal organs, and it relieves that monotonous utterance which becomes very unpleasant to the congregation. This ordinary pitch, with variations

[8] Horton, *op. cit.*, pp. 19–20.
[9] Charles Reynolds Brown, *The Art of Preaching*, p. 163.

above and below, gives the character of naturalness. Distinctness of syllabic utterance imparts the quality termed penetration, or of carrying the sound to the greatest possible distance without intermingling with other sounds.[10]

Horton spoke of the cultivation of the voice.

> But so far as the voice can be produced by careful cultivation, and modulated by study and practice, the preacher should see to it that, like a good workman, he shall never mar his message by a flaw in the instrument, but shall give to all the truths he has to communicate the added charm of a musical and appropriate delivery.[11]

The element of loudness was discussed by Hall.

> If the *voice* be too low and indistinct the ear grows tired in catching the words. If it be occasionally loud and rough, the ear is offended, as is the eye with grotesque, awkward, or constrained action. If the words come too rapidly the sense is confused: if very slowly, like minute-guns at sea, the hearer grows impatient. A dull monotone is soporific: so is a continuous shout. There ought to be naturalness in the voice, and along with that periods of repose. Then there is room for emphasis, for expression, for variety of modulation.[12]

The disadvantage of a weak voice was pointed out by Crosby.

> And yet I can not but hold that one whose most prominent function it is to use his voice in a large assembly, must be a man neither of obscure or feeble utterance. His words should be both clear and loud, that the illiterate and the old may not be left in doubt as to his meaning.[13]

Beecher discussed the voice in its relationship to persuasion.

> You may fire an audience with a loud voice, but if you wish to draw them into sympathy and to win them by persuasion, and are near enough for them to feel your magne-

10 Simpson, *op. cit.*, pp. 182–83.
11 Horton, *op. cit.*, p. 274.
12 Hall, *op. cit.*, p. 167.
13 Crosby, *op. cit.*, p. 18.

tism and see your eye, so that you need not have to strain
your voice, you must talk to them as a father would talk
to his child. You will draw them, and will gain their
assent to your propositions, when you could do it in no
other way, and certainly not by shouting.[14]

The problem of the monotonous voice was also introduced
by Beecher.

A great many men commence preaching under a
nervous excitement. They very speedily rise to a sharp
and hard monotone; and then they go on through their
whole sermon as fast as they can, never letting their
voices go above or below their false pitch, but always
sticking to that, until everybody gets tired out, and they
among the rest.[15]

Burton added, "A monotonous voice makes length, enor-
mously. There is nothing that gives such a sense of eternity as
a well continued sober monotone." [16] Jefferson's view of the
matter was that, "The best thing that a preacher can do with
his voice is to hide it. The best voice for preaching is the voice
that no one ever hears." [17]

APPEARANCE

Several of the speakers discussed the physical aspects of the
preacher which meet the audience's eye. Beecher called for the
audience's unobstructed view of the preacher.

When a man is made by God he is made *all over,* and
every part is necessary to each and to the whole. A man's
whole form is a part of his public speaking. His feet
speak and so do his hands. You put a man in one of these
barrelled pulpits, where there is no responsibility laid
upon him as to his body, and he falls into all manner of
gawky attitudes, and rests himself like a country horse
at a hitching-post. He sags down, and has no conscious-

14 Beecher, *op. cit.,* I, 132.
15 *Ibid.,* p. 130.
16 Burton, *op. cit.,* p. 119.
17 Jefferson, *op. cit.,* p. 284.

ness of his awkwardness. But bring him out on a platform, and see how much more manly he becomes, how
much more force comes out! The moment a man is
brought face to face with other men, then does the influence of each act and react upon the other.[18]

A moment later he elaborated the advantage which is to be
gained by the preacher's standing directly before the congregation.

A man who speaks right before his audience, and without notes, will speak, little by little, with the gestures
of the whole body, and not with the gestures of one finger
only.[19]

Horne spoke in favor of simple gestures.

It is always easier in this matter to enforce the truth
by precept than by practice; but nothing is more certain
than that the man who has learned early . . . to be content with those simple gestures which are natural and
dignified, has mastered what is fundamental to the art
of pulpit oratory.[20]

"Gestures which are striking," according to Jefferson, "make
an impression the first few times, but if they keep on striking they give pain." [21]

IMITATION

Buttrick, Jowett, Beecher, and Scherer commented upon
the danger of imitating another man's delivery. Buttrick
merely expressed the principle, when he said, "A wise
preacher will study the masters, but he will not mimic them;
he will be himself." [22] Jowett elaborated the principle, demonstrating the danger out of his own early experience.

Be yourself, and slavishly imitate nobody. . . . When
we begin to imitate we nearly always imitate the non-

18 Beecher, *op. cit.*, I, 71.
19 *Ibid.*, pp. 71–72.
20 Horne, *op. cit.*, p. 206.
21 Jefferson, *op. cit.*, p. 284.
22 Buttrick, *op. cit.*, p. 175.

essentials, the tertiary things that scarcely count. In my own college there was a peril of our turning out a species of dwarfed or miniature Fairbairns. We could so easily acquire the trick of his style,—that sharp antithetical sentence, doubling back upon itself, and which we fashioned like standardized pieces of machinery cast in a foundry! I believe I became rather an expert in the process, and for some time I carried the Fairbairn moulds about with me, only unfortunately there was nothing in them! [23]

From his own early efforts at preaching Beecher illustrated the danger of imitation.

There was never anything that so nearly killed me as trying to be Jonathan Edwards. I did try hard. Then I tried to be Brainard; then I tried to be James Brainard Taylor; then I tried to be Payson; then I tried to be Henry Martyn; and then I gave up, and succeeded in being nothing but just myself.[24]

Still another to point out the danger of imitation was Scherer.

No famous preacher ever lived without having his style and even the tones of his voice borrowed, without interest, be it said, by whole generations of theological students. Much of this sincerest of all flattery is no doubt unconscious; but it is none the less objectionable. And I never have been able to understand how anybody's wife or friends would or could let him get away with it. They ought to sandpaper him down to the quick! Deliberate imitation of the masters in strategy and approach may be, in fact, I believe it is, a most helpful discipline. In his early days, and for many years after, Dr. Jowett used to practice the analysis of texts and the outlining of sermons in the mood now of Spurgeon, now of Dale, now of Bushnell, or Maclaren, or Whyte. But habitually to assume, even though unintentionally, the pose of another, to take on his accents, to pattern after his mind, some-

[23] Jowett, *op. cit.,* pp. 128–29.
[24] Beecher, *op. cit.,* III, 275.

times after even his gestures—this is to be no one truly, with no claim upon anybody's respect.[25]

STYLE

Of the lecturers who spoke most fully concerning the preacher's style of preaching, all were in favor of the natural style, as opposed to the artificial style. Jefferson spoke rather freely upon the subject.

It is because preachers do not come close enough to individuals that they sometimes form an unhuman style of speaking. To speak naturally ought to be the ambition of every preacher. He cannot afford to subtract from the force of his message by tones which repel or by intonations which offend. He ought to speak in the pulpit as a gentleman speaks when addressing his friends on matters of importance. If he uses tones never heard in the home, and cadences which would bring a laugh if used in any circle of society, he hurts the chances of his truth. The Christian pulpit has been a hotbed for the growth of all sorts of curious and unearthly tones. Twangs of various twists, singsongs of divers melodies, howls of different degrees of fury, and roars of many types of hideousness have tarnished the fame of the pulpit and caused the ungodly to blaspheme. The cause of these vocal monstrosities and outrages is that the preacher forgets he is talking to individual men.[26]

Kelman joined in the condemnation of the unnatural pulpit manner.

However it may have arisen, there can be no question as to the fact that preaching has suffered to a most lamentable extent by the habitual assumption of a pulpit manner which is felt by the hearers to be unreal. Against this habit I wish to enter my strong protest. The formality of language and of bearing—sometimes even of voice—which is often assumed by the preacher under the delusion that it is the suitable and proper thing for preaching, is not real dignity and it is not impressive solemnity.[27]

"Would that we had the courage to slough off the traditional mannerisms of the pulpit and to do the natural thing in the natural way," [28] was Sperry's expression on the subject. Speaking on the positive side of the subject, Charles Reynolds Brown described the desirable manner of speaking.

> The tone of dignified conversation furnishes the staple method for effective delivery. It wears better than any other style of speech. The men who shout and roar in the pulpit are not the men who speak to the human heart the words of eternal life.
> . . . There need be nothing tame or spiritless about this method of delivery—the highest art is to be found ever in the right use of that which is simple and natural.[29]

Kelman had recommended the same style of speaking a few years prior to Brown's lectures.

> Take the sermon as essentially a conversation with your hearers, and converse with them, instead of either bellowing at them or wailing to them. Above all, be good-natured in manner and in tone. There is a "curate *contra mundum*" way of preaching which gives the impression of a young man standing up alone on behalf of eternal truth, and at the risk of his life defying every member of the congregation to his or her face, even when he is uttering sentiments which it is inconceivable that any sensible person would dispute. It is wiser and more effective to hold your welcome for granted, to take your congregation into your confidence, and speak to them as to people with whom you are on friendly terms.[30]

Behrends declared that the natural manner of speaking is not to be achieved without effort, and proceeded to suggest means of acquiring the style.

[27] Kelman, *op. cit.*, pp. 10–11.
[28] Sperry, *op. cit.*, p. 114.
[29] Charles Reynolds Brown, *The Art of Preaching*, p. 168.
[30] Kelman, *op. cit.*, p. 164.

Now, there is an artificial cultivation of manners. It infects the tone, the attitude, the dress. The elocution becomes pompous. The dress becomes prescribed and official. Mannerism is the worst of manners. When primary or undue attention is given to the form, the life suffers and shrivels. And yet, to be perfectly natural, observing always that outward decorum which befits the occasion, demands the severest and most unremitting self-discipline. It requires the culture of the heart, until the spirit in you obtains such clearness of vision, such intensity of grasp, such an intuitive perception of what the occasion requires, such a fixed purpose to meet every emergency as it arises, that the proprieties will almost take care of themselves, as fragrance radiates from the rose and light from the sun. Keep the central fires burning.[31]

METHODS OF DELIVERY

Twenty-two of the Yale lecturers discussed the relative desirability of the three most widely used methods of delivering the sermon: reading from manuscript, speaking from memory, and extemporaneous preaching. The broadest difference of opinion in the entire series of lectures occurred on this question. There was found to be a clearly discernible trend toward one of the three methods, a trend which became more evident as succeeding lectures were given. So that this trend may be apparent, the ensuing discussion is presented in chronological order. Beecher, in his first series of lectures, attributed to extemporaneous preaching the meaning later given to impromptu preaching.

No man can speak well, the substance of whose sermons has not been prepared beforehand. Men talk of "extemporaneous preaching," but the only part that can properly be extemporaneous is the external form. Sometimes, indeed, one may be called to preach off-hand,—*ex tempore,*—and may do it with great success; but all such sermons will really be the results of previous study.[32]

[31] Behrends, *op. cit.,* pp. 65–66.
[32] Beecher, *op. cit.,* I, 211.

In the same lecture he indicated that it might not be necessary to decide in favor of one method to the exclusion of all others.

> Many considerations have been urged for and against written and unwritten sermons; and there are advantages in both kinds, and both have their disadvantages; so that a true system would seem to require sometimes one mode, and sometimes the other.[33]

Still later in the same lecture, however, he evidenced his own leaning toward the unwritten method.

> But, considered ideally, he who preaches unwritten sermons is the true preacher; however much you may write, the tendency of all such mechanical preparation should be towards the ideal of the unwritten sermon; and throughout your early training and your after labor, you should reach out after that higher and broader form of preaching.[34]

Hall, in the 1874–1875 series, firmly recommended the written method, though he did approve the delivery of the sermon without the manuscript. It might be inferred, from the language used by Hall, that he was more opposed to impromptu speaking than to extemporaneous speaking.

> Write every word, or an equivalent for every word, and set down every idea you ought to give to the people, and in its relative place. . . . Write regularly, conscientiously, and at your best. I urge this on you all the more because I am myself described, in a way that may mislead, as an *extempore* speaker, and I should be extremely vexed if my supposed method should ensnare any one into the delusion that any purely *extempore* plan is likely to be permanently effective with ordinary men. Whether you take your manuscript to the pulpit, or burn it when you have done your best upon it, or leave it in some *limbus sermonum* to be be [sic] burned by ungrate-

[33] *Ibid.*, p. 212.
[34] *Ibid.*, p. 218.

ful posterity, is of secondary, that you write is of the first, importance.[35]

Taylor, who delivered the 1875–1876 series, was the chief exponent of the carefully prepared manuscript. He felt that writing is a necessity.

> I have very strong convictions upon this point [the careful writing of every discourse], and as a different opinion has been recently advanced by one whose views must be always received with deference and respect, you will forgive me if I seek, with some measure of fullness, to set forth my reasons for the advice which I have ventured to offer.
>
> It seems to me that the importance of the work we are engaged in demands this exactness of written preparation at our hands.[36]

He summarized his own feelings, thus:

> If I might speak from my own experience, therefore, I would say, that *memoriter* preaching is the method which has the greatest advantages, with the fewest disadvantages; extempore preaching is the method in the employment of which success is hardest, and failure commonest; and preaching from a manuscript is the method in which, if he choose to train himself in it, the man of average ability will make, on the whole, the best of his talents, and make the fewest failures.[37]

In one of his lectures of the 1876–1877 series, Brooks gave each of the methods credit for the possession of certain virtues and certain faults.

> With regard to the vexed question of written or unwritten sermons I have not very much to say. I think it is a question whose importance has been very much exaggerated, and the attempt to settle which with some invariable rule has been unwise, and probably has made stumbling speakers out of some men who might have

35 Hall, *op. cit.*, p. 123.
36 Taylor, *The Ministry of the Word*, p. 114.
37 *Ibid.*, p. 150.

been effective readers, or stupid readers out of men who might have spoken with force and fire. The different methods have their evident different advantages.[38]

He spoke further on the same subject, concluding with the following paragraph:

It is easy . . . to characterize the two methods, but, when our characterizations are complete, what shall we say? Only two things, I think, and those so simple and so commonplace that it is strange that they should need to be said, but certainly they do. The first is that two such different methods must belong in general to two different kinds of men; that some men are made for manuscripts, and some for the open platform; that to exclude either class from the ministry, or to compel either class to use the methods of the other, would rob the pulpit by silencing some of its best men. The other remark is that almost every man, in some proportion, may use both methods; that they help each other; that you will write better if you often speak without your notes, and you will speak better if you often give yourself the discipline of writing. Add to these merely that the proportion of extemporaneous preaching may well be increased as a man grows older in the ministry, and I do not know what more to say in the way of general suggestion. The rest must be left to a man's own knowledge of himself and that personal good sense which lies behind all homiletics.[39]

In 1877–1878, Dale spoke in favor of the extemporaneous method.

Gentlemen,—About the comparative advantages of preaching from a manuscript and preaching extemporaneously, I have some difficulty in speaking. It seems to me that the overwhelming weight of the argument is on the side of extemporaneous preaching; but I have very rarely the courage to go into the pulpit without carrying with me the notes of my sermon, and occasionally I read every sentence from the first to the last.[40]

38 Brooks, *op. cit.*, pp. 169–70.
39 *Ibid.*, pp. 171–72.
40 Dale, *op. cit.*, p. 151.

One year later, in the 1878–1879 lectures, Simpson gave this subject a very full treatment. First, he explained his conception of extemporaneous preaching.

> Strictly speaking, extemporaneous preaching is impossible. A minister may select a text without having his thoughts specifically arranged, and may depend upon his memory and imagination for the utterances he is about to make; but his power of speech he received in infancy; the words he employs he has used from childhood. If he quote Scripture, or refer to any incident within his experience or observation, he is using his memory. The extemporaneousness of the speech lies only in the order in which his thoughts are presented, or in such suggestions as at the moment may occur.[41]

Later, he mentioned some of the disadvantages of reading the sermon from a manuscript, saying:

> . . . it seems to me the advantages are not so great as the disadvantages. In reading closely, little of the preacher's personal power, except his voice, is added to the written words. Even that is restrained, as the reading voice is not so full as the speaking one. The power of the eye, the play of the features, the light of the countenance, and the freedom of movement, are either lost to the audience or greatly restricted. This personal power being a great factor in preaching, what impairs it inevitably weakens the impression of the sermon.[42]

Concluding his analysis of the manuscript method, he said:

> If we consider the advantages carefully, we find that they inure to the preacher rather than to his hearers. But is the comfort or convenience of the speaker the chief end of preaching?[43]

Turning to the extemporaneous method, he pointed out its true nature and some of its advantages.

[41] Simpson, *op. cit.*, pp. 98–99.
[42] *Ibid.*, p. 170.
[43] *Ibid.*, p. 171.

Once for all, let me say, that extemporaneous speaking, or direct address, as I prefer to call it, does not exclude the most thorough and perfect preparation. It may be abused by ignorant and indolent men; but it is not designed to diminish the necessity for extensive reading and careful thought. The order and the parts of the discourse should be clearly fixed in the mind; illustrations may be selected and arranged; suitable language for certain portions may be well studied, or the whole sermon may be written; yet at the time of delivery, with the heart full of the subject, and with the outlines clearly perceived, let the speaker rely on his general knowledge of language and his habit of speaking for the precise words he may need. If he be deeply in earnest he will, as he proceeds, feel a glow of enthusiasm which will give a warmth and vigor to his expression.[44]

Still later, however, he opened the door to the use of reading in certain situations.

It may also be fairly admitted that where sermons are delivered purely for instruction, reading may not only be allowable, but may even be preferable; yet persuasion, rather than instruction, is the great end of preaching. Instruction is essential, but without persuasion the sinner is never moved or saved.[45]

The next man to broach the subject was Robinson in the 1881–1882 series. He was enthusiastically in favor of the extemporaneous method.

In unwritten sermons, spoken freely and freshly from the mind and heart, the preacher comes into an immediateness of relation with his auditors that never is attainable by him who is dependent on his manuscript. There exists a nameless something acting and re-acting on the hearers and the speaker as they look into each other's eyes, that no skill in reading with stolen glances at the audience, can ever render possible. The hearers catch the speaker's thoughts and emotions, and he, from their re-

[44] *Ibid.*, p. 173.
[45] *Ibid.*, p. 174.

sponsive looks, gathers new inspiration as he advances. The extempore speaker, who is master of both his subject and himself, has at the same time a mastery over his audience, such as no other can ever possess.[46]

Broadus, in the 1888–1889 series of lectures commended the extempore method; yet, he did so with a rather light touch.

Public speaking is one of the noblest exercises of the human powers; preaching is its highest form; and if extemporaneous speaking be the best method of preaching, it is surely worth labor to attain excellence in this,— diligent and faithful self-cultivation, resolute determination always to do our best, as long as we live.[47]

In the 1889–1890 series, Behrends suggested the use of the extemporaneous method.

Talk in the pulpit as earnest men talk to each other, and as they talk to you. That will be almost sure to lead you to cultivate what is called extemporaneous preaching,—which is neither memoriter recitation, nor loose, unconnected, unpremeditated speech,—but the free utterance of clear and thoroughly mastered thought.[48]

In the 1890–1891 lectures, Stalker approved the extemporaneous method, but only for preachers trained in a certain way.

The preacher, having thought of two or three lines of remark and got hold of two or three stories, enters the pulpit with these materials lying loosely in his mind, and trusts to the moment for the style of the sermon. Of course, if a man has trained himself to preach in this way always, it is all right; but, if not, it is a mistake.[49]

Horton pointed out one of the weaknesses of the written sermon in one of his 1892–1893 lectures.

A sermon is not only relative to the preacher, and relative to the Truth which is to be delivered, but it is also

---

46 Robinson, *op. cit.*, p. 194.
47 Broadus, *op. cit.*, p. 476.
48 Behrends, *op. cit.*, p. 222.
49 Stalker, *op. cit.*, p. 174.

relative to the audience. It is the peculiar weakness of written sermons when they are composed for general use, and not with a view to a stated audience or a special occasion, that they generally fail to grapple the hearers in a way to secure attention.[50]

Greer, in 1894–1895, indicated the reasons behind his own choice of the extemporaneous method of preaching.

My own practice is to preach without notes; and of course I prefer that practice, otherwise I should not practice it. It has proved itself for me to be the better way; though I am far from saying that it is the better way for everybody. I am satisfied, however, after having tried both ways, that preaching without notes is the better way for me. I can in that way put myself more fully into my preaching; and however it may seem to the people who hear me, it seems to me, at least, as though I came in that way nearer to the people, and could speak with greater freedom and more directness to them.[51]

He also pointed out some of the weaknesses of the manuscript method.

A manuscript fetters and binds me, and I seem when speaking from it, to be speaking also to it. It gets in my way, and I become impatient of it, and I long to push it aside and look away from it, and not to look back at it again, but to continue to look at the people; and every time I do look back at it again, I feel as though something had come between us, and broken the current between us. And something *has* come between us,—the manuscript has come between us; and I experience then the truth of what Dr. Storrs says, that paper is a nonconductor, and does not easily let the electric current go through.[52]

In his 1896–1897 lectures, Watson reported the man in the pew as favoring the extempore method.

[50] Horton, *op. cit.*, pp. 279–80.
[51] Greer, *op. cit.*, pp. 177–78.
[52] *Ibid.*, p. 178.

The exact question is, whether, after the average man has studied his sermon, and done his best by it, he ought to read the result or say what is in him to his hearers face to face. The pew is unanimous in favour of delivery, and the pew is right.[53]

Tucker stated his conclusions, in 1897–1898, in this fashion:

. . . either method [reading or memoriter], though extremely forcible in itself, is by comparison with the extempore method unnatural. The aim being oratorical, the method is not so true to the aim.[54]

In setting forth his own view, John Brown, in the 1899–1900 series quoted Alexander Maclaren as favoring the extemporaneous method.

He says: "I began my ministry with the resolution that I would not write sermons, but would think and feel them, and I have stuck to it ever since. It costs quite as much time in preparation as writing, and a far greater expenditure of nervous energy in delivery; but I am sure that it is best for me, and equally sure that everybody has to find out his own way." [55]

Jowett, in the lectures for 1911–1912, broke with his immediate predecessors, in saying that the method of delivery is immaterial.

There are some questions about the sermon on which I am comparatively indifferent. Whether it shall be preached from a full manuscript or from notes, whether it shall be read, or delivered with greater detachment; these questions do not much concern me. Either method may be alive and effective if there be behind it a "live" man, real and glowing, fired with the passion of souls.[56]

In the series of 1912–1913, Parkhurst couched his feelings in very moderate terms, beginning his comments with an "if."

53 Watson, *op. cit.*, p. 59.
54 Tucker, *op. cit.*, p. 97.
55 John Brown, *op. cit.*, p. 266.
56 Jowett, *op. cit.*, pp. 170–71.

If the preacher's use of a manuscript is such as to deaden his consciousness of those whom he is supposed to be addressing, such, that is to say, that either he or his hearers feel that the manuscript forms a barrier between the pulpit and the pew, then certainly the manuscript ought to be dispensed with. Preaching proper, like any other kind of teaching, involves an interchange of personalities, and anything that embarrasses the exchange and interrupts the circuit is fatal.[57]

In the lectures of 1913–1914, Horne made reference to Calvin's emphasis on extemporaneous preaching.

It is remarkable that one who was so scholarly in all his tastes should be the determined champion of extempore preaching. Indeed he went so far as to declare that the power of God could only pour itself forth in extempore speech.[58]

Kelman was another to express his leaning toward the extemporaneous method in rather moderate language. He delivered the Yale lectures in 1918–1919.

It must be remembered, however, that in order to make it powerful as preaching, the reading of a discourse will always require severe effort and attention. Notes, whether taken into the pulpit or left at home, seem to offer the fullest opportunity for self-expression to the preacher. He brings only his structure of thought, and finds his language in the hearts and eyes of his congregation. His sermon will doubtless be a rougher-edged and less literary production than that of him who writes it out at leisure beforehand, but there may be a positive advantage in that. Our aim is not literary polish or completeness, but direct hits upon men's conscience, intellect, and heart; and the rougher edge may give the deeper wound.[59]

No one was more certain in his conclusion than was Sclater, in the 1926–1927 series, when he said, "The verdict is in

57 Parkhurst, *op. cit.*, p. 53.
58 Horne, *op. cit.*, p. 181.
59 Kelman, *op. cit.*, pp. 163–64.

favour of the spoken and against the read sermon: and it is no use arguing about it." [60] Buttrick, in the series of 1930–1931, strongly favored the writing of the sermon.

> Then must come the writing of the sermon. But must a man write? For ourself (we would not dogmatize for any other man) that question is answered in emphatic assent. The sermon must be written—not as an essay is written, but as a sermon is written; that is to say, with the eyes of a congregation (wistful, hungry, sad, or gayly indifferent) looking at the writer over his desk.[61]

He indicated in the same lecture, however, that his own method was somewhat of an extemporaneous delivery of a written sermon.

> A read sermon is doubtless preferable to extemporaneous speech if the latter is slipshod and ill-prepared; but in most churches a manuscript even dramatically read would be a barrier between preacher and people. . . . the manuscript can be mastered (not by rote but in substance) and left at home; or it can be taken into the pulpit as a guide-map; or it can be condensed into notes brief or full and the notes used as a prompter. In any event the preparation must be painstaking, and the sermon must be mastered.[62]

Scherer's comment in the 1943 lectures forms an appropriate conclusion to this discussion of the most effective method of delivery.

> But whatever you do, whether you take with you into the pulpit what you have written or lay it aside, whether you cultivate the art of unobtrusive reading or the art of free delivery, memoriter or otherwise, give yourself wholly in that thirty minutes. Learn to forget everything but your message, and the God Whose truth it is, and the people who sit there needing it, and the love you have for them. Let it be done urgently and warmly and calmly,

[60] Sclater, *op. cit.*, p. 117.
[61] Buttrick, *op. cit.*, pp. 156–57.
[62] *Ibid.*, pp. 162–63.

as a friend would speak with his friend. My own habit is to begin with a sentence prayer and to close with another. I think I shall always continue it.[63]

SUMMARY

Just as the manufacturer knows that, no matter how excellent his product, there are no profits until after delivery, so the thoughtful preacher knows that, no matter how fine the sermon, there is no profit until after the sermon is actually delivered to the minds and hearts of the people. Successful delivery is not universal. Only after long years of constant attention and continued practice does one achieve the art of delivering sermons effectively.

Voice and appearance play important parts in the process of delivery. The voice is best when without calling attention to itself it presents the message to the listener loudly enough to be heard and clearly enough to be understood, and yet without noticeable strain. Artificiality of voice, while unbelievably common to the pulpit, possesses no advantages and many disadvantages. The appearance is best when, without calling attention to the person of the speaker, it reinforces his vocal delivery. Appropriate gestures, meaningful facial expression, and proper platform movement are of value to the preacher.

Each preacher has a personal style of his own which should be retained. Slavishly to imitate another, even though he be a master of the preaching art, usually spells disaster.

The best of all the speaking styles is the plain, natural style of animated conversation. While the formal, artificial manner of speaking leaves congregations cold, the warm, personal, conversational mode enables the preacher to reach the hearts of his hearers.

Finally, the method of delivery which is most widely used by successful preachers is the extemporaneous method. This

63 Scherer, *op. cit.*, pp. 204–5.

method means neither that there has been no preparation of the sermon, nor that the preparation has been sketchy and haphazard. The extemporaneous sermon is best when it has been preceded by the written sermon. Rather than read from the manuscript, the extemporaneous preacher leaves it at his desk, delivering his message with eye and body as well as with voice.

Chapter X

SETTING FOR THE SERMON

Every sermon is delivered in some kind of setting. Something has preceded it in the service; something will follow; it is delivered amid certain physical surroundings. All of these elements make up the background or setting for the sermon. A great many of the Yale lecturers spoke of the influence which the setting has upon the effectiveness of the sermon. The comments of those who spoke of the elements surrounding the sermon in the worship are here presented first, and are followed by the comments of those who spoke of the physical setting of the sermon.

THE SERVICE

Thirteen of the men who addressed the divinity students at Yale University were concerned with the order of worship and its influence upon the sermon. Beecher stressed the importance of the music service. His comments are of special interest to those who use instrumental music.

Why do they begin the service with the organ? What uses do you yourselves conceive in it? I will tell you what I think about it. I think that when the family comes to church, having been hurried and flurried in getting the children ready,—when the little brood have been looked after, and the five or the six are combed and curled and hooked and shoed, and all got in order, the house shut up and secure, and the little throng safely housed in the pew,—the mind all fluttered with those sweet domestic cares,—it is a great relief if something can quietly, imperceptibly, smooth those cares away. Some come from their houses, heavy with the lassitude of oversleeping on

Saturday night and Sunday morning. Having been exces-
sively pressed during the week, they get up drowsy and
sleepy, eat their nine o'clock or ten o'clock breakfast,
come away to church, and are spent. There is nothing in
them. Others come in, frivolous and gay and genial.[1]

In the same lecture he further elaborated his point.

Now, that is what the organ undertakes, or should
undertake, to do. It should take up the congregation and
wash them clean in sound. It should disperse all these
secular and worldly impressions, associations, thoughts,
and feelings, and lift them up into the aesthetic,—the
imaginative. "Very well; but is that worship? is that religion?" No, but it is that state of mind out of which comes,
more easily than from any other, the next stage, of positive religious feeling. When a congregation are set free
from the entanglements and burdens of the world, and
brought into the higher realms of imagination, fancy,
and feeling, they are ready for the plastic touch, they
are ready to listen, to take part indeed. If an organ be
well played in the beginning, as soon as its tones cease,
the congregation is reasonably prepared to join with the
choir in the singing of the opening hymn or anthem.[2]

Finally, Beecher showed that his task in the sermon was
greatly lessened by the preliminary tuning of the congregation.

. . . If I can bring the congregation, before I come
personally to handle them, into a triumphant, jubilant
state, a cheerful, hopeful, genial state, my work among
them will be made easier by one half than if they were in
a very depressed, sad state.[3]

Charles Reynolds Brown also spoke of the aid which the sermon receives from the order of worship.

The sermon may also add immeasurably to its strength
by being set in a well-arranged and well-conducted order

[1] Beecher, op. cit., II, 120.
[2] Ibid., p. 121.
[3] Ibid., p. 134.

of worship. In all our non-liturgical churches the sermon is commonly regarded as the outstanding feature of the service, but it had best not stand aloof in lonely detachment from other vital elements in that hour appointed for the satisfying worship of God.[4]

Earlier in his series of lectures Brown had spoken of the importance of a spiritual atmosphere in the worship service.

> If they are to hear the softer and more intensive notes in the message you bring, there must be that atmosphere where spiritual sound waves will carry. There must be a suitable sustaining medium so that your words and your purpose and your feeling may indeed reach the hearts of those for whom the message is intended. Your own high mood of devotion as people see it in your face, as they hear it in the deeper undertones of your voice, as it finds expression in your reading of the Scripture lesson and in your prayer, that mood of devotion will, if it be full and strong, create and maintain that atmosphere where the voice of the Spirit as He speaks through you will reach and find the attentive souls of those who hear.[5]

At another point in his lectures he spoke of the dis-service rendered the preacher by the insertion of distracting elements into the service.

> The preacher will be aided in his delivery by seeking to develop also the right mood in the congregation just before the sermon is to begin. It is bad psychology to have the taking of the collection, or a long list of confusing notices, or the singing of a choir number, which may frequently prove to be a misfit, come immediately before the sermon. The best thing that the people in a congregation can do to prepare their minds for the reception of a sermon is to sing together in hearty fashion some suitable hymn which shall prepare the way for the message of the hour.[6]

[4] Charles Reynolds Brown, *The Art of Preaching*, p. 198.
[5] *Ibid.*, p. 93.
[6] *Ibid.*, pp. 165–66.

Jefferson was another who spoke of the importance of the preparation of the congregation for the sermon.

> The sermon goes forth in vain unless the congregation is unified and hearts have become responsive and docile. Music and prayer are God's instruments for the taming of lawless impulses, and for the creation of spiritual unities and harmonies. A reverent mood is indispensable to the victory of a sermon.[7]

Of prayer he further said, "In the building of a reverential mood, no form of worship is so efficacious as public prayer." [8] "Music is also a form of power," he added, "which may be used for the creation of those particular tempers in which the Christian religion finds delight." [9] He named the Bible as an additional source to be used in creating the proper mood in the congregation, when he said, "It creates moods and chastens tempers as no other book in all the world. It produces a climate in which sermons come to luxuriant growth." [10] Jefferson concluded his remarks upon this subject with an emphatic statement concerning the importance of moods.

> Moods, then, are the preacher's first concern. His earliest work is to bring his people into a Christian frame of mind. What men are willing to believe depends largely upon their mental mood. A preacher forgets this at his peril.[11]

Taylor also spoke of the influence which the service has upon the sermon.

> But, to look at the matter in another light, every one must perceive that the sermon and the service act and react upon each other. The preacher who begins his discourse after a fervent prayer and an inspiring hymn, is always more animated and earnest than he would have

[7] Jefferson, op. cit., pp. 125–26.
[8] Ibid., p. 128.
[9] Ibid., p. 134.
[10] Ibid., p. 145.
[11] Ibid., p. 148.

been if the devotional exercises had been languid and formal. And after an impressive sermon, even the most careless worshiper must have been moved by the hush of reverence with which the people join in prayer, and the enthusiasm of soul and voice with which they sing the closing hymn.[12]

Taylor's main emphasis was upon the vital place of Scripture reading in the service.

The reading ought not to be subordinate to your sermon, but your sermon ought to be subordinate to it. Indeed, the end of your preaching will be secured, in a large measure, when you have stirred up the hearers to search the Scriptures, whether the things which you have spoken are confirmed by them or not; but if, in your public treatment of the Word of God, you are listless and mechanical, you cannot hope to interest any one in the study of it. The eloquent McAll, of Manchester, England, is reported to have said: "If the Lord had appointed two officers in His Church, the one to preach the Gospel and the other to read the Scriptures, and had given me the choice of these, I should have chosen to be a reader of the inspired Word of God," and with such an opinion, we are not surprised to learn that he excelled in that exercise; nay, it is not improbable that his deep reverence for the Bible so manifested, contributed largely to the power of his discourses.[13]

Brooks was still another who gave attention to the influence of the service upon the sermon. He said, "You never can make a sermon what it ought to be if you consider it alone. The service that accompanies it, the prayer and praise, must have their influence upon it." [14] That the other elements of the service are of value in the delivering of God's message to the people was also suggested by Jowett, when he said, "And so with these mighty allies of prayer, and Scripture, and

[12] Taylor, *The Ministry of the Word*, pp. 208–9.
[13] *Ibid.*, p. 220.
[14] Brooks, *op. cit.*, p. 142.

202 THE HEART OF THE YALE LECTURES

music, all pulsing with the power of the Holy Ghost, we shall give to a prepared people the message of the sermon." [15] Park spoke of various types of ritual.

> Happy is that preacher who addresses an audience already moved and impressed by the dignity and beauty of the services which precede the sermon. Some kind of ritual seems necessary in all services of worship, whether it be of the "I'm a regular guy" type, "Well, fellows! Here we are again! What do you say to Hymn 198?" or the solemn stereotyped Protestant form "Let us join in reading Responsive Reading number 68," or the Catholic approach to God with "Lift up your hearts," "We lift them up unto the Lord." All are equally ritual, because it is impossible to vary them every time they are used, the only difference is that the first two brothers think they are not ritualistic because what they say every Sunday is not beautiful.[16]

Freeman emphasized the essential place of music in the preparation of the audience for the sermon.

> I would not undertake to preach a sermon or conduct a service as a pastor without determining beforehand the hymns and frequently the anthems to be sung. A service should be symphonic in character, and music is one of its primary elements. A secularized organist and a secularized choir, wholly out of sympathy with the spiritual implications of the ministry of music, impair if they do not destroy the reverence and dignity of corporate worship. Here I would make the leader of worship, the messenger in the pulpit, an autocrat.
>
> Music compels the members of a congregation to coalesce. As a unifying power, rightly and reverently used, it is quite incomparable. Some choirs and some choirmasters are the enemies of both preacher and congregation, and neither worship nor message can survive their baleful influence.[17]

15 Jowett, *op. cit.*, p. 170.
16 Park, *op. cit.*, p. 113.
17 Freeman, *op. cit.*, p. 153.

Burton was impressed by the influence of music upon men.

> A great advance in expression is made when words are joined to music and they together, carry a theme. I am not going to say anything against the possibilities of expression and impression that are in preaching; but I have been made to know a thousand times in my own experience that music can beat us all, especially in its play on the feelings and in its power to voice the feelings.[18]

Sclater spoke of the place which the sermon should occupy in the worship, relative to the other items of the worship.

> Now, this puts the sermon where it belongs. It has a place, a great place and a place all its own, in the scheme of worship: but it is a supplementary place. It gives an opportunity for "particularizing" Vision; and therefore it is an act of great dignity. But it is not the crown of worship: and the other parts of the service are not "preliminaries." Protestantism did a great service when it reëxalted preaching: but it went off the rails when it did so at the expense of praise and prayer. Preaching will not lose, but gain, when it is seen in proper proportion, and when it is rightly related to other acts, in which worship obtains a more complete expression.[19]

Merrill noted the added power which the sermon receives by reason of its association with the other elements of the worship.

> In fact, however, the preacher has in the details of worship amid which his sermon is set a wonderful asset. If he is willing to restrict slightly his unlicensed freedom, and patiently plan to give to prayer and praise full scope, he will find these elements of worship giving wings to his words; greater power and greater freedom will come to his preaching for thoughtful and eager use of the values that lie in liturgy and music.[20]

[18] Burton, *op. cit.*, p. 173.
[19] Sclater, *op. cit.*, p. 45.
[20] Merrill, *op. cit.*, pp. 39–40.

AUDITORIUM

Six of the lecturers were concerned with the physical environment in which the sermon is delivered. Beecher and Brown were the most prolific on this subject. In describing the planning of Plymouth Church, Beecher evidenced a high regard for the building's effect upon the effectiveness of his sermons.

> Brother Day, the son of old President Day, of Yale College, was one of my right-hand men in founding the Plymouth Church in Brooklyn; and being a civil engineer, and the church having voted to build, he went into my study with me to plan the edifice. He asked me what I wanted, in the first place, and how many people I wanted the church to seat. I told him. "Very good," he said; "and how do you want them located?" "I want them to surround me, so that they will come up on every side, and behind me, so that I shall be in the centre of the crowd, and have the people surge all about me." The result is, that there is not a better constructed hall in the world for the purposes of speaking and hearing than Plymouth Church. . . . It is perfect, because it was built on a principle,—the principle of social and personal magnetism, which emanates reciprocally from a speaker and from a close throng of hearers. This is perhaps the most important element of all the external conditions conducive to good and effective preaching.[21]

Charles Reynolds Brown's conception of an ideally arranged church building was very similar to that of Beecher.

> The ideal auditorium for speaking would be shaped something like a horseshoe, with the minister located midway between the two corks of the shoe. This might not be impressive architecturally, but it would lend itself admirably to the purposes of public address.[22]

[21] Beecher, *op. cit.*, I, 73–74.
[22] Charles Reynolds Brown, *The Art of Preaching*, p. 156.

The distance between pulpit and pews was important to
Beecher.

> The next point you should look to is to have your pews
> as near as possible to the speaker. A preacher must be a
> man among men. There is a force—call it magnetism, or
> electricity, or what you will—in a man, which is a per-
> sonal element, and which flows from a speaker who is *en
> rapport* with his audience. This principle should be uti-
> lized in the work of preaching. I do not say that Jonathan
> Edwards could not have preached under the pulpit dis-
> advantage. He could have preached out of anything. But
> there are not many men like Jonathan Edwards. The
> average man needs all the extraneous advantages he can
> press into his service.[23]

Beecher gave an example of a poorly placed pulpit.

> In Dr. Storrs's church in Brooklyn (The Church of the
> Pilgrims) there was formerly a space of from fifteen to
> twenty feet between the pulpit and the pews. It has been
> changed. But formerly you could see the minister only
> down to his chest. He stood in that box, stuck up against
> the wall, and then came a great space, like the desert of
> Sahara; and over on the other side of it began to be his
> audience. Before he can fill such a space the magnetic
> influence of the man is all lost. He has squandered one
> of the best natural forces of the pulpit.[24]

Charles Reynolds Brown agreed with Beecher on the necessity
of the pulpit's being near the pews.

> The pulpit had best be located as near as possible to
> the front pews. If there is a wide open space of twenty or
> thirty feet between the pulpit and the first row of people,
> a kind of Nevada desert without even sage brush and
> Jack rabbits in it to liven it up, this empty interval
> serves as a non-conductor of spiritual power. It serves to
> insulate the preacher from those to whose needs he would
> minister.[25]

[23] Beecher, *op. cit.*, I, 72–73.
[24] *Ibid.*, p. 71.
[25] Charles Reynolds Brown, *The Art of Preaching*, pp. 157–58.

Brown was opposed to the Gothic style of architecture for churches.

> The physical conditions in the church itself affect the delivery of any sermon. The architects seem to have forgotten oftentimes that Protestant churches are built primarily to speak in, to sing in, and to hear in. The Gothic church, with its high arches and long aisles, with its stately, obstructing columns and its defective acoustics, may have been adapted to a spectacular service which was meant to be seen rather than heard. The Gothic church as a rule is not well adapted to the work of preaching.[26]

This feeling was concurred in by Taylor.

> We complain of the architect who, forgetting that we are living in the nineteenth century, will insist on building churches for us in the beautiful, yet cold, inconvenient, and dimly-lighted Gothic of the past, and we say to him: "These were all well for former days, but give us something suited to our present requirements."[27]

Burton furnished an example of an expensive, but poorly built, church building.

> Bishop Potter, of New York, went to dedicate a very fine church;—and after the service, when the people were gathered about in a bubble of happification over the goodly edifice now completed and sanctified, it was noticed that he was silent. And when some one at last ventured to inquire: "Do you not like our Church," he said:—"O yes, it is a grand establishment,—and has only three faults." Of course they wanted to know right off, what those were. "You can neither see, nor hear, nor breathe in it," said the Bishop. As good a description of a first-class, modern, gothic meeting-house, as was ever given perhaps—so far as it goes.[28]

26 *Ibid.*, p. 156.
27 Taylor, *The Ministry of the Word*, p. 251.
28 Burton, *op. cit.*, pp. 118-19.

Beecher mentioned another building as being unfortunately built.

> We will take the church in New York called the Broadway Tabernacle. In it there are two lines of columns which hide a range of six pews, on each side straight from the pulpit clear through to the corner of the church, where the men and women cannot see the preacher on account of these architectural adjuncts which run up to the ceiling and make the church so beautiful. There the people can sit and look at the columns during the whole of the sermon-time.[29]

Both Simpson and Charles Reynolds Brown noticed the lack of proper ventilation in many churches. Brown said, "The presence of an abundance of fresh air contributes steadily to the effective delivery of a sermon." [30] On the subject of the lighting of the building, he added:

> The church should be sufficiently light for the minister to be able to look into the faces of the people, and to know something as to what is going on in their minds. It should be light enough for the people to follow the changing expression in his own face.[31]

By way of further emphasis, he concluded that:

> These are all little things but they affect for good or for ill the delivery of the sermon. When the surgeon is about to perform a major operation, he insists upon having all the physical conditions as perfect as they can be made. His own white antiseptic dress and that of the nurse, the tiled room which reduces to a minimum the danger of infection, the sterilized instruments, sponges and bandages to be employed,—all these have to do with the success of the operation. You are undertaking something much more difficult and delicate in every way— you cannot afford to neglect any of those conditions

[29] Beecher, *op. cit.*, I, 70–71.
[30] Charles Reynolds Brown, *The Art of Preaching*, p. 158.
[31] *Ibid.*, p. 159.

which will aid or retard you in accomplishing the desired
spiritual result.[32]

Simpson mentioned the need for fresh air.

> The principles of ventilation are generally but poorly
> understood by sextons. They usually confound warm air
> with pure air, and keep the rooms closed to have them
> warm. The interest of many a service is destroyed by this
> means. People wonder what is the matter with their
> preacher and with themselves. They have no life, no en-
> thusiasm. They cannot have any when their lungs are
> loaded with impure exhalations, and the brain is op-
> pressed with imperfectly oxygenated blood.[33]

Beecher indicated the added effect to be gained from a close
seating of the congregation.

> People often say, "Do you not think it is much more
> inspiring to speak to a large audience than a small one?"
> No, I say; I can speak just as well to twelve persons as
> to a thousand, provided those twelve are crowded around
> me and close together, so that they touch each other.
> But even a thousand people, with four feet space between
> every two of them, would be just the same as an empty
> room. Every lecturer will understand what I mean, who
> has ever seen such audiences and addressed them. But
> crowd your audience together, and you will set them off
> with not half the effort.[34]

Concerning the size of the audience, Watson said, "It does
not matter for effect upon the worshippers or preacher how
many are present, but only that the place be full." [35]

SUMMARY

Just as a precious stone takes on new beauty when set in
a beautiful mounting, so the sermon takes on new power
when set appropriately amid the various elements of worship.

[32] *Ibid.*, pp. 159–60.
[33] Simpson, *op. cit.*, pp. 271–72.
[34] Beecher, *op. cit.*, I, 73.
[35] Watson, *op. cit.*, p. 171.

Music, prayer, and the reading of the Scriptures are the best means of preparing the minds of the congregation for the presentation of the sermon. Although some would seek to achieve this preliminary tuning of the congregation by allowing them to listen to the playing of beautiful music, others are confident that an active participation in the singing of hymns is even more productive of the proper attitude of mind for the hearing of the sermon. Still others look to periods of meditation and prayer as a means of opening the minds of the congregation to the message. The proper reading of the Scriptures is also supremely important in the achievement of an atmosphere in which sermons may thrive.

The building in which the sermon is preached also influences the success of the sermon. It ought to be a building in which preacher and congregation are close together without deadening vacant spaces between. It ought to be a building in which the congregation can see and hear without strain. Plenty of light and an abundance of fresh air are also desirable. Finally, the service will be most effective if the audience is of sufficient size to fill the auditorium.

CHAPTER XI

MISCELLANEOUS ELEMENTS

In addition to the elements already discussed in this section there were several other elements suggested by the various lecturers which did not fall into any of the previous chapter classifications. They include such matters as types of sermons, the divine element in preaching, the length of the sermon, and the maturing of sermon ideas. The discussion concerning each is set forth in the following pages in the above-mentioned order.

TYPES OF SERMONS

Wide differences of opinion concerning the type of sermon most likely to succeed were discovered among the eight Yale lecturers who discussed this phase of preaching. Brooks expressed a feeling of indifference to such a discussion.

I am inclined to think that the idea of a sermon is so properly a unit, that a sermon involves of necessity such elements in combination, the absence of any one of which weakens the sermon-nature, that the ordinary classifications of sermons are of little consequence. We hear of expository preaching and topical sermons, of practical sermons, of hortatory discourses, each separate species seeming to stand by itself. It seems as if the preacher were expected to determine each week what kind of sermon the next Sunday was to enjoy and set himself deliberately to produce it. It may be well, but I say frankly that to my mind the sermon seems a unit, and that no sermon seems complete that does not include all these elements, and that the attempt to make a sermon of one sort alone mangles the idea and produces a one-sided thing. One element will preponderate in every sermon according to the nature of the subject that is treated, and the structure of the sermon will vary according as you choose to announce for it a topic or to make it a commentary upon some words of Christ or His apostles. But the mere preponderance of one element must not exclude the others, and the difference of forms does not really make a difference of sermons.[1]

In agreement with Brooks was Scherer, who also expressed the opinion that the traditional sermon types are not mutually exclusive.

You are familiar with the different types of sermon: doctrinal, expository, ethical, pastoral, evangelistic. Let me only say again that I have never preached or heard or read a sermon worthy of the name which was not to a greater or less degree all five of these together, precisely as a good novel is made up of narrative, description, characterization, and dialogue. . . . We would better see to it that the sermon is too. A sermon without exposition, with nothing which leads to a clearer understanding of God's Word, is without its highest sanction. A sermon without doctrine, with nothing which leads to a clearer understanding of the cardinal tenets of the Christian faith, is without foundation. A sermon without the ethical is pointless. . . . A sermon without the pastoral is spiritless. And a sermon without the evangelistic is Christless and useless altogether![2]

Day urged the young preachers at Yale to adopt the method which Christ used.

He did not take a passage from the law or the prophets, unravel its general principles, and then look about to discover if there were some place where those principles might be having an immediate application. Rather did he address himself to the human situation before him, guided by familiarity with the moral vision of yesterday but also by his own fresh and unique insight. He was, if anything, a topical preacher, talking about themes of

---

[1] Brooks, *op. cit.*, pp. 129–30.
[2] Scherer, *op. cit.*, p. 165.

immediate interest to the people before him. He had what we moderns call the problem approach. His homilies were suggested by incidents of the day, incidents which he always lifted into the light of eternity, but still incidents of the day, not the indictments of some far yesterday.[3]

Sperry declared himself against several widely accepted sermon practices:

There shall be no Bible passage as a point of departure; there certainly shall be no text, since that is one of the most deadening devices handed down from the past; there shall be no attempt at anything like introductions and conclusions; there shall be a wholly colloquial vocabulary and a most conversational· manner.[4]

Charles Reynolds Brown commended the text sermon, although he may have had in mind a longer passage than is ordinarily meant.

The habit of taking texts is more than a mere convention. In my judgment the best sermons grow directly out of texts. The best sermon themes are suggested mainly by the habitual, thoughtful, devotional reading of the Scriptures. The varied literature of the Bible covers a wide range of human need and privilege. The Bible is like a broad, thick slice of human experience which has found expression here in superb literary form. All the sins men commit are there; all the virtues, all the vital interests, all the high opportunities for fellowship with the Eternal are there wrought out in terms of life and in words that glow with meaning. They are all there in principle if not in detail because the spirit of all the duties in the calendar is there, even though the letter of exact direction may in some cases be lacking.[5]

Broadus indicated his own preference for the sermon built around a text.

3 Day, op. cit., p. 249.
4 Sperry, op. cit., p. 115.
5 Charles Reynolds Brown, The Art of Preaching, pp. 34-35.

It is manifest that to take a text gives a tone of sacredness to the discourse. But more than this is true. The primary idea is that the discourse is a development of the text, an explanation, illustration, application of its teachings. Our business is to teach God's word. And although we may often discuss subjects, and aspects of subjects, which are not presented in precisely that form by any passage of Scripture, yet the fundamental conception should be habitually retained, that we are about to set forth what the text contains.[6]

Forsyth also commended the use of the text in preaching.

The Bible is still the preacher's starting-point, even if it were not his living source. It is still the usual custom for him to take a text. If he but preach some happy thoughts, fancies, or philosophies of his own, he takes a text for a motto. It was not always so; but since it became so it is a custom that is fixed. And this from no mere conservatism. The custom received ready, nay inevitable, confirmation from the Reformers. It corresponded to the place they gave the Bible over the Church, on the one hand, and the individual on the other. It is the outward sign of the objectivity of our religion, its positivity, its quality as something given to our hand. Even when we need less protection against the Church, we still need it against the individual, and often against the preacher. We need to be defended from his subjectivity, his excursions, his monotony, his limitations. We need, moreover, to protect him from the peril of preaching himself, or his age. We must all preach *to* our age, but woe to us if it is our age we preach, and only hold up the mirror to the time.[7]

Brooks warned against too strong a demand for text sermons.

For over six hundred years now it has been the almost invariable custom of Christian preachers to take a text from Scripture and associate their thoughts more or less strictly with that. For the first twelve Christian centuries there seems to have been no such prevailing habit.

6 Broadus, *op. cit.*, p. 21.
7 Forsyth, *op. cit.*, p. 8.

This fact ought to be kept in mind whenever the custom of a text shows any tendency to become despotic or to restrain in any way the liberty of prophesying.[8]

Several of the preachers spoke very favorably of the expository sermon. Taylor set forth his own interpretation of expository preaching as follows:

> By expository preaching, I mean that method of pulpit discourse which consists in the consecutive interpretation, and practical enforcement, of a book of the sacred canon. It differs, thus, from topical preaching, which may be described as the selection of a clause, or verse, or section of the inspired Word, from which some one principle is evolved and kept continuously before the hearer's mind, as the speaker traces its manifold applications to present circumstances, and to human life; from doctrinal preaching, which prosecutes a system of Biblical induction in regard to some great truth, such as justification, regeneration, the atonement, or the like, gathering together all the portions of holy writ that bear upon it, and deducing from them some formulated inference; from hortatory preaching, which sets itself to the enforcement of some neglected duty, or the exposure of some prevalent iniquity; and from biographical preaching, which, taking some Scripture character for its theme, gives an analysis of the moral nature of the man, like that which Bishop Butler has made in his wonderful discourse on Balaam, and points from it lessons of warning or example.[9]

Charles Reynolds Brown referred to his own pleasant experience with expository preaching.

> I have used for some years, with growing satisfaction to myself and with increased interest and profit secured to my congregation, the method of expository preaching, devoting at certain seasons months and months together to the exposition of single books in the Bible. I wish here to indicate strongly my sense of the value of this

8 Brooks, *op. cit.*, p. 160.
9 Taylor, *The Ministry of the Word*, p. 155.

method and to speak of its special appropriateness and utility in presenting that social message which is my main theme.[10]

In another lecture he gave concrete evidence of the extensive use of expository preaching in his own practice.

> In the last church I served, . . . where I was pastor for nearly fifteen years, I find from an examination of my record book that during those years, I preached courses of expository sermons to that one congregation as follows:—From the Old Testament, six months on Genesis, three months on Exodus, three months on Joshua, three months on Judges, two months on the life of Elijah as recorded in Kings, two months on Job, six months on Isaiah, two months on the minor prophets. And I had in preparation a six months' course of sermons on first and second Samuel.
>
> In the New Testament, I preached for six months on Matthew, six months on Mark, twelve months on Luke, which to me is the greatest and dearest book in all the Bible, six months on John, six months on Acts, two months on Romans, three months on first and second Corinthians, and two months on the Book of Revelation. When this is added up it means that there was some course of expository sermons in process of delivery for six entire years of my pastorate there. And I believe that the testimony of at least two-thirds of the people in that church would confirm my own belief that this was the most profitable portion of my preaching from that pulpit.[11]

He further enumerated seven advantages of expository preaching: (1) it was the type of preaching done by the apostles; (2) it insures the preacher's thorough knowledge of the Bible; (3) it also insures the people's more thorough knowledge of the Bible; (4) it develops the Scriptural point of view; (5) it results in a more honest use of the Bible; (6)

---

[10] Charles Reynolds Brown, *The Social Message of the Modern Pulpit* (New York: Charles Scribner's Sons, 1912), pp. 37–38.
[11] Charles Reynolds Brown, *The Art of Preaching*, pp. 53–54.

the systematic study of book after book of the Bible guarantees
order in preaching; and (7) this method also insures the inclusion of certain difficult themes which the preacher might
otherwise tend to avoid.[12] Forsyth admonished the young
ministerial students of Yale to preach more sermons of this
type.

> Preach more expository sermons. Take long passages
> for texts. Perhaps you have no idea how eager people are
> to have the Bible expounded, and how much they prefer
> you to unriddle what the Bible says, with its large ut-
> terance, than to confuse them with what you can make
> it say by some ingenuity. It is thus you will get real
> preaching in the sense of preaching from the real situa-
> tion of the Bible to the real situation of the time. It
> is thus you make history preach to history, the past to
> the present, and not merely a text to a soul.[13]

Hall enumerated still other advantages of the exposition of a
single, long passage of Scripture:

> And this suggests the wisdom of taking to a larger
> extent than we do, chapters, or parts of chapters, and
> expounding them. We set out bits of Scripture in great
> beauty, like the separate tiles of a mosaic floor. Let us
> be expository to a greater extent, and the people will
> have the opportunity to see the pattern. We are liable
> to distort separate texts, and to misplace their messages.
> Let us help the people to look at groups of truths as they
> are set side by side by the Holy Ghost.[14]

Day's was the dissenting voice on the subject of expository
preaching.

> Some things which are said about expository preaching
> do not greatly impress me. It certainly has little au-
> thority from the greatest of all preachers. He did not
> proceed, as far as we are able to determine, either by
> quotation or exegesis. He came to a people who were

12 *Ibid.*, pp. 43–47.
13 Forsyth, *op. cit.*, p. 166.
14 Hall, *op. cit.*, p. 68.

saturated with expositions of ancient authorities and he came with a fresh approach to reality and to specific life problems.[15]

Twelve of the Yale lecturers spoke of an element which comes from God and which is essential to the success of the sermon. Taylor made a rather full explanation of it.

> That is effective preaching which convinces the intellect, stirs the heart, and quickens the conscience of the hearer, so that he is moved to believe the truth which has been presented to him, or to take the course which has been enforced upon him.
>
> This result cannot be produced, in any case, without the agency of the Holy Ghost; yet it is never to be forgotten that, in bringing it about, that Divine person works by means, which have, even in themselves, a fitness to secure the end in view. Now of these means, so far as they are connected with the Christian ministry, the sermon is the most important; and the preacher ought always to seek that his discourse shall have in it special adaptation to effect the result which, at the moment, he has set before him.
>
> There is no inconsistency between his faith in the necessity of the agency of the Spirit, and his exertion to have his sermon such as shall be signally fitted to impress his hearers; nay, rather the more intelligently [he] believes that he is a "laborer together with God," the more diligently will he work to make his discourse as excellent as possible.[16]

Broadus said on this point, "After all our preparation, general and special, for the conduct of public worship and for preaching, our dependence for real success is on the Spirit of God." [17] Dale suggested the means by which the preacher is to seek for this divine aid.

[15] Day, op. cit., p. 248.
[16] Taylor, The Ministry of the Word, p. 107.
[17] Broadus, op. cit., p. 540.

I know that to preach the gospel so as to reach the hearts and consciences of men, we need a special gift of the Holy Ghost: this gift we ought to seek in earnest prayer. I know, too, that the preaching of even an apostle will be powerless apart from the direct action of the Spirit of God upon the souls of men; and the manifestation of the presence and power of the Spirit is not to be expected unless we pray for it.[18]

Still another to mention the divine element in preaching was Charles Reynolds Brown.

But all this detailed preparation, taken by itself, is mere dust of the ground. It has little worth until the Spirit of the Lord shall move upon the face of it and breathe into it the breath of his own mighty life, bestowing upon your sermon a living soul.[19]

He called it the most important asset the preacher has.

You will find that in the number of conversions made, in the range and power of your inspirational appeal, in the measure of comfort and help afforded to your people, and even in the sheer attractiveness you may exhibit as a popular preacher, there is no other one asset which will bear comparison for a moment with the sense of this divine element operating in all your work.[20]

Several of the speakers mentioned a slightly different, yet closely related, element. They indicated that God's assistance comes through the preacher's close association with Him. They felt that the sermon will have the stamp of God upon it, if the preacher had an experience of God in his own life. Calkins made his explanation of the matter quite full.

Preaching is simply an effort to give words and outward content to that inward and spiritual experience. A sermon has been defined as the overflow of the soul. If the soul itself be empty, there can be no overflow. A

18 Dale, *op. cit.*, p. 203.
19 Charles Reynolds Brown, *The Art of Preaching*, p. 222.
20 *Ibid.*, p. 243.

preacher may possess every other qualification. He may have a fine presence, and his elocution may be perfect. He may be well trained and intellectually the master of his subject; he may have a good set of ideas and a healthy grasp of the practical problems with which he has to deal. He may have all this and much else. But if he lacks, or in proportion as he lacks, a deep vital and personal experience of God and of the Christian revelation of God, he is sure to fail as a preacher. For preaching is simply the uttering of one's own experience. And if one has no experience, neither can one utter it.[21]

John Brown referred to an outstanding preacher of the past as an example of one who achieved much of his power through intimate relationship with God.

I have explained Baxter's marvellous success at Kidderminster by calling attention to his direct and powerful speech, his close contact with his people, and his going on steadily year after year urging men to come into the Kingdom of God. But may I not now say that all these things rested on something deeper still—that they gathered point, fire and force from the deep heart experiences revealed in the confessions I have read to you? This man got his power by being alone with God and by looking into the face of God! And it is there we must get power too. There is no substitute for this power and no other way of getting it. It is the soul that has caught fire from the altar which sets other souls on fire.[22]

Jowett noticed the loss of power resulting from the preacher's separation from God.

But a second thing happens when, for any cause, we are separated from the Lord whom we have vowed to serve. Our speech lacks a mysterious impressiveness. We are wordy but we are not mighty. We are eloquent but we do not persuade. We are reasonable but we do not convince.[23]

[21] Calkins, *op. cit.*, p. 120.
[22] John Brown, *op. cit.*, p. 194.
[23] Jowett, *op. cit.*, p. 59.

Horne spoke of the change wrought in the preacher by divine assistance.

> Something has got to happen to us; some magic change must pass over our spirits; and beneath the inspiration of the new revelation of Deity and Humanity our speech will clothe itself with colour and beauty as naturally and inevitably as the spring adorns and decorates the earth.[24]

Forsyth attributed much of the power of the Gospel to this divine element.

> Its [the Gospel's] authority is not that of the preacher's personality, nor even of his faith, nay, not even of his message alone, but that of the divine action behind him, whereof he himself is but as it were the sacramental element, and not the sacramental Grace.[25]

LENGTH OF SERMONS

Eight speakers drew attention to the element of sermon length. Simpson gave two reasons against the preaching of long sermons:

> The question then arises: "How long should the sermon be?" . . .
> . . . The only safe rule is, to quit before taxing the attention and patience of the congregation so that they will be unwilling to return again to the house of God. Long sermons, also, are a strain upon the minister who delivers them, which, if he possesses earnestness of manner, will very likely unfit him for a protracted ministry.[26]

Taylor was another who was opposed to long sermons.

> I only add, in this connection, that a sermon, to be effective, must not be inordinately long. When weariness begins to be felt by the hearer, edification ends, and sometimes the latter portion of a discourse only effaces the impression which the earlier has made.[27]

[24] Horne, *op. cit.*, p. 149.
[25] Forsyth, *op. cit.*, pp. 84–85.
[26] Simpson, *op. cit.*, pp. 138–39.
[27] Taylor, *The Ministry of the Word*, p. 125.

Watson suggested:

> When the sermon has culminated after a natural fashion, it ought to end, leaving its effect to rest not on rhetoric but on truth. There may be times when for effect the sermon may cease suddenly some letters before Z, because the audience has surrendered without terms and the sermon has served its purpose.[28]

Of the length of sermons, Beecher said:

> One word as to the length of sermons. That never should be determined by the clock, but upon broader considerations,—short sermons for small subjects, and long sermons for large subjects. It does not require that sermons should be of any uniform length. Let one be short, and the next long, and the next intermediate. . . . The true way to shorten a sermon is to make it more interesting.[29]

John Brown mentioned Alexander Maclaren as one who sometimes ended his sermons earlier than expected.

> Further, that his [Alexander Maclaren's] mode of preparation had this effect sometimes, that his material did not always last as long as he expected. In such cases, when his wool was done, he had the courage to leave off spinning. He would never condescend to empty talk merely for the sake of filling up what has come to be regarded as the canonical time. He has been known to sit down at the end of twelve minutes, simply remarking that he had no more to say. And I do not know why a minister should go on talking when he has no more to say, though there are some ministers who do.[30]

Abbott named several elements which should be considered in the determining of the length of the sermon.

> How long should a sermon be? This is like asking how large should a gateway be. The size demanded of the

[28] Watson, *op. cit.*, pp. 30–31.
[29] Beecher, *op. cit.*, I, 234.
[30] John Brown, *op. cit.*, p. 268.

gateway depends on the size of the load to be carried through; the length of the sermon depends on the largeness of the idea of which it is a vehicle. People do not object to long sermons, they object to lengthy sermons. If what the minister wants to say can be said in three minutes, the sermon is too long if it takes four minutes. If the minister is full of a theme which for its adequate presentation would require an hour, the sermon seems short if it occupies forty-five minutes. There is, however, an important fact which the modern minister should realize, but does not always,—the change which has been produced within the last twenty-five years by the telegraph and the newspaper. Men think much more quickly than they used to think. Contracts which they would take hours to talk over, they now complete, save for the legal phrasing, in five minutes. They read the daily newspaper by the headlines, or, glancing the eye down the column of the editorial, extract its significance by a kind of instantaneous intellectual process. Accustomed to this rapidity of mental action through the week, they go to church, and are wearied by hearing a minister hold a single thought before them, possibly a rather commonplace thought, for fifteen or twenty minutes, or even half an hour, while he is hoping to keep their attention upon it by the beauty with which he attires it, or even insisting that it is the duty of the hearer to continue to listen after he has learned all that the minister has to say.[31]

Burton agreed with Beecher on the length of sermons.

A short sermon is a sermon that seems short; it may be fifteen minutes long or it may be an hour. Time has nothing to do with it. If a man is unconscious no speech seems long to him. The hearer fast asleep is willing you should go on till you are tired out. And, what is the same thing, the hearer so absorbed by what you are saying as to be unconscious, does not charge the sermon with being prolix. Time is measured, not by clocks, nor even by the rotation of the earth, but by the state of our

31 Abbott, op. cit., pp. 213–14.

minds, and the things going on therein. All experience proves that.[32]

According to Charles Reynolds Brown, the size of the man is more important than the time involved in the determining of the correct length of a sermon.

> There is no reason in the nature of the case why a sermon should be just so long. Why should a sermon be just thirty minutes, or forty minutes, or if by reason of unusual powers of endurance and of attenuation, sixty minutes in length? There is no more reason that a man's sermon should be just so long, than there is that a man's trousers should be just so long. It all depends on the length of the man. In one case it depends upon the length of the man's legs, and in the other case it depends on the length of the man's mind.[33]

Brown [34] also listed the following elements which he said will make the sermon seem long: (1) long introductions; (2) lack of arrangement; (3) dwelling too long upon the obvious; (4) a steady monotone; (5) lack of variety; and (6) long conclusions.

MATURATION

Twelve of the Lyman Beecher lecturers indicated the importance of the sermon's growth and development through a long period of time before it is finally delivered. Charles Reynolds Brown named some of the advantages of such a procedure:

> If a minister can hold a certain truth in his mind for a month, for six months perhaps, for a year it may be, before he preaches on it he will find new ideas perpetually sprouting out of it, until it shows an abundant growth. He may meditate on it as he walks the streets,

[32] Burton, *op. cit.*, p. 118.
[33] Charles Reynolds Brown, *The Art of Preaching*, p. 95.
[34] *Ibid.*, pp. 102–11.

or as he spends some hours on a train, when his eyes are too tired to read.[35]

Merrill said on the same subject that:

> . . . a man may get surprising results if he keeps his prospective sermon floating in his mind, somewhere between the conscious and the subconscious, amid his varied doings through the day and the week.
>
> It is good for a man that he get his theme very early, if possible before the previous Sunday is past. For if it lie in his mind thus for a few days, it will come up with a surprising amount of valuable material gathered out of the corners of his brain.[36]

Stalker incorporated the element of maturation into his rules for sermon preparation.

> Let me mention one more rule for the composition of the sermon which appears to me to be the most important of all. It is, to take time. Begin in time and get done in time—this, I often say to myself, is the whole duty of a minister. . . . The process of thinking especially should be prolonged; it is not so important that the process of writing should be slow. It is when the subject has been long tossed about in thought that the mind begins to glow about it; the subject itself gets hot and begins to melt and flash, until at last it can be poured forth in a facile but glowing stream.[37]

Pepper suggested the desirability of the preacher's discussing the sermon with others during its period of growth.

> A sermon should be long in preparation. It should grow rather than be made and there should be several under way at once. It would be well if a preacher were on such terms with his men that it were possible even to talk over a sermon in the course of its preparation. Nothing draws people closer to one another than to think things out together. It would be an interesting situation

35 *Ibid.*, p. 64.
36 Merrill, *op. cit.*, p. 89.
37 Stalker, *op cit.*, pp. 116–17.

if when the sermon were finally preached a little group of men should have toward it a sense of co-proprietorship.[38]

About hastily-prepared sermons, Jowett said:

> It may be that a word will lay hold of you so imperatively as to make you feel that its proclamation is urgent, and that its hour has come. But I think it frequently happens that we go into the pulpit with truth that is undigested and with messages that are immature. Our minds have not done their work thoroughly, and when we present our work to the public there is a good deal of floating sediment in our thought, and a consequent cloudiness about our words. Now it is a good thing to put a subject away to mature and clarify.[39]

A few moments later he added that:

> . . . this will mean that the preparation of Sunday's sermons cannot begin on Saturday morning and finish on Saturday night. The preparation is a long process: the best sermons are not made, they grow: they have their analogies, not in the manufactory, but in the garden and the field.[40]

Agreeing that maturation is necessary in sermon preparation, Dale said that:

> There is still another reason for delay when we think we have a grasp of new truth. We shall not be able at once to do justice to our new discovery. At first we shall not handle it firmly and with any freedom. The kind of mastery over a doctrine which is absolutely necessary to effective exposition can only come when by repeated and prolonged meditation we have made it perfectly familiar to us.[41]

Watson distinguished between the time required to write a sermon and the time necessary to create it.

[38] Pepper, *op. cit.*, p. 87.
[39] Jowett, *op. cit.*, p. 130.
[40] *Ibid.*, p. 134.
[41] Dale, *op. cit.*, p. 15.

"How long does it take to prepare a sermon?" is an ambiguous question. If you mean to write the manuscript, then a day may suffice; if you mean to think a sermon, then it may be ten years.[42]

Jefferson pointed out the ease with which sermons are prepared after a period of maturation.

Men who carry sermon themes long in their mind are always surprised by the ease with which the sermons, when called for, come forth. The mind has queer ways of working below consciousness, and a theme once given to it is probably unfolding day after day, although we ourselves are unconscious of its growth. One never knows what is going to happen when he puts a truth to soak in the juices of the mind.[43]

Brooks contrasted special preparation of sermons with general preparation.

I think that the less of special preparation that is needed for a sermon, the better the sermon is. . . . One preacher depends for his sermon on special reading. Each discourse is the result of work done in the week in which it has been written. All his study is with reference to some immediately pressing occasion. Another preacher studies and thinks with far more industry, is always gathering truth into his mind, but it is not gathered with reference to the next sermon. It is truth sought for truth's sake, and for that largeness and ripeness and fullness of character which alone can make him a strong preacher. Which is the better method? The latter beyond all doubt.[44]

SUMMARY

For many generations the text sermon has held a very prominent place among the several sermon types. Although it is still held in honor, there is a growing tendency toward the

[42] Watson, *op. cit.*, p. 14.
[43] Jefferson, *op. cit.*, p. 256.
[44] Brooks, *op. cit.*, p. 157.

two other leading types—the subject sermon and the expository sermon. The expository sermon was recommended with unusual zeal by several of the leaders among the Yale lecturers. It was also suggested that a single sermon might possess in its several parts characteristics of the several different sermon types.

In addition to his own power as evidenced in the preparation and the delivery of the sermon, the minister of God must have the assistance of God's power. Through earnest prayer and communion with God, through constant meditation upon his word, the preacher receives the power of God which is able to make his sermons reach deep into the hearts of men. God's power operates through the sermon and through the preacher to change the lives of men.

Sermons must submit to certain limitations of time. However, it was somewhat generally agreed that the size of the man in the pulpit and the importance of the particular message at hand should determine the length of the sermon, rather than the hands of the clock. It was also generally agreed that sermons should be started a great while before the date of delivery so that the ideas will have ample opportunity to grow.

PART III

THE CONGREGATION

Chapter XII

TAKING AIM

The third major factor in preaching is the congregation. The preacher and the sermon are without meaning unless there is a congregation, for preaching exists for the sole purpose of influencing men. The aim of preaching is to move the people from a lower to a higher plane of living. The final test of the effectiveness of all preaching is this: What changes have occurred in the lives of the people because of the preaching?

This section of the book deals with the following three important phases of preaching as it relates to the congregation: (1) taking aim, (2) analysis of the audience, and (3) approach to the audience. Each is discussed in a separate chapter.

Twenty-one of the Lyman Beecher speakers discussed in their lectures the importance of thoughtful consideration of the purpose of the sermon. The feeling was unanimous that a proper realization of the purpose for which the sermon is to be preached is essential to success in the pulpit. There was no dissenting voice on this point.

Beecher gave no subject greater emphasis, in the thirty-three lectures which he delivered in the first three years of the Lyman Beecher series, than the subject of taking aim. Because of that emphasis, the first several pages of the present chapter are devoted to a presentation of some of Beecher's most forceful comments upon this subject. He began by picturing the evils of the preacher's lack of purpose.

It is hardly an imaginary case to describe one as approaching the Sabbath day somewhat in this way: "O

dear me, I have got to preach! I have beat out pretty
much all there is in that straw, and I wonder what I
shall preach on next"; and so the man takes the Bible and
commences to turn over the leaves, hoping that he will
hit something. He looks up and down, and turns forward
and backward, and finally he does see a light, and he says,
"I can make something interesting from that." Interesting, why? For what purpose? What, under heaven, but
that he is a salaried officer expected to preach twice on
Sunday, and to lecture or hold the prayer-meeting in the
middle of the week; and the time has come round when,
like a clock, it is his business to strike, and so he does
strike, just as ignorantly as the hammer strikes upon the
bell! He is following out no intelligent plan. He is a perfunctory preacher, doing a duty because appointed to
that duty.[1]

In characteristic fashion, he next summoned a convincing
illustration to aid him in driving home his point.

What would you think of a physician in the house-
hold who has been called to minister to a sick member of
some family, and who says, "Well, I will leave something
or other; I don't know; what shall I leave?" and he looks
in his saddle-bags to see what he has yet got the most of,
and prescribes it with no directions; the father, mother,
and children may all take a little, and the servants may
have the rest. Another physician, and a true one, comes,
and the mother says, "Doctor, I have called you in to
prescribe for my child." He sits down and studies the
child's symptoms; traces them back to the supposed
cause; reflects how he shall hit that case, what remedial
agents are supposed to be effective, what shall be the form
of administration, how often; he considers the child's temperament and age, and adapts himself to the special necessity of the individual case.[2]

A second illustration was drawn from his own experience.

I used to go out hunting by myself, and I had great
success in firing off my gun; and the game enjoyed it as

[1] Beecher, *op. cit.*, I, 4-5.
[2] *Ibid.*, pp. 5-6.

much as I did, for I never hit them or hurt them. I fired off my gun as I see hundreds of men firing off their sermons. I loaded it, and bang!—there was a smoke, a report, but nothing fell; and so it was again and again. I recollect one day in the fields my father pointed out a little red squirrel, and said to me, "Henry, would you like to shoot him?" I trembled all over, but I said, "Yes." He got down on his knee, put the gun across a rail, and said, "Henry, keep perfectly cool, perfectly cool; take aim." And I did, and I fired, and over went the squirrel, and he didn't run away either. That was the first thing I ever hit; and I felt an inch taller, as a boy that had killed a squirrel, and knew how to aim a gun.[3]

In the several pages which immediately followed this illustration, Beecher [4] told of his first successful sermon. He had been preaching for two years and a half when it happened. Because of discouraging results from his work he had undertaken a careful study of the methods employed by the apostles. He concluded that their success resulted from a complete understanding of the people to whom they spoke, and from a careful adaptation of their sermons to those people. He resolved to imitate their methods, and carefully planned a sermon to fit the people who would sit in his audience. In describing the results of that sermon, he said, ". . . there were seventeen men awakened under that sermon. I never felt so triumphant in my life. I cried all the way home. I said to myself: 'Now I know how to preach.' " [5] Later in his series of lectures, he touched again upon the subject of the purpose of preaching.

> Sermons are mere tools; and the business that you have in hand is not making sermons, or preaching sermons,— it is *saving men*. Let this come up before you so frequently that it shall never be forgotten, that none of these

[3] *Ibid.*, p. 10.
[4] *Ibid.*, pp. 10–12.
[5] *Ibid.*, p. 12.

things should gain ascendency over this prime controlling element of your lives, that you are to save men.[6]

A moment later he described the ideal way to plan for the
preaching of each subsequent sermon.

You will very soon come, in your parish life, to the
habit of thinking more about your people and what you
shall do for them than about your sermons and what you
shall talk about. That is a good sign. Just as soon as you
find yourself thinking, on Monday or Tuesday, "Now,
here are these persons, or this class,"—you run over your
list and study your people,—"what shall I do for them?"
you will get some idea what you need to do.[7]

Noyes also spoke of taking aim.

The Master of one of the Yale colleges observed after
a Sunday service in Battell Chapel: "Preaching is like
shooting quail. If you aim for all the birds, you hit none,
but if you aim for one, you are likely to get several."
He was right. . . .[8]

Charles Reynolds Brown joined Beecher in emphasizing the
need for the preacher to concentrate upon the people and
their needs.

The leaves of the sermon are for the healing of the
people. The eyes of your head may be upon your pulpit
and upon your paper, if you are a manuscript preacher,
but the eyes of your mind and the attention of your
heart must be upon those plain and needy people there in
the pews. Not here behind the sacred desk nor upon it
where your homiletic work of art lies in all its learned
beauty, but out there among the lives of men, tempted,
struggling, doubting, sorrowing, failing, is the place of
your supreme concern.[9]

In another place, the same author said, "Your supreme concern then in the pulpit will not be your sermon but the souls

6 *Ibid.*, pp. 38–39.
7 *Ibid.*, p. 41.
8 Noyes, *op. cit.*, p. 105.
9 Charles Reynolds Brown, *The Art of Preaching*, p. 23.

of your people." [10] The same consideration of the audience was recommended by Jefferson, when he said, "A doctor's business is not to know books, but to cure people. Your supreme business is not to build sermons, but to build characters." [11] Brooks explained the reason for some of the poor preaching of his day in terms of a lack of purpose.

> The first thing for you to do is to see clearly what you are going to preach for, what you mean to try to save men from. By your conviction about that, the whole quality of your ministry will be decided. To the absence of any clear answer to that question, to the entire vagueness as to what men's danger is, we owe the vagueness with which so many of our preachers preach.[12]

Several lectures later, Brooks again emphasized the importance of the purpose of the sermon.

> A sermon exists in and for its purpose. That purpose is the persuading and moving of men's souls. That purpose must never be lost sight of. If it ever is, the sermon flags.[13]

In naming a list of qualities which the sermon should possess, Taylor spoke of definite aim.

> Every sermon should have a distinct object in view. One must preach, not because the Sabbath has come round, and he has to occupy the time somehow, but rather because there is something pressing upon his mind and heart which he feels impelled to proclaim. . . .
> Ever, therefore, as you sit down to prepare your discourse, let your question be, "What is my purpose in this sermon?" and do not move a step until you have shaped out before your mind a definite answer to that inquiry.[14]

10 *Ibid.*, pp. 239–40.
11 Jefferson, *op. cit.*, p. 106.
12 Brooks, *op. cit.*, p. 33.
13 *Ibid.*, p. 110.
14 Taylor, *The Ministry of the Word*, p. 110.

Abbott spoke in almost identical language a few years later.

> The first condition of an effective sermon is a definite object. Mark the difference between subject and object. In preparing a sermon the minister should define his object in his own mind before he select either his subject or his text. What do I want to accomplish this Sunday morning, in this congregation, with this discourse? This is the first question for the preacher to ask himself.[15]

The same advice concerning the purpose of the sermon was given by Burton.

> So you must ask yourself, in every case—what do I wish to accomplish with this sermon-stock that I have on hand. When that is settled, the form of the organization to be made begins to be settled. Get your aim, and every least item of your stock of material spontaneously shapes itself to that aim; as all things followed the music of Orpheus. A clear aim, firmly held, works . . . results.[16]

Burton confessed that the greatest weakness of his preaching was in regard to the matter of taking aim.

> It has been the sin of my life that I have not always taken aim. I have been a lover of subjects. If I had loved men more and loved subjects only as God's instruments of good for men, it would have been better, and I should have more to show for all my labor under the sun.[17]

Robinson was another to give the consideration of the sermon purpose a place of primary importance.

> Suppose a topic with its text to have been chosen. What shall be the next step? Manifestly, it should be to decide, as definitely as possible, just what we propose to accomplish by the discourse. And, the more exactly that purpose can be defined, the better. And better still, the more specific the theme, the greater the likelihood of

15 Abbott, *op. cit.*, p. 208.
16 Burton, *op. cit.*, p. 53.
17 *Ibid.*, p. 55.

freshness and fullness in the treatment of it, and of distinctness of impression and conviction with the hearers.[18]

In one of his lectures Jowett described an interesting technique for the preacher's use in keeping the sermon purpose in mind during the period of sermon preparation.

> When I have got my theme clearly defined, and I begin to prepare its exposition, I keep in the circle of my mind at least a dozen men and women, very varied in their natural temperaments, and very dissimilar in their daily circumstances. These are not mere abstractions. Neither are they dolls or dummies. They are real men and women whom I know: professional people, trading people, learned and ignorant, rich and poor. When I am preparing my work, my mind is constantly glancing round this invisible circle, and I consider how I can so serve the bread of this particular truth as to provide welcome nutriment for all. . . . You may not like my method: it probably would not suit you, and you may devise a better: but at any rate it does this for me,—in all my preparation it keeps me in actual touch with life, with real men and women, moving in the common streets, exposed to life's varying weathers, the "garish day," and the cold night, the gentle dew and the driving blast. It keeps me on the common earth: it saves me from losing myself in the clouds. Gentlemen, our messages must be related to life, to lives, and we must make everybody feel that our key fits the lock of his own private door.[19]

Jowett also had a concrete recommendation to make to the young minister concerning the sermon purpose.

> To this end I think it is needful, before we go into the pulpit, to define to ourselves, in simple, decisive terms, what we conceive to be the purpose of the service. Let us clearly formulate the end at which we aim. Let us put it into words. Don't let it hide in the cloudy realm of vague assumptions. Let us arrest ourselves in the very midst of our assumptions, and compel ourselves to name

18 Robinson, *op. cit.*, p. 142.
19 Jowett, *op. cit.*, pp. 136–37.

and register our ends. Let us take a pen in hand, and in
order that we may still further banish the peril of vacuity
let us commit to paper our purpose and ambition for the
day.[20]

Like Jowett, Scherer suggested keeping the people of the congregation in mind while preparing the sermon.

With regard to the actual writing, there is hardly an
end to the suggestions one could offer. Perhaps the most
essential thing is that you keep always before your mind's
eye the people to whom you shall speak. Not that you are
to introduce something here for this man's benefit, or
something there which may have some particular bearing
upon that woman and the way she acted at the congrega-
tional meeting; but you should visualize, while you write,
as many living, needy, real people as you can, and say to
them straightforwardly what is in your heart. The farther
away you can get from embroidered essays on fascinating
fancies, the better; and the nearer you can get to the spirit
and the manner of an earnest and private conversation,
the more effective will your sermon become.[21]

A moment later in the same lecture he added:

I mean to make everything subservient to one purpose,
and that purpose not the writing of a great sermon or the
elaboration of some mighty and puissant theme, but the
ministering to human souls of the redemptive power of
God. Do bear that forever in mind. Principal Denney
used to say, "No man can give at once the impression that
he himself is clever and that Christ is mighty to save."
You are preaching not to make clear what good preaching
is or ought to be; you are preaching to lay hold desperately on life, broken life, hurt life, soiled life, staggering
life, helpless life, hard, cynical, indifferent, willful life,
to lay hold on it with both hands in the high name of the
Lord Christ and to lift it toward his dream.[22]

20 *Ibid.*, pp. 147–48.
21 Scherer, *op. cit.*, p. 180.
22 *Ibid.*, p. 181.

Simpson mentioned the necessity of consideration of the sermon purpose.

> Decide what end you propose to reach by the sermon. Is it for the impenitent, for the inquirer, or for the edification of believers? Is it to enforce some pressing duty, to guard against some danger, or to afford comfort and hope to the suffering and sorrowing? According to the object proposed, let the text be selected.[23]

Merrill was still another who thought the sermon purpose worthy of consideration. He said that:

> . . . we need to bear in mind that in preaching the object is even more important than the subject. Every sermon aims at definite action. It is meant to make a difference in the lives of the hearers, or it is no true sermon. Here also there is need of skill in orderly treatment, human as well as logical skill, that the object may be enforced at the end with full and compelling effect.[24]

Dale spoke emphatically of the need for a purpose behind the sermon:

> . . . you should first of all come to a clear understanding with yourself about the precise object of your sermon.
> *What is the sermon to do?* The answer to this question determines the whole method of preparation.[25]

"We shall preach to no purpose unless we have a purpose in preaching," [26] was another of Dale's statements. Buttrick referred to a technique used by another of the Yale lecturers, Henry Sloane Coffin, in his effort always to keep his sermon aim before himself.

> Doctor Coffin has told that for years it was his practice to write at the head of his manuscript the aim of that sermon: "I wish and am required in this sermon to . . ."

23 Simpson, *op. cit.*, pp. 134–35.
24 Merrill, *op. cit.*, p. 35.
25 Dale, *op. cit.*, p. 131.
26 *Ibid.*, p. 24.

Such clarity of aim will blaze a straight trail through many a listening mind.[27]

In a discussion of effective preaching, Broadus said, "Unless it aims at real and practical results, it is spurious." [28]

SUMMARY

Before a man begins to erect a building he pauses to consider the services which the building must render when completed. Is it to house a chemistry laboratory at a large university? Is it to serve as a dwelling for a small family of modest income? Or, is it to furnish office space in an overcrowded city? Only when he has determined the purpose for which the building is to be erected can he choose the most appropriate type of architecture, the most suitable materials, the best size and arrangement for the building.

In like manner, the wise preacher carefully considers the use to which his sermon is to be put before he chooses the materials with which to build the sermon and determines the arrangement of those materials. Just as there is little possibility that a building constructed without thought of its eventual use could be of much value, so it is likewise improbable that a sermon constructed without thought of its effect could have much influence. The wise speaker first decides what the purpose of his sermon is to be, and then bends every effort to accomplish that purpose.

[27] Buttrick, *op. cit.*, pp. 160–61.
[28] Broadus, *op. cit.*, p. 5.

CHAPTER XIII

ANALYSIS OF THE AUDIENCE

In order to accomplish his basic purpose, that of moving men, the preacher must possess a thorough knowledge of mankind in general and of his own congregation in particular. Thirty-eight of the Lyman Beecher lecturers found occasion to mention this need. In addition, many of the speakers suggested methods of attaining this knowledge. Both the announcements of the principle and the suggestions for carrying it into effect are presented in succeeding pages.

Because of Taylor's rather full discussion of this subject in his lectures, several of his comments are included here. The following quotation shows the importance which he placed upon the preacher's knowledge of men.

> Another prerequisite to success in the pulpit is *a good knowledge of the human heart*. The physician must understand, not merely the nature of the remedies which he is to employ, but also the symptoms and workings of the diseases which he desires to cure. He must "walk the hospitals" as well as study the pharmacopeia. Now, the gospel is a remedial measure, and therefore it is essential that its preachers should be acquainted with the nature of man, as well as with the means which, as the instrument in the hands of God's spirit, he is to use for its transformation and renewal. Hence, he who wishes to become an efficient minister, will be a diligent student of men.[1]

Taylor proceeded to suggest four avenues through which the young minister might secure a knowledge of men. The first which he named was the study of the many characters of the

[1] Taylor, *The Ministry of the Word*, pp. 35–36.

Bible, which, he said, represent "every phase of human nature." [2] The second area of source material was the field of
human literature or history.[3] The third source of information indicated by Taylor was "the dramatic works of Shake-
speare." [4] His final suggestion was "to mingle much among
men themselves." [5]

Brooks laid down three rules which bear upon the
preacher's need of a knowledge of his people.

> These three rules seem to have in them the practical
> sum of the whole matter. I beg you to remember them
> and apply them with all the wisdom that God gives you.
> First. Have as few congregations as you can. Second.
> Know your congregation as thoroughly as you can. Third.
> Know your congregation so largely and deeply that in
> knowing it you shall know humanity.[6]

Beecher also suggested the importance of a thorough study of
people.

> If I might be allowed to criticise the general theological
> course, or to recommend anything in relation to it, I
> should say that one of the prime constituents of the train-
> ing should be a study of the human soul and body from
> beginning to end.[7]

A brief insight into Beecher's own method of analysis of
people is given in the following paragraph.

> When I see a man I instinctively divide him up, and
> ask myself, How much has he of the animal, how much
> of the spiritual, and how much of the intellectual? And
> what is his intellect, perceptive or reflective? Is he ideal,
> or apathetic, or literal? And I instinctively adapt myself
> to him.[8]

2 *Ibid.*, p. 41.
3 *Ibid.*, pp. 41–42.
4 *Ibid.*, p. 42.
5 *Ibid.*, p. 44.
6 Brooks, *op. cit.*, p. 190.
7 Beecher, *op. cit.*, I, 86.
8 *Ibid.*, p. 51.

Beecher's own practice, described in the following quotation, gives some hint as to the reason why he was one of the most effective preachers of his time.

Now, I take great delight, if ever I can get a chance, in riding on the top of an omnibus with the driver, and talking with him. What do I gain by that? Why, my sympathy goes out for these men, and I recognize in them an element of brotherhood,—that great human element which lies underneath all culture, which is more universal and more important than all special attributes, which is the great generic bond of humanity between man and man. If ever I saw one of those men in my church, I could preach to him, and hit him under the fifth rib with an illustration, much better than if I had not been acquainted with him. I have driven the truth under many a plain jacket. But, what is more, I never found a plain man in this world who could not tell me many things that I did not know before. There is not a gatekeeper at the Fulton Ferry, or an engineer or deckhand on the boats, that I am not acquainted with, and they help me in more ways than they know of. If you are going to be a minister, keep very close to plain folks; don't get above the common people.[9]

Elaborating further on this suggestion, he said:

Begin your ministry with the common people. Get seasoned with the humanity and sympathies which belong to men; mix with farmers, mechanics, and laboring men; eat with them, sleep with them; for, after all, there is the great substance of humanity.[10]

Watson also thought it desirable for the minister to be well acquainted with life.

The minister ought to be soaked in life; not that his sermons may never escape from local details, but rather that, being in contact with the life nearest him, he may state his gospel in terms of human experience.[11]

[9] *Ibid.*, pp. 97–98.
[10] *Ibid.*, p. 147.
[11] Watson, *op. cit.*, p. 55.

Along the same line of thought, Horne called attention to a field of practical study which he would include in the seminary curriculum.

> The course of study I would fain include in the curriculum of every modern school of the prophets would be conducted in a tenement district, or some area where men and women live—or exist—doing unending tasks for starvation wages. If to that could be added a brief course of study of the actual lives of the wealthy dilettantists and neurotics who make up so large a portion of what is called Society, we should breed a race of prophets who would be our leaders in a new exodus towards a new land of promise.
>
> When the great masses of our peoples are made to understand that our preachers are those who know the inwardness of their life and lot, and have entered into close brotherhood with them to champion their right to fullness of life and opportunity, then faith will revive in our lands even as we read in the time of Moses, "And the people believed, for when they saw that the Lord had visited His children, and had seen their afflictions, then they bowed their heads and worshipped." [12]

Freeman noted the preacher's need for an exact knowledge of the conditions of men in slightly different terms.

> Our first work as ministers is that of diagnosis. Diagnosis goes before treatment. Remedial work is based upon accurate knowledge of the conditions it is designed to treat. All this comes within the sphere of our pastoral ministry.
>
> To so identify ourselves with the lives of men and women that we shall know their susceptibilities, their tendencies, their weaknesses, gives us not only an accurate and sympathetic knowledge, but equips us to deal with them specifically and scientifically. [13]

[12] Horne, op. cit., pp. 77–78.
[13] Freeman, op. cit., p. 77.

At this point the analytical method employed by Coffin, as reported in *The Presbyterian Tribune* and quoted by Scherer is appropriate.

> What ranges of Christian experience seem unknown to this congregation?
> To what Christian principles do they appear blind?
> What spiritual needs seem unmet?
> What areas of individual and social life in this community seem to lie outside Christ's Kingdom?
> What is lacking or defective in the Church's effect on the community?
> What Christian resources are nominally listed by this congregation but not used?
> What aspects of the Gospel have most immediate appeal to those not yet Christians? [14]

Pointing to the preacher's need for a knowledge of his people, Parkhurst also compared the preacher's work with that of the physician.

> Healthy prescription always depends on safe diagnosis, and a preacher who does not know both the ideal man and the man actual, is no more fitted to preach than a physician is qualified to practice who is not familiar with anatomy and physiology, both normal and abnormal.[15]

Greer was another to draw this analogy between the physician and the preacher.

> The physician who prescribes without an adequate knowledge of the case for which he prescribes will not prescribe well; and the preacher who preaches without an understanding of the society to which he preaches, its prevailing temper or distemper, will not preach well.[16]

Still another to make the same comparison was Broadus, who said, "The preacher, like the physician, ought in addition to

[14] Scherer, *op. cit.*, p. 157.
[15] Parkhurst, *op. cit.*, p. 65.
[16] Greer, *op. cit.*, p. 39.

what is learned from books, to 'study cases,' as they arise in his practical labors." [17] Pepper put the matter epigrammatically in saying that "The preacher who does not know his people might as well be haranguing a deaf and dumb asylum." [18]

Tucker mentioned the necessity of the preacher's knowing the minds of men.

> The interpretation of religious truth involves the understanding of the mind to be reached as well as of the truth to be declared. A preacher may have a clear and right understanding of religious truth, but he will still fail in the interpretation of it if he does not know and estimate the state of mind before him. [19]

Faunce also affirmed that need.

> We want a working knowledge of men, whether the knowledge comes from laboratory or library or farm or factory, and whether we call such knowledge psychology or common sense. [20]

He went further to name Charles Haddon Spurgeon and Dwight L. Moody as men who were successful largely because of their psychological insight. He concluded that:

> . . . the successful preachers and leaders of men have always been psychologists, whether consciously or not. The essence of psychology is insight into the workings of other men's minds—and such insight has marked all great orators, teachers, and organizers. [21]

Sperry expressed emphatically his feeling of a need for audience analysis.

> Preaching is, for the man who does it, a dual transaction which must reckon with Christian truth on the one hand and with the mind of the hearer on the other

17 Broadus, *op. cit.*, p. 97.
18 Pepper, *op. cit.*, p. 76.
19 Tucker, *op. cit.*, pp. 129–30.
20 Faunce, *op. cit.*, pp. 157–58.
21 *Ibid.*, pp. 156–57.

hand. Most of us who have been preaching for some time will agree that technically it is mainly a task of finding the exact range. The successful preachers of any day—successful in the best sense of the word—are by no means its ablest scholars; they are men who succeed because they can match their understanding of religion in the abstract by a knowledge of human nature in the concrete. That means speaking to men and women living under particular circumstances at a given time in history.[22]

Burton expressed a similar thought.

They [the people] do not like to be fired at by a glib expert who knows guns perfectly but does not know men,—who makes first-rate arguments but does not hit anybody, because nobody stands just where he aims. Every preacher's eyes are more or less askew, for shooting, until he has been over among the people, and appreciates their situation.[23]

Jowett was sure that the possession of this quality is the secret of moving men.

Gentlemen, we need to know men, and when our men know that we know them, and respect and revere them, you may depend upon it we have got the key into the lock which will open their most secret gate.[24]

Stalker gave consideration of the audience a place in one of his lectures.

One [rule] often recommended is to keep the audience in view to which the composition is to be addressed. If by this is meant that the writer, as he sits at his desk, should try to conjure up in his imagination the benches of the church and their occupants, I do not know whether it is a practicable rule or not. But, if it means that the preacher, as he composes his sermon, should keep in view the circumstances of his hearers—their stage of culture, the subjects in which they are interested, the Scriptural

[22] Sperry, *op. cit.*, pp. v–vi.
[23] Burton, *op. cit.*, p. 96.
[24] Jowett, *op. cit.*, p. 222.

attainments which they have already made, and the like—
it is one of the prime secrets of the preacher's art. . . .[25]

Hall was another lecturer who emphasized the preacher's
need of knowing the people.

> Now, to make the most of himself, what, on the ordi-
> nary principles of common sense, which the Scriptures
> never contradict, ought he to do? Obviously he *ought to
> know the people*.[26]

He defended the practice of visitation a little later in the
same lecture, largely upon the ground that it will give the
preacher the knowledge of the people which he must have in
order to preach effectively to them.[27] Sclater also emphasized
the necessity of the preacher's visiting among the people for
the same reason.

> "The proper study of mankind is man." The preacher
> will obtain his best material from his reading in human
> nature. The pastoral and the preaching offices are in-
> dubitably intertwined. We must know some people to
> preach to anybody: and we must know our own people
> to preach to *them*. And there is no way of getting to know
> them, but by coming into personal contact with them.
> Somehow, sometime, the preacher must visit.[28]

Calkins added his word of commendation to that of those
above upon the subject of visitation.

> Moreover it is such work which makes real preaching
> possible. People want good preaching. But how can a
> man preach effectively to people whom he does not know?
> How can he bring the Gospel he is commissioned to de-
> clare to bear upon experiences he knows nothing what-
> ever about? It is an ignorant notion that parish visita-
> tion takes the time which ought to be devoted to sermon-
> writing. The most helpful preachers are always the best
> pastors.[29]

25 Stalker, *op. cit.*, pp. 112–13.
26 Hall, *op. cit.*, p. 35.
27 *Ibid.*, pp. 41, 42, 44.
28 Sclater, *op. cit.*, pp. 100–1.
29 Calkins, *op. cit.*, p. 185.

Still another to speak of the necessity of visiting the members of the congregation was Scherer.

> The day may come—I hope it will—when we shall not
> be required or expected to be expert in half a dozen dif-
> ferent directions. Others with more special training may
> relieve us of dancing continual attendance on all the
> enterprises of religious education, social service, and
> church management; but no one can ever make unneces-
> sary for us that contact with men and women which some-
> times goes disrespectfully by the name of "bell-pushing"
> or "the front-door ministry." There is no other road into
> the knowledge of human life and human need; and there
> is no other road down which you may travel half so effec-
> tively, if not toward the heart, then toward the crown of
> your ministry, which is the pressing home of the gospel
> of Jesus Christ to the individual souls of your people.[30]

In his picture of the ideal preacher Simpson enumerated many of the advantages to be gained from visitation.

> The families in which he visits, the social companies
> he attends, the men he encounters in business, and the
> children on the streets, furnish him matter for thought.
> He is God's messenger to benefit every one of them.
> Hence he studies their habits of life, their progress in
> knowledge, their aptitudes, besetments, and controlling
> influences. He searches for a key that shall open the wards
> of their hearts, for knowledge which shall instruct them,
> and for consolation which shall alleviate their sorrow.
> His business is more with men than with books.
> . . . Human nature spreads out before him. It is the
> staple on which he works. He must study the laws of
> mind, of the associations of thought, of the origin of emo-
> tions, the manner in which they strengthen or antagonize
> each other, and the influence which they exert upon the
> will. For this purpose he needs not only to read the best
> authors, and to study the best systems, but to study man
> for himself—especially to study his own congregation,

[30] Scherer, *op. cit.*, p. 22.

that he may know how to apply to them the word of God.[31]

Concerning the subject of analysis, Albert Parker Fitch said, ". . . I sincerely believe that the most fateful undertaking for the preacher at this moment is that of analyzing his own generation." [32]

Although most of the lecturers recommended the study of mankind directly, there were several who also commended the indirect study of humanity through the pages of literature. The following paragraph from Oxnam is representative of this emphasis.

I am pleading for a scholarship that will bring the preacher into an understanding of the experience of the race. Consequently, I would stress the place of literature and drama in his preparation. I am assuming that he will be trained in the scientific method. But he must know man. William Lyon Phelps, in his little volume *The Excitement of Teaching,* said:

A treatise on chemistry published in 1904 is as useless as the almanac of that year, whereas Hamlet, published in 1604, and a play by Euripides, produced in 406 B.C. are as true [now] as they were for their own age and generation. . . . It is a curious thing that we call novels "works of fiction, when they are works of eternal truth." [33]

SUMMARY

In his parables Christ often spoke of the hearts of men as the soil in which his gospel was to be planted. It would seem legitimate, then, to draw an analogy between the farmer's need for a knowledge of the soil and the preacher's need for a knowledge of the hearts and minds of men. In addition to

[31] Simpson, *op. cit.,* p. 82.
[32] Albert Parker Fitch, *Preaching and Paganism* (New Haven: Yale University Press, 1920), p. 32.
[33] Oxnam, *op. cit.,* p. 139.

his knowledge of the planter and the seed, the farmer must also know something of the soil, for a particular soil may not respond favorably to the growing of one kind of crop while it may be specially responsive to the growing of another. Sometimes the addition of a single chemical element will change an unproductive field into one which is productive. The farmer must know his soil; the preacher must know mankind.

This knowledge of mankind may come from many sources —the characters of the Bible, the men whose lives are described in secular history, the characters of secular literature —but the most productive source of all is man himself. To know men deeply the minister must live among them, observing every phase of human behavior. Only by living close to men can he learn the innermost workings of their minds, and only then does he know how to take aim with the message of God. Of the criticisms leveled at the ministry, none is more serious than that which charges that the minister is too exclusively concerned with books.

CHAPTER XIV

APPROACH TO THE AUDIENCE

The manner in which the preacher approaches his hearers
would seem to have an important bearing upon his success or
failure in influencing them. The subjects of the two preceding
chapters—audience analysis and taking aim—are important
only as they prepare the ground for an effective approach
to the audience. The importance of this psychological approach was rather generally felt by the Lyman Beecher lecturers, for no less than forty-four of them dealt with the subject. Their remarks covered an exceptionally wide range of
material; however, the essential points presented fall into
eight groups which are discussed under the following head-
ings: rapport, reason-emotion, direction-indirection, life-
situations, positive-negative, motives, repetition, and humor.

RAPPORT

Of the sixty-six Yale lecturers, twenty-two discussed the
factors which have to do with the creation of a favorable
audience-speaker relationship. These factors are discussed
under the heading "rapport," a term used by Stalker and
Beecher. Stalker said:

Some preachers have an extraordinary facility of putting themselves at once, and every time, *en rapport* with
the audience, so that there is from first to last, whilst
they speak, a commerce between the mind in the pulpit
and the minds in the pews. To others this is the most difficult part of preaching. The difficulty is to get down
amongst the people and to be actually dealing with them.
Many a preacher has a thought, and is putting it into

good enough words, but somehow the people are not listening, and they cannot listen.[1]

The statement of Beecher concerning the desirability of this quality was in agreement with that of Stalker.

> The first thing you want in a neighborhood is to get *en rapport* with the people. You want to get their confidence, to induce them to listen to you. It is a part of the intuition of a true preacher to know how to get at men.[2]

Speaking of the same element, Dale said, "One of your first objects should be to secure the confidence of your people. They will get very little good from your preaching unless they trust you."[3] Merrill was another to comment upon the subject of the audience's confidence in the preacher.

> It may be laid down as an absolute law, that, given clear confidence on the part of the hearers that the speaker seeks first their spiritual upbuilding, that his main concern is with the spiritual life and not with the propagation of certain views, and he can say anything he honestly believes, and carry the wholesome respect and attention of practically all in the congregation.[4]

John Brown turned to history to secure further emphasis for the importance of this quality.

> A great analyst of the art of public speaking as it was brought to perfection in Greece said that a speaker must convince his hearers at the very outset: first, that he has their interests at heart, next, that he is competent to interpret these interests, and, thirdly, that he is free from the taint of self-seeking. It is scarcely likely that Richard Baxter gathered the precepts of the art of speaking from the great work of Aristotle, for Greek was not much in his way, but he certainly always had these purposes before him.[5]

[1] Stalker, *op. cit.*, pp. 118–19.
[2] Beecher, *op. cit.*, I, 51.
[3] Dale, *op. cit.*, p. 223.
[4] Merrill, *op. cit.*, p. 67.
[5] John Brown, *op. cit.*, p. 173.

Several of the speakers indicated that much of the responsibility for the audience-speaker relationship depends upon the attitude with which the preacher approaches the congregation. A number of suggestions were made, therefore, concerning the preacher's mental approach to his people. In regard to this phase of the discussion, Williams said:

Let us speak our "truth in that love" which "suffereth long and is kind, which beareth all things, believeth all things, hopeth all things." And if the truth brings us persecution and even the cross as it brought Him, let us face it as He did, saying, "Thy will be done." But often as I see it, it is the manner of our delivery and not the matter of our message that brings us hatred and antagonism. It is not the truth but the lack of love in its utterance that provokes and irritates. Many that imagine that they are persecuted for righteousness' sake are simply persecuted for their own sakes because they are what they are, egotistical, intolerant, without understanding or sympathy, simply ugly in temper and disposition.[6]

Taylor also spoke of the proper feeling for the preacher to sustain toward the man in the pew.

There is a way to every man's heart if you can only find it. Study him, therefore, until you discover it, and then enter in by it, and take possession of him for your Lord. Let him feel and know that you come to assist him in his conflict with himself; that you are in alliance with those aspirations after something higher and nobler than he is, which are the strongest yearnings of his heart; that you are desirous of helping him to withstand those temptations with which every day he has to contend, and you will gain not his ear only, but his heart, almost before he is aware of it.[7]

Beecher, in picturing the effective preacher, named the same quality as an important element in the preacher's approach.

6 Williams, *op. cit.*, p. 180.
7 Taylor, *The Ministry of the Word*, p. 46.

It is not the man who has the most profound sense of the glory of God; it is not the man who has the most acute sensibility to the sinfulness of sin; it is the man who carries in his heart something of the feeling which characterized the atoning Christ,—it is he that is the most effectual preacher. It is the man who has some such sorrow for sin that he would rather take penalty upon himself than that the sinner should bear it. It is not the man who is merely seeking the vindication of abstract law, or the recognition of a great, invisible God; it is the man who is seeking in himself to make plain the manifestation of God as a Physician of souls, sorrowing for them, calling to them, and yearning to do them good. It is the compassion of men who, while they know how to depict the dangerousness of sin, oftentimes its meanness, and always its violation of Divine law, yet recognize that they can never bring men so easily to an admission of their sinfulness by representing God's wrath and producing in them a feeling of terror, as by holding up before them the Divine compassion and kindness.[8]

Approaching the subject from the negative side, Hall indicated the way in which the audience should not be approached.

A man may set out the doom of the wicked in a tone of human threatening and bravado, as though he said, "This is what you will come to for disregarding *my* advice, and you well deserve it." This is enough to mar the truest sermon. . . . My brethren, remember two words spoken to masters (and the reason of them applies to you), "forbearing threatening, knowing that your Master also is in heaven." . . . I also know that the first place in which the terrors of the Lord are to make their impression is on the heart of the preacher, and that their true effect there is to make him not terrible, or terrific, but tender and persuasive.[9]

8 Beecher, *op. cit.*, III, 224–25.
9 Hall, *op. cit.*, pp. 165–66.

Jowett spoke of *"the peril of dictatorialism"* in preaching.[10]

For the securing of a good feeling between audience and speaker, it was further suggested that the discourses must be carefully adapted to the people who make up the audience. Beecher spoke of this matter.

> There is another question which I have barely hinted at, and that is, in attempting to address the truth in different forms to men, so as to meet the wants of a whole community, must not a man be universal like Shakespeare? [11]

Gunsaulus put the matter briefly when he said, "We must go where men are, touch them where they are, seek them for what they are, if we are to be soul-winners like Andrew." [12] To impress the same truth John Brown used the example of John Bradford.

> "He [John Bradford] was," he says, "in those times a master of speech; but he had learned from his Master not to speak what he could speak, but what his hearers could hear. He knew that clearness of speech was the excellency of speech; and therefore resolved with a good orator to speak beneath himself rather than above his auditory. . . ." [13]

In speaking of the preacher's approach to his congregation, Broadus said, "We are not to speak *before* the people, but *to* them, and must earnestly strive to make them take to themselves what we say." [14] John Brown used almost the identical sentence in one of his lectures.

> An important rule to bear in mind is that you must keep touch with your audience and carry them along with you. . . . There is nothing so unreal as to see a man speaking *before* his hearers but not *to* them.[15]

10 Jowett, *op. cit.,* p. 104.
11 Beecher, *op. cit.,* I, 61.
12 Gunsaulus, *op. cit.,* p. 252.
13 John Brown, *op. cit.,* p. 47.
14 Broadus, *op. cit.,* p. 245.
15 John Brown, *op. cit.,* p. 147.

Parkhurst emphasized the need to fit the material to the congregation.

> A highly educated congregation is not to be dealt with in a manner different from that to be pursued in addressing an uneducated one, except so far as the mode of address is concerned, but not so far as relates to its matter and the object had in view.[16]

Freeman spoke of the need for adaptation, also.

> Both technique and method must adapt themselves to the peculiar needs of those to whom we minister.
> We do not for a moment hold that there is a gospel for the rich and another gospel for the poor, we do affirm that the form of its expression must recognize conditions and circumstances that are too evident to be ignored. There are places where the refinements of liturgical forms do not fit.[17]

The results of the failure to adapt the sermon to the audience were pointed out by Simpson.

> From some cause literary men and able thinkers do not always draw the masses. Their language is too learned, or their sympathy not apparent. It not unfrequently happens that some man of the people, some mechanic or day-laborer, will gather around him an audience which the man of culture cannot hold. The reason is, they understand him; his language is the language of their lives; he speaks in their habits of thought; he seems to sympathize with them, and their very souls cleave to him.[18]

Horton said of the state of preparation of the audience:

> If the congregation is prepared, the sermon may immediately plunge *in medias res;* but if not, the minds of the hearers must be first wooed, and won, grappled, interested, opened. A true pastor knows the state of the people's thought.[19]

[16] Parkhurst, *op. cit.,* p. 37.
[17] Freeman, *op. cit.,* p. 143.
[18] Simpson, *op. cit.,* p. 154.
[19] Horton, *op. cit.,* p. 281.

Speaking of the same matter, Sockman said, "The timing of shots is as important in the pulpit as in presidential fireside chats." [20]

The need of beginning upon common ground was expressed by Faunce.

> The orator who begins by reminding a hostile or suspicious audience of some conviction that he and they hold in common, may never have heard of "apperception," but he has the essence of the doctrine. The speaker who rests his audience at regular intervals, by pause or change of subject, or the insertion of something in lighter vein, may never have studied "voluntary attention," but he has learned by experience what such attention is and how to hold it. [21]

Park also recommended the common-ground method.

> It is clear that mere scolding is out of place in the pulpit. Under a rain of denunciation most modern hearers put up their umbrellas and let the drips run on to their neighbors' shoulders. It is better to lead the congregation along, starting with certain general principles to which they gladly assent and then applying these to unexpected special instances, and modestly inferring how is it possible to escape the obvious applications. It is not a question of cowardice or courage, it is a question of method. [22]

Jefferson illustrated the advantages of the common-ground approach.

> Some churches are in a shell. The new preacher sees this at a glance. He proceeds forthwith to drive into it a series of logical and pointed discourses on the particular doctrine upon which the church in his judgment needs enlightenment, whereas he ought first by the patient exposition of old truths in which every one believes create an atmosphere under whose genial influence the shell

[20] Sockman, *op. cit.*, p. 58.
[21] Faunce, *op. cit.*, p. 157.
[22] Park, *op. cit.*, p. 46.

will open of itself. Men cannot be driven into believing things by argumentative sermons, but are made hospitable to new truths by the gradual transforming of their minds. It is not by mental force or brilliant argument that inadequate or erroneous conceptions are gotten rid of, but by elevating the whole plane of thinking and raising the temperature of the life of the heart. A church will believe what it ought to believe only when it is in the right mood.[23]

REASON—EMOTION

Twenty-four of the lecturers discussed the desirability of the preacher's appealing to reason, or to emotion, or to both. Among those who introduced this subject into their lectures, there were several who did so in a general manner, naming a number of possible appeals in the same paragraphs. Others discussed the appeal to reason and the appeal to emotion separately.

Ten of the speakers did little more than name the possible appeals which the preacher may make. Dale was one of these.

I believe in the duty of consecrating to the exposition and defence of Divine truth every faculty and resource which the preacher may happen to possess. There is no power of the intellect, no passion of the heart, no learning, no natural genius, that should not be compelled to take part in this noble service. The severest and keenest logic, the most exuberant fancy, the boldest imagination, shrewdness, wit, pathos, indignation, sternness, may all contribute to the illustration of human duty and of the authority and love of God.[24]

Brooks called for the use of a number of elements in the approach to the audience.

And so that preaching which most harmoniously blends in the single sermon all these varieties of which men make their classifications—the preaching which is

[23] Jefferson, op. cit., p. 149.
[24] Dale, op. cit., p. 25.

strong in its appeal to authority, wide in its grasp of truth, convincing in its appeal to reason, and earnest in its address to the conscience and the heart, all of these at once—that preaching comes nearest to the type of the apostolical epistles, is the most complete and so the most powerful approach of truth to the whole man; and so is the kind of preaching which, with due freedom granted to our idiosyncracies, it is best for us all to seek and educate.[25]

Another to name a number of appeals which may be used was Faunce.

The aim of preaching is to appeal to the primary instincts and interests of the soul, to address the entire nature of man with all its passions, appetites, inarticulate hungers, blind reactions, and subconscious strivings, as well as its perception of logical validity. Men are indeed to be uplifted and moulded through the presentation of the truth; but this truth is addressed not merely to the reasoning power, but to the entire personality.[26]

Beecher further indicated the breadth of area in which appeals can be made.

If a man can be saved by pure intellectual preaching, let him have it. If others require a predominance of emotion, provide that for them. If by others the truth is taken more easily through the imagination, give it to them in forms attractive to the imagination. If there are still others who demand it in the form of facts and rules, see that they have it in that form. Take men as it has pleased God to make them; and let your preaching, so far as concerns the selection of material, and the mode and method by which you are presenting the truth, follow the wants of the persons themselves, and not simply the measure of your own minds.[27]

The same thought was developed by Horton.

25 Brooks, *op. cit.*, p. 132.
26 Faunce, *op. cit.*, p. 174.
27 Beecher, *op. cit.*, I, 58–59.

And if the diversity of intellectual conditions must constantly be remembered, it is equally necessary to consider the wide difference of temperaments, and to preach with some adaptation to these differences. Some are moved only by reason, and become stolid and resentful directly an emotional key is struck. Some are moved only by emotion, and grow apathetic and fidgety whenever the discourse moves on the lines of pure thought. Each of these classes must be sought and won. Still more striking is the divergence between the ethical or practical mind on the one hand, and the mystical or spiritual on the other. The first will be reached by the Sermon on the Mount, and in some plain discourse about keeping the passions under control, or the like, will be led to the secret of God; the other, unmoved by the strong appeal of duty, will see nothing in Christ until He is being tortured and crucified, and will only be stirred to repentance, amendment, and a new life by some clear and sharp doctrine in the metaphysics of Redemption. It is a one-sided and ineffectual ministry which overlooks these endless varieties, and the man who would make full proof of his ministry, and speak faithfully the Word of God, must suffer his mind and heart to expand until he can, to some extent, at any rate, realise the numberless states and conditions and requirements which are represented in even a very ordinary congregation of modern worshippers.[28]

Charles Reynolds Brown was still another to mention the several avenues of approach together.

When you undertake to preach a sermon you set yourself the task of convincing the judgment, of kindling the imagination, of moving the feelings, and of giving such a powerful impulse to the will that this finer quality of being may find expression in finer forms of action.[29]

Fifteen of the Lyman Beecher speakers gave a somewhat full discussion of the preacher's use of appeal to reason. Crosby was one of these.

28 Horton, *op. cit.*, pp. 293–94.
29 Charles Reynolds Brown, *The Art of Preaching*, p. 2.

Now, a very large part of the preacher's work is argumentative. God in His Word reasons with man. His holy service is a reasonable service, and every man should be able to give a reason for the hope that is in him. Men are to be *convinced,* for it is the *truth* that makes men free from the bondage of sin and condemnation, and conviction is the result of argument. The heart can be impressed and the life changed only where the reason is convinced, and, however ignorant a man may be of "Barbara Celarent," he is moved by syllogistic processes. A mere declamation or rhapsody carries no converting power with it, however it may excite or inflame the mind. There must be truth as the initiative of all true life, and all truth runs in rational forms. When we say the argumentative preacher is the convincing preacher, we are not advocating a dry skeleton argument for a sermon. Far from it. We have already endeavored to show that variety of illustration should mark every discourse. Not only should the joints be perfect, but the flesh and skin should exhibit the fullness and outlines of health and beauty. The argument will be the more cogent when thus adorned, and the adornment will be the more satisfying when beneath it is recognized the solid structure of a correct and complete argument. The preacher will thus often conceal his argument while making it, but, nevertheless, the argument is there, and the efficient force of the sermon, *ceteris paribus,* will be in proportion to the value of the argument.[30]

Sclater also gave appeal to reason a leading place in his conception of preaching.

To make our faith credible: to convince the minds of our hearers that God and sin and love and the indwelling spirit are *facts*—here is the dignified enterprise on which we may embark Sunday by Sunday, knowing that, if we can succeed, the immediate object of preaching has been achieved. Once a man is convinced of a truth he is strengthened with might. And have we not sadly to admit that our modern preaching is weak here, compared with the standards of former days? No doubt, we have a

30 Crosby, *op. cit.,* pp. 69–70.

harder task than our fathers, who could clinch a doubtful
argument with a "proof-text." No doubt, knowledge has
grown from more to more, and the modern, intelligent
congregation cannot be put off with half-reasoning. But
have we not shrunk from our task because it is hard, instead of regarding its difficulty as a challenge? The fact
remains that the condition of sustained, effective preaching is wide knowledge and good, hard thinking: and
that young ministers must scorn the sophistry that tells
them that their congregations will not listen to theological sermons. The truth is the exact opposite—they will
not listen long to anything else. Of course, the language
must not be the technical language of the class-rooms of
a by-gone age: but theology expressed in comprehensible
speech is essential. After all, what is theology but considered commonsense applied to the meaning of life and
the relations of God and man? Let us pay our congregations the very slight compliment of believing them to be
rational beings who want to know, and who hold that
"Thought is the citadel." Unless we stiffen our preaching,
and replace the iron of argument in it, the Reformed
Church will die of pernicious anaemia.[31]

Broadus named argument as an important element in preaching.

Now argument, in the logical, and at the same time
popular, sense of the term, forms a very large and very
important department of the materials of preaching.
There are preachers, it is true, who seem to consider that
they have no occasion for reasoning, that everything is to
be accomplished by authoritative assertion and impas-
sioned appeal. . . . But preachers really have great use
for argument, and there are many reasons why its importance in preaching should be duly considered.[32]

Stalker showed the importance of the intellect in religion.

But the intellect is a noble faculty and has an important office in religion. It is, properly speaking, ante-

31 Sclater, op. cit., pp. 81–82.
32 Broadus, op. cit., p. 168.

cedent to both feeling and will; and what is put into it determines both what feeling and choice will be.[33]

Robinson expressed the same view.

> The truth is, all sound minds at bottom are rational. Every man's self-respect is appealed to when his reason is addressed; and every man, however much he may for the moment be pleased with the mere tickling of his fancy, will resent it in the end with revulsion of feeling, as if he had been imposed upon.[34]

Parkhurst was of quite a different opinion as to the importance of reasoning in preaching.

> Presumably my point of view upon entering into the work of the ministry was not markedly different from that of most inexperienced preachers, in supposing that men could be syllogized into the kingdom of heaven; that they could be snared in a sort of logical trap and transported at the impulse of an inevitable conviction.
>
> One lesson that a theologue ought thoroughly to have learned prior to ordination is that while people have convictions they are not very much given to making use of them, and treat them—especially moral and religious ones—very much as they do bric-a-brac, which is designed rather for decoration than for consumption.
>
> So that logically to have fastened a truth upon a hearer's mind is no slightest guarantee of practical religious results.[35]

Day agreed with the opinion expressed by Parkhurst.

> There is no greater fallacy in dealing with people than the assumption that the logical presentation of ideas, especially about personal conduct and social institutions, will make of people persons. Too much of our preaching and teaching and church organization assume that.[36]

McDowell issued a warning concerning the use of argument.

[33] Stalker, *op. cit.*, p. 246.
[34] Robinson, *op. cit.*, p. 149.
[35] Parkhurst, *op. cit.*, pp. 9–10.
[36] Day, *op. cit.*, p. 60.

. . . Do not overestimate the value of religious argument, or the difficulty of persuading men by other measures. Men are not, as a rule, influenced so much by an argument as they are by an interest and a testimony.[37]

Hall indicated that preachers sometimes assume unnecessary burdens of proof.

Gentlemen, we are heralds, rather than logicians. We announce the Lord's will; many truths of the Word we may fearlessly declare without waiting to argue. They will do their work. Some of them instantly connect themselves with convictions or demands in the human soul, and fit them as the key fits the lock. Some of them can afford to await proof. Some of them get their proof as other Scriptures are explained, as the stones hold one another in the arch. But to be able to echo the triumphant and authoritative utterances of God's word, we must know them.[38]

Beecher also spoke of the overuse of argument.

Do not *prove* things too much. A man who goes into his pulpit every Sunday to prove things gives occasion for people to say, "Well, that is not half so certain as I thought it was." . . . Do not employ arguments any more than is necessary, and then only for the sake of answering objections and killing the enemies of the truth. . . . Take things for granted, and men will not think to dispute them, but will admit them, and go on with you and become better men than if they had been treated to a logical process of argument, which aroused in them an argumentative spirit of doubt and opposition.[39]

In his third series of lectures, Beecher repeated what he had said earlier in regard to this point.

As has been said by Joubert (whose wisdom is of a high order, and whose writings I wish could be trans-

[37] McDowell, *op. cit.,* p. 171.
[38] Hall, *op. cit.,* p. 89.
[39] Beecher, *op. cit.,* I, 124–25.

lated), there is danger of exciting unbelief by attempting
to argue things which are not within the sphere of argument, the effect being to stir up combativeness in men,
and the gladiatorial spirit. A man may be led to meet
your arguments,—by which, as it were, you defy investiga-
tion,—with a skepticism which otherwise would slum-
ber.[40]

Agreeing with this point of view, Broadus said, "We often
belabor men with arguments and appeals, when they are much
more in need of practical and simple explanations, as regards
what to do, and how to do it." [41] Charles Reynolds Brown
shared this opinion of argument.

> The sermon seems shorter where the minister does
> not stop to prove everything, nor to explain everything.
> Jesus never stopped to prove anything. He spoke about
> God, and about duty, about prayer, and about redemp-
> tion, about the kingdom of heaven and the future life,
> as great valid certainties. He was so sure of them that he
> made others sure of them. He did not argue; he pro-
> claimed.[42]

Fourteen of the Yale lecturers discussed rather thoroughly
the preacher's use of appeal to the emotions of his hearers.
One of those who dwelt longest on this subject was Parkhurst.

> I have . . . undertaken to say something respecting
> the dynamic efficiency of the heart, moved thereto by the
> conviction that in our attempts to arrive at the secret
> of things, human and divine, an over-emphasis is laid
> upon educated thought and an under-emphasis laid upon
> cultivated affection, and that the brain is allowed to crowd
> out the heart in the process of arriving at truth and in
> the work of making truth effective in individual life and
> in social relation.[43]

40 *Ibid.,* III, 70.
41 Broadus, *op. cit.,* p. 153.
42 Charles Reynolds Brown, *The Art of Preaching,* p. 121.
43 Parkhurst, *op. cit.,* p. 72.

He developed his view of the place of emotional appeal in his first lecture.

> This is no plea for sentimentality, which is simply sentiment run riot, undisciplined hysteria, emotionalism gathered about no fixed intelligent point of crystallization. It is a demand rather for a cultivated and developed faculty of affection which shall be an easy match for a cultivated and developed faculty of thought, so that, while the action of the brain shall give support to the play of the heart, the play of the heart shall add luster and warmth to the action of the brain.[44]

Of the lack of training in emotional development, he said that:

> . . . while the college curriculum is constructed with a definite view to building up the student on his intellectual side, I do not recall in my four years' submission to that curriculum a single suggestion as to the serious part played in life and in service by the emotive energies or to the necessity of developing them in parallelism with the cultivation of the powers of thought.[45]

Faunce defended the widespread use of the emotional appeal in preaching.

> For centuries Christian teachers have apologized for the emotional element in religion. . . . The truth is that our feelings are the mainspring of all we have and are. The feelings are not signs of weakness, they are the motive power in all our living. If they are wrongly directed, we become slaves of passion or caprice. If they are strong and steadfast, then the intellectual and social life becomes potent and progressive. Every feeling tends to vent itself in action, and when strong enough issues in deeds without any conscious choice. That habitual currents of feeling wear channels in the very substance of the brain, that through those channels feeling discharges itself with ever increasing swiftness and ease, that the

[44] *Ibid.*, pp. 11–12.
[45] *Ibid.*, p. 9.

slightest desire tends to eventuate in deeds, and that no human being can permanently desire one thing and act another—these are the psychological facts that reënforce the ancient insight: "As a man thinketh in his heart so is he." [46]

Beecher also set forth his view of the place that emotion should play in the work of the minister.

> If a man undertake to minister to the wants of his congregation purely by the power of feeling, without adequate force in the intellect, there are valid objections to that; but every man who means to be in affinity with his congregation must have feeling. It cannot be helped. A minister without feeling is no better than a book. You might just as well put a book, printed in large type, on the desk where all could read it, and have a man turn over the leaves as you read, as to have a man stand up, and clearly and coldly recite the precise truth through which he has gone by a logical course of reasoning. It has to melt somewhere. Somewhere there must be that power by which the man speaking and the men hearing are unified; and that is the power of emotion. [47]

Charles Reynolds Brown turned to the writing of the Bible for his justification of the use of emotion.

> The men who wrote the Bible wrote with their pens and with their minds up to a certain point, but when they would have us see visions and dream dreams they wrote with their hearts. "Out of the heart are the issues of life" because men and women do mainly those things which they feel like doing. "With the heart man believeth unto righteousness"—he cannot achieve that high end in any other way. Therefore any one who ignores sentiment or makes light of feeling in order to leave more room for the chilly dictates of a coldly calculated expediency makes a sorry trade. [48]

[46] Faunce, *op. cit.*, pp. 172–73.
[47] Beecher, *op. cit.*, I, 118.
[48] Charles Reynolds Brown, *The Art of Preaching*, p. 173.

Horne indicated the high regard in which he held the preacher's use of the emotions when he said that:

> . . . if my protest were the last word ever to be said in a Lyman Beecher lecture in favour of "human preaching" and the cultivation of the art of popular oratory, I would venture to say it. You have every chord of the human heart to play on. Surely the art of eliciting their music is worthy of your study and cultivation. Men and women, after all their history and education, are still human beings, compounded of laughter and tears, sunshine and shadow. Humanity is still, as it has always been, capable of the heights of heroism, and the depths of shame. Not one of the elemental human passions has been eradicated by all our philosophies. No process of evolution has carried us, or ever will, beyond their grip. Life and death are just as poignant experiences as in the early days of our race; and if our refinements have done anything for us, they have made us more sensitive and not more stoical. We may, of course, ignore these facts, and assume that those to whom we preach are above all things engrossed with metaphysics, and have an inward craving for the critical probability that there were two Isaiahs. But if that is our attitude we have much to learn. Nobody ought ever to go into a pulpit who can think and talk about sin and salvation, and the Cross of Christ, which is for all true men the symbol of hope and service, without profound emotion and passion.[49]

"Phillips Brooks," according to Sperry, "has said that he who lacks emotion lacks expression, and it is true that the utterances of the prophet are shot through with feeling." [50] "Without passion no pulpit can be a throne of light," [51] was Calkins' opinion on this subject. Sclater differentiated between a high and noble use of emotional appeal and a base, unworthy use of it, in saying that:

49 Horne, *op. cit.*, pp. 255–56.
50 Sperry, *op. cit.*, pp. 32–33.
51 Calkins, *op. cit.*, p. 147.

> . . . the immediate object of preaching is achieved
> by *awaking the emotions*. This sounds the simpler
> method, and most men try it. Congregations are curiously
> sentimental; and sometimes seem to like to have their
> emotions stirred by fat fingers. The audiences that are
> attracted by praters, who pull out the *vox humana* stop
> at the beginning and keep it on all the time, are depress-
> ingly large. "Sob-stuff" is almost a synonym for much
> preaching today. But the degradation of emotive pulpit
> work must not blind us to its possible splendour. For
> preaching of this sort, at its height, is poetry. Here,
> preaching becomes an art, fit to rank with the noblest
> arts of them all. Imagination and feeling have to be
> blended with the glory of words in a delicate and sensi-
> tive mind. Nor is thought to be neglected; poems are
> thought transfused with feeling and conveyed through
> images portrayed rhythmically. He that proposes to
> preach in this way is set on a road that seeks the hill-tops.[52]

Sclater also named several of the basic emotions toward which
appeals are often directed by preachers.

> A curious change is to be observed in this type of work
> in recent times. A generation ago, a sermon, designed to
> appeal to the emotions, would, three times out of four,
> have appealed to the emotion of fear: whereas, nowadays,
> you will search far before you find a minister using the
> "hangman's whip." "Hold them over the pit," is advice
> which, today, only brings a smile. Do you think that it
> is a justified smile? Do you find life so bereft of the stern
> and the tragic, that we can afford not to be frightened?
> Does God, in His strong mercy, never scare us? We shall
> do well to remember that He, at least, plays upon the
> whole of the ascending emotive scale of fear, awe, joy and
> love: and that preachers are not loyal to all they should
> have learned in experience, if they are never afraid them-
> selves, and, consequently, compelled to communicate
> their fear to their hearers. However, it is doubtless best
> to touch mostly upon the strings at the upper end of the
> emotive scale, remembering "the expulsive power of a

[52] Sclater, *op. cit.*, pp. 82–83.

new affection"; and knowing that, though reason may fail to change a man, if you "touch the lever of his affections, you move his world." [53]

Broadus clearly indicated that he felt that emotional appeal has a place in preaching.

> But while ignorant people often value too highly, or rather too exclusively, the appeal to their feelings, cultivated people are apt to shrink from such appeals quite too much. . . . The prophets made the most impassioned appeals. Our Lord and the apostles manifestly strove not merely to convince their hearers, but to incite them to earnest corresponding action, and their language is often surcharged with emotion.
> Yet we should never wish to excite feeling for its own sake, but as a means of persuasion to the corresponding course of action.[54]

Stalker referred to the emotional state in which the apostle Paul addressed his hearers.

> One of the subtlest students of his [the apostle Paul's] life, the late Adolphe Monod, of the French Church, has fixed on this as the key to his character. He calls him the Man of Tears, and shows with great persuasiveness that herein lay the secret of his power.
> It is certainly remarkable, when you begin to look into the subject, how often we see St. Paul in the emotional mood, and even in tears. In his famous address to the Ephesian elders he reminded them that he had served the Lord among them with many tears, and again, that he had not ceased to warn everyone night and day with tears. It is not what we should have expected in a man of such intellectual power. But this makes his tears all the more impressive. When a weak, effeminate man weeps, he only makes himself ridiculous; but it is a different spectacle when a man like St. Paul is seen weeping; because we know that the strong nature could not have been bent except by a storm of feeling.[55]

[53] *Ibid.*, pp. 83–84.
[54] Broadus, *op. cit.*, pp. 252–53.
[55] Stalker, *op. cit.*, p. 159.

Charles Reynolds Brown spoke of the degree of emotion which the preacher must feel in order to move his congregation.

> All these deep and precious states of feeling enter into the very warp and woof of religious experience. You cannot address yourself to those more delicate and intimate emotions, you cannot mold them or utilize them in the formation of finer types of character unless you have already entered into them yourself. The heart knows the language of the heart as no other faculty ever can.[56]

DIRECTION—INDIRECTION

Seven of the Yale lecturers spoke of the use of indirection in preaching. "The greatest teaching," said Park, "is never direct." [57] Sockman said of the indirect influence:

> . . . the prevalence of propaganda has made minds increasingly deaf to direct appeal. The per capita cost of conversion through preaching is increasing. But at the same time, it would seem that as men steel themselves against direct appeal they are becoming more susceptible to indirect influence. Never did fashion and "atmosphere" seem more pervasive and potent than now. Stylesetting in mental and moral attitudes is as rapid and subtle as in manners and dress. In the realm of religion this means that the power of personality increases as the force of direct appeal diminishes. We may frankly admit that the word "preaching" has an unpopular connotation. The word suggests a form of propaganda, an effort to put something over, to make others "be good." [58]

Still another to comment upon the preacher's effectiveness through indirection was Behrends.

> There is in this a practical hint of the greatest importance, that the minister's best work is always done

---

[56] Charles Reynolds Brown, *The Art of Preaching*, p. 173.
[57] Park, *op. cit.*, p. 43.
[58] Sockman, *op. cit.*, p. 109.

when no one can suspect that he is posing as a special pleader.[59]

Kelman clearly indicated his preference in the matter.

> If, however, the main object be appeal, it will often be more effective to begin with data of experience which have no apparent connection with the text at all, and to show a deeper meaning in these, which leads back to the text in the end, surprising the hearers with the religious significance of the ordinary facts of their lives.[60]

Robinson suggested a source of materials for the preacher's use as an aid in indirect enforcement of truth.

> But in casuistical preaching, the cases dwelt on should be neither the actual well-known ones of the hearers, nor the imaginary ones of the preacher. The first would be personal, and, as such, offensive, and so fail of their object; the second, from their very unreality, would be profitless. Amplest materials are found in the bits of personal history scattered throughout the Bible. The Bible is a mirror for all men through all time. Human nature being the same in every age, the preacher, who paints the real portrait of Scripture personages, presents what all recognize as genuine; and if he dissects a Scripture character, showing the difficulties, the trials and triumphs or defeats, through which it was formed, he cannot fail to throw a most useful light on existing conflicts in the hearts of his hearers. This kind of casuistry in the pulpit is always useful.[61]

Beecher also suggested a means of preaching by indirection.

> So there are thousands of persons in the world that you will take if they do not know that you are after them, but whom you could not touch if they suspected your purpose. Illustrations are invaluable for this kind of work, and there is nothing half so effective.[62]

[59] Behrends, *op. cit.*, p. 229.
[60] Kelman, *op. cit.*, p. 151.
[61] Robinson, *op. cit.*, pp. 176–77.
[62] Beecher, *op. cit.*, I, 168.

In explaining his own use of this technique, he said that:

> . . . in using an illustration pointed at a certain fault or weakness among your people, as I have done a thousand times (and I speak within bounds), never let it be known that you are aiming at any particular individual. . . . They do not suppose that I know anything about their difficulty, because, when I am hitting a man with an illustration, I never look at him. But such a man or woman will go home, and say, "Why, if somebody had been telling him of my case, he could not have hit it more exactly." They take it to heart, and it is blessed unto them. I have seen multitudes of such cases.[63]

In another lecture, Beecher spoke of indirection as the method to be used in arousing emotions.

> . . . You can never make people feel by scolding them because they don't feel. You can never move anybody by saying, "Feel!" Feeling is just as much a product of cause as anything else in the world. I could sit down before a piano and say, "A, come forth"; and it won't. But if I put my finger on the key it will, and that is the only way to make it. The human soul is like a harp; one has but to put his hand to a chord and it will vibrate to his touch, according as he knows how. It is the knowing how that you are to acquire. It is the very business that you are going out into the world for; it is to understand human nature so that you can touch the chords of feeling.[64]

A moment later he showed how feeling is developed.

> In general, feeling results from the presentation of some fact or truth that has a relation to the particular feeling you wish to produce. If I wanted to make you weep, I would not tell you an amusing story; I would, if I wanted to make you laugh, and that story had a relation to laughing. If I wished to make you weep, I would tell you some pathetic incident, the truth embodied in which had some sympathetic relation to feeling. Charge yourself with this: "If these people are to feel, I, as the

[63] *Ibid.*, pp. 167–68.
[64] *Ibid.*, II, 94–95.

minister of the Holy Ghost, am to be the cause of it by applying to their minds such treatment, such thoughts, as stand connected with the production of feeling." If they do not feel, it is because you do not play well. If they do feel, it is because you are a master of your business,—*quoad hoc*.[65]

A few years later Behrends expressed the same thought in regard to the creation of emotional states.

You do not deal directly with your feelings; something comes in to change the direction of your thoughts, until by attention they are diverted and riveted, and as these new thoughts master you, the feelings change without effort on your part. Now, this fact is of the highest practical importance. If you want to change your own feelings, or the feelings of others, there must be a change in the thoughts; you must give to the mental vision a different direction.[66]

The same view was held by Broadus.

Apart from sympathy with our own emotion, we can excite emotion in others only by indirect means, not by urging them to feel, though we should urge with the greatest vehemence. We must hold up before the mind considerations suited to awaken emotion, and let them do their work.[67]

LIFE SITUATIONS

Nine of the lecturers at Yale included in their discussions remarks upon life-situation preaching. At the very beginning of the Lyman Beecher series, Beecher spoke of it.

Now, the school of the future (if I am a prophet, and I am, of course, satisfied in my own mind that I am!) is what may be called a *Life School*. This style of preaching is to proceed, not so much upon the theory of the sanctity of the Church and its ordinances, or upon a pre-existing

[65] *Ibid.*, p. 95.
[66] Behrends, *op. cit.*, p. 143.
[67] Broadus, *op. cit.*, p. 255.

system of truth which is in the Church somewhere or somehow, as upon the necessity for all teachers, first, to study the strengths and the weaknesses of human nature minutely; and then to make use of such portions of the truth as are required by the special needs of man, and for the development of the spiritual side of human nature over the animal or lower side—the preparation of man in his higher nature for a nobler existence hereafter. It is a life-school in this respect, that it deals not with the facts of the past, except in so far as they can be made food for the present and factors of the life that now is; but rather studies to understand *men,* and to deal with them, face to face and heart to heart,—yea, even to mold them as an artist molds his clay or carves his statue.[68]

Nearly seventy years later Sockman also spoke of this method of preaching.

The Lord's roadmaker who watches and works for openings into the hearts of his people will naturally find that concern conditioning his messages. He will prepare his sermons with the needs of his people in mind. He will visualize individuals whose secret cares have been revealed to him. His messages will grow out of life situations. . . .

"Life-situation preaching" strikes a responsive chord in clergy and people because of its realism. It confronts not theories but conditions.[69]

He explained the method more fully a few moments later.

If sermons aim at solving the life situations of actual persons, they will not fall into the traditional classifications of topical, expository, doctrinal and the like. When we start with life situations we start where men live, then lead the questioning soul to the doctrinal and Biblical sources. Instead of the traditional expository type of preaching which spends the first paragraphs explaining the Hebrew and Greek roots while the listeners' minds rove over greener pastures, the sermon will arrest the attention of the hearer with a real issue and then direct

68 Beecher, *op. cit.,* I, 77–78.
69 Sockman, *op. cit.,* pp. 118–19.

the quest to the ever-satisfying Scriptures. It is the project method applied to the Bible. Such preaching will combine the teaching quality with the intensely practical.[70]

Something akin to the same method was discussed by Bowie.

> The most characteristic modern preaching has taken its cue from the psychological approach. It is not deductive, but inductive. It does not begin with large religious doctrines and then bring these down to their particular applications. It begins with the living person, and his confused but vital impulses; and it explores the possibilities for these, until at last it shows the frustration of the irreligious life, and reveals the great highroads of religious faith as the way in which the man himself must choose to go when he has found the real direction of his soul.[71]

In one of the lectures of Horne there is a suggestion of this approach to the audience.

> If only young preachers knew today the power of a "mighty application" of their sermons, and the supreme art of training all their guns upon actual temptations and tendencies, upon actual sins and selfishnesses of their hearers, we should not have as much cause as we have, to lament the decline of pulpit influence and authority.[72]

Tucker said, "The preacher must learn to think toward men, not away from them." [73] Concerning Jesus, Williams said, "He ever approached society through the concrete individual as every effective ministry must." [74]

The opposite of this approach received the comment of Jefferson.

> Men sometimes are blown out of their pulpit by working from their note-books toward the church, instead of

[70] *Ibid.*, p. 123.
[71] Bowie, *op. cit.*, p. 28.
[72] Horne, *op. cit.*, pp. 185–86.
[73] Tucker, *op. cit.*, p. 105.
[74] Williams, *op. cit.*, p. 151.

from the church toward their note-books. Let a man find
out what the church is able to digest and assimilate, and
then go to his books in search of it. A physician always
looks at his patient before he goes to the medicine chest.
A wise preacher begins, not with his books, but with his
church.[75]

Tucker illustrated this fault with an incident from his own
experience.

I may be pardoned if I refer to an experience of this
sort in my own early ministry. I had prepared a sermon
which had been, I doubt not, profitable to me, but which
was so utterly ineffective as a sermon that I took the
liberty of asking a very discerning friend what was the
difficulty with it. His reply was the best criticism I ever
received. "You seemed to me," he said, "to be more concerned about the truth than about men." Yes, that was
the difficulty. I saw it in a moment. I had no right as
a preacher to be concerned about the truth. I should have
had the truth in command, so that I could have given
my whole concern to men. As it was, the sermon lacked
authority.[76]

John Brown quoted Dale's confession of weakness in this
same regard.

"I have been thinking much, and with much concern
about my preaching. It has a fatal defect. It is wanting
in an element which is indispensable to real success.
I do not think that I should state the exact truth if I
said that I was not anxious for the conversion and per-
fection of individual men, and cared only for setting
forth the truth. But I fear that the truth occupies too
large a place in my thought, and that I have been too
much occupied with the instrument—the divine instrument—for effecting the ends of the ministry." [77]

Brooks also spoke of the weakness resulting from the wrong
approach to the audience.

[75] Jefferson, op. cit., p. 15.
[76] Tucker, op. cit., pp. 20–21.
[77] John Brown, op. cit., p. 256.

I am sure that one great source of the weakness of the pulpit is the feeling among the people that these men who stand up before them every Sunday have been making up trains of thought, and thinking how they should "treat their subject," as the phrase runs.[78]

POSITIVE—NEGATIVE

Seven Lyman Beecher lecturers spoke of affirmative preaching, comparing its merits with those of negative preaching. Kelman clearly indicated his preference in the matter. He said that:

. . . our preaching must be mainly positive and not negative. . . . Negative preaching, occupied mainly with threatening and invective, is far easier than the positive inculcation of virtue and of faith. It requires less thinking. The evil is naturally interesting, and it is abundantly ready to one's hand. It thrusts itself upon one's notice and easily seizes one's imagination. The good is seldom so evident, and perfect things are hidden, and must be sought and found. . . . Positive preaching is more difficult than negative, but in the main it is infinitely more effective.[79]

Jefferson commended the positive approach.

Many publications rail constantly at evildoing, and not a few ministers have caught this denunciatory spirit. But evil is most certainly overwhelmed, not by fixing the eyes on the things that are bad, but by turning the heart to the things that are good.[80]

Still another to point out the advantages of the positive approach was Oxnam.

The voice of the preacher is too often the voice of protest. It is positive proposal that is needed more than negative prohibition. The religious forces of the nation must become influential at the place decision is made be-

[78] Brooks, op. cit., p. 15.
[79] Kelman, op. cit., pp. 253-55.
[80] Jefferson, op. cit., p. 103.

fore it is made. Their convictions must be presented as creative and cooperative contributions. Protests may estop wrong action; proposals are necessary to inaugurate right action. Negatives are easy to discover; and this is not to object to those corrective and coercive actions that are required to keep a community clean and healthy but to point out the higher necessity of organizing the group life itself upon those positives consonant with the moral law, or, as the preacher prefers to put it, the will of God, and of discovering and applying measures expressive of that law and will.[81]

Watson compared the results of negative preaching with those of positive preaching.

It seemeth to us, when we are still young, both clever and profitable to make a hearer ashamed of his sin by putting him in the pillory and pelting him with epithets. Such is the incurable perversity of human nature, that the man grows worse under the discipline, and even conceives an unconscionable dislike to the officer of justice. As we grow older and see more of life it seems easier to put a man out of conceit with his sin by showing him the winsome and perfect form of goodness. So full of surprises is human nature that he will loathe himself and be drawn to the preacher, and, best of all, love righteousness. He that scolds in the pulpit, or rails, only irritates; he that appreciates and persuades wins the day.[82]

Beecher indicated that his preference was the positive method.

The approach which we make to men's consciences and feelings in religion must be made in such a way as to excite in them, not combativeness, not resistance, but hope and aspiration.[83]

Going still further in the direction of positive preaching, Broadus had a suggestion to offer.

When one has argued some general duty, as that of family or private prayer, of reading the Bible, or of

81 Oxnam, *op. cit.*, p. 52.
82 Watson, *op. cit.*, pp. 57–58.
83 Beecher, *op. cit.*, III, 241.

relieving the needy and distressed, it is exceedingly useful to add hints as to the actual doing of the particular duty, so as to make it seem a practical and a practicable thing, so as to awaken hope of doing better, and thus stimulate effort. Many a Christian duty seems to most people impracticable for *them;* and the most effective application in such cases is to show that it is practicable.[84]

Early in his series of lectures Hyde gave a definition of preaching which is built out of the positive approach.

Preaching is the art of keeping constant and urgent before men Christ's expectation that in every relation of life they are to do and be what absolute Good Will requires.[85]

MOTIVES

Eight of the preachers who spoke before the young men at Yale introduced the subject of appeal to motives or desires. Robinson indicated the importance of this subject.

But, to the busy and on-rushing people of this generation, the gospel must be so preached as to reach and control them in their hidden springs of action; yielding not one iota of its original demands, nor changing in the minutest particular its original method of saving men, it yet should be so preached as to exorcise or sanctify the ruling spirit of a false civilization.
. . . The gospel, to do its work, must take society at the level where it finds it; must address it in language it can understand, plying it with motives it can appreciate, and penetrating to the heart of it through every open avenue. It must deal with the motives of men, with the morals of society and of private life, and with the duties of citizens, and of the state.[86]

Broadus also mentioned the use of motives in moving men.

Persuasion is not generally best accomplished by a mere appeal to the feelings, but by urging, in the first

[84] Broadus, *op. cit.,* pp. 248–49.
[85] Hyde, *op. cit.,* p. 27.
[86] Robinson, *op. cit.,* pp. 22–23.

place, some motive or motives for acting, or determining to act, as we propose.[87]

Dale emphasized the importance of motives.

> I doubt whether we sufficiently consider the variety of motives which bring men to Christ, or the kind of preaching which is likely to call these motives into vigorous and effective action. There is room for a treatise on the Philosophy of Conversion, in which questions of this order might be investigated.[88]

Dale [89] named the following motives which lead men to Christ: (1) a sense of duty; (2) a desire to escape from a dissatisfaction with their own lives; (3) an inner urge to find God; (4) a sense of shame and self-disgust; and (5) a desire to receive divine help in perfecting their own lives. Sockman quoted a list of basic desires which the preacher may use in his preaching.

> In a religious journal [Zion's Herald, March 13 and 27, 1940], a specialist in business salesmanship essayed recently to advise the pulpit how it could reach a larger public by appealing to the twelve basic emotional hungers which the business world capitalizes. He listed these hungers as follows: security, progress, health and beauty, superiority, companionship, acquisition, activity, competition, group urge as in family and race, curiosity, sex, and religion. That people will go where they think these hungers can be satisfied, is not to be denied.[90]

Then he warned, "But let us remember that it is one thing to cater to popular hungers, it is another thing to feed the soul through them." [91] Another set of findings concerning people's desires and interests was reported by Sockman:

> Dr. Harold Ruopp, who has rendered such valuable service through his analysis of this preaching form, col-

87 Broadus, *op. cit.*, p. 249.
88 Dale, *op. cit.*, p. 204.
89 *Ibid.*, pp. 204–7.
90 Sockman, *op. cit.*, pp. 35–36.
91 *Ibid.*, p. 36.

lected the expressions of interest from some four thousand church attendants. His classification of their concerns is revealing and significant. The problems dealing
with "the individual and his inner self" constituted 48.7
per cent of the total expressions. These included personality problems, such as the feeling of futility, dis-
harmony, frustration, insecurity, fear, anxiety, loss of a
sense of significance; life decisions about education, vocation, marriage, personal moral problems, arising from
jealousy, hatred, greed, anger, sex, alcoholism, misfortune, with the questions growing out of accidents, sick-
ness, suicide, death. A second group of problems having to
do with "the individual in his relationship to the family"
accounted for 21.2 per cent of the responses. The third set
of questions, numbering 16.7 per cent of the total, dealt
with "the individual in his relationship to larger social
groups and society," involving problems of "social in-
equality, unemployment, the profit motive, Christian
citizenship, internationalism and conflicting loyalties."
The fourth classification, only 13.4 per cent, dealt with
"the individual in his relationship to God and the uni-
verse," consisting of such issues as the meaning of religion,
what is involved in following Jesus, the conflict between
science and religion.[92]

Day listed still another natural desire of mankind.

Men often seek the satisfaction of the need for self-
respect by identification with a group, whether it be
racial, political, social, or religious. If one shares the glory
of the group, then the more glorified the group the greater
the luster which results from belonging.[93]

Freeman named another motive.

A religious appeal that has in it nothing of the demand
for sacrifice, or the surrender of self to the high claims
of the heroic Christ, gathers few adherents to His
standard.[94]

The same general thought was also expressed by Jacks.

92 *Ibid.*, pp. 120–21.
93 Day, *op. cit.*, p. 161.
94 Freeman, *op. cit.*, pp. 47–48.

And here I will say, though it is anticipating what I have to say at greater length later on, that the preacher will be well advised to address his congregations on the same assumption that I am now making in regard to you. Assume that they are composed of brave men and women, and assume it especially in regard to the young. You will not fill your churches by appealing to the love of comfort, ease and safety. You are far more likely to empty them. One of the reasons why so many churches are empty today is that the appeal has been pitched too low. Psychology is teaching us many things; but if it leads us to think, as I am afraid it sometimes does, that human nature always demands the easiest paths and is most attracted by the line of least resistance, then we shall find that psychology has led us astray, led us, indeed, to a region where the things of the spirit have no foothold at all.[95]

REPETITION

Three of the speakers at Yale mentioned the desirability of repetition. Hall was first.

A superficial person is apt to suppose that to tell a thing once is sufficient for all purposes. A thoughtful person knows the contrary, knows that in the common affairs of life we often repeat and reiterate the instructions we wish to be remembered and acted upon. So a thoughtful teacher soon finds; and one of the main objects of the preacher is to teach. The teacher varies his phraseology, puts his points variously, asks questions, illustrates, suggests, employs shifts and expedients to insinuate definite ideas into the mind.[96]

Several years later Watson expressed the same view.

If any one desires to lodge an idea in the minds of his hearers he must learn the secret of artistic repetition, by which the same thing is said over and over again, but cast into a new dress on each reappearance.[97]

95 Jacks, *op. cit.*, pp. 4-5.
96 Hall, *op. cit.*, pp. 100-101.
97 Watson, *op. cit.*, p. 42.

Still later, Sockman said, ". . . I find that by repeated pricks some persons are aroused to action who take a major operation unmoved because under the anaesthetic of disagreement!" [98]

Four of the Yale lecturers spoke of the use of humor in preaching. Broadus mentioned it and gave a warning concerning its use.

When humor is employed in preaching it ought to be an incidental thing, and manifestly unstudied. It is so natural for some men to indulge in quaint, and even in very odd sayings, they so promptly and easily fall back into their prevailing seriousness, that the humorous remarks are unobjectionable, and sometimes, through the well-known relation between humor and pathos, they heighten the effect. But an *effort* to be amusing, anything odd that appears to have been calculated, is felt to be incompatible with a genuine seriousness and solemnity.[99]

Kelman spoke of humor in almost exactly the same way that Broadus had mentioned it.

Humour is admissible in preaching, and it may be one of the finest and most penetrating swords of the Spirit. . . . Yet an awful doom awaits that preacher who allows his sense of humour to master him, and to leave itself upon the memory of the congregation as the main impression of his work.[100]

Charles Reynolds Brown was freer in speaking of the advantages to be gained through the use of humor.

The wise, guarded, and tasteful employment of humor now and then will aid in keeping alive in the minds of

[98] Sockman, *op. cit.*, p. 125.
[99] Broadus, *op. cit.*, p. 26.
[100] Kelman, *op. cit.*, p. 161.

your hearers a full sense of the fact that you too are a man. The uniformly solemn and excruciatingly pious parson who proclaims the fact that he has no sense of humor is hopeless. His people are likely to look upon him as our great-grandparents looked upon certain drastic spring medicines—not pleasant to take, but in some mysterious way "good for the system." [101]

The subject was also mentioned by Tucker.

It is impossible to discuss the question of the introduction of humor into the pulpit, apart from the knowledge of the man. The humor of one preacher may be as reverent as the solemnity of another.[102]

SUMMARY

One of the chief prerequisites of persuasion is a congenial audience-speaker relationship. Without such a feeling strong arguments and normally convincing proofs may fall upon deaf ears. The preacher's first task is to present himself to his hearers in such a way that their reaction will be favorable. In order to succeed in this undertaking he must have the audience's interest at heart, must be competent to interpret that interest, and must be free from self-seeking. His attitude toward the audience must be one of genuine sympathy; he must adapt all that he says to the peculiar requirements of his group; he must begin his discourse upon common grounds of belief. Then, perhaps, he may be *en rapport* with his audience.

In his approach to the congregation the effective minister will use both the appeal to reason and the appeal to emotion, since both appeals are held to be legitimate. Some men respond better to one, some to the other. A warning should be sounded against the misuse of either type of appeal. Sometimes preachers have undertaken to prove propositions which did not require proof. In such cases the offering of proof often

101 Charles Reynolds Brown, *The Art of Preaching*, pp. 141–42.
102 Tucker, *op. cit.*, p. 122.

has served to create more doubt than confidence. Sometimes preachers have allowed their use of emotional appeal to degenerate into sentimentalism or sensationalism. Both practices should be avoided. Let it be remembered, however, that many of the greatest preachers have been men who exhibited a high degree of emotion in their own natures.

Still another approach is that of indirection. In persuading men, the indirect appeal is often more effective than the obvious, direct appeal. In addition, indirection often sets the stage for the effective use of other techniques of persuasion by creating the desired audience mood or emotional state. The relating of Biblical narratives and illustrations is a favorite means of securing indirection. Life situation preaching is one of the more widely used methods of the present day. Rather than use the subject-matter approach, the preacher begins with a consideration of the problems and needs which are present in life situations of the members of the audience. He then turns to the Scriptures to find help in meeting these needs.

Again, the preacher's approach should be more often positive than negative. Although there are numerous occasions when evil must be soundly denounced, the positive setting forth of good is more likely to inspire the people to reach upward toward the better life. In moving men the basic human motives, urges and desires should not be forgotten, for in them are the springs of response. A judicious appeal to the proper motives will assure effectiveness.

Repetition of the important points of the sermon is also a means of making their acceptance by the audience more certain. Finally, the use of incidental and appropriate humor may be of value in the sermon. A warning should be given, however, against the extended use of humor, especially when it attracts attention to itself.

Taken together, these suggestions should serve to guide the preacher in his approach to the congregation.

CHAPTER XV

CONCLUSIONS AND EVALUATIONS

"What is the secret of real influence in the pulpit?" was the question asked as this volume began. Now, after an examination of the principles of effective preaching as set forth in the sixty-six published volumes of the Lyman Beecher Lectures, it is possible to draw certain conclusions which go far in answering this question.

In order that these conclusions may be even more meaningful, a comparison with the principles of effective secular speaking is undertaken. The theory of persuasion set forth by the Yale lecturers is compared to the theory of persuasion set forth by secular rhetoricians both ancient and modern. The rhetoricians whose writings were chosen as a basis for comparison are: Aristotle (384 B.C.–322 B.C.), Cicero (106 B.C.–43 B.C.), Quintilian (c. A.D. 35–95), George Campbell (1719–1796), Richard Whately (1787–1863), Arthur Edward Phillips (c. 1870–   ), James Albert Winans (1872–   ), William Norwood Brigance (1896–   ), Ray K. Immel (1885–1945), and Alan H. Monroe (1903–   ). It is widely agreed that history has accorded to Aristotle, Cicero, and Quintilian the leading places in the development of ancient rhetoric, and to Campbell and Whately the distinction of forming the bridge between ancient rhetorical traditions and modern tenets, while contemporary educators of the field of speech recognize Phillips, Winans, Brigance, Immel and Monroe as leaders in the public speaking of today.

1. *The most vital element in the persuasion of a congregation is the person who stands in the pulpit. In turn, the*

paramount qualification of the man in the pulpit is his Christian character.

In naming the man as the prime factor in persuasion, the Yale lecturers did not necessarily relegate the preacher's message to a place of secondary importance, for his material was not considered in their discussions at this point. No effort was made to determine the relative value, in the persuasive process, of the preacher as compared with his message. Among the elements which were considered, the man who speaks was declared to be the most vital element in persuasion. He is far more important than the language or the illustrations of the sermon, far more essential than the order of worship or the physical setting in which the sermon is delivered, far more necessary than the style of the discourse or the technique of presentation, for upon the man all these elements depend. If he be a great man, these factors are eminently successful; if he be a small man, these factors have little effect. The superlative language which the Yale lecturers used in describing the importance of personality in preaching was at first somewhat startling. After more mature thought, however, one feels that they are correct in naming the person of the preacher as the prime element in persuasion.

Less startling was the high degree of emphasis given to the preacher's need of character. As early as the time of Aristotle, among the ancient rhetoricians, this element was mentioned.

> The instrument of proof is the moral character, when the delivery of the speech is such as to produce an impression of the speaker's credibility; for we yield a more complete and ready credence to persons of high character not only ordinarily and in a general way, but in such matters as do not admit of absolute certainty but necessarily leave room for difference of opinion, without any qualification whatever. . . . For so far from following the example of some authors of rhetorical handbooks, who in their "art" of Rhetoric regard the high character of the speaker as not being itself in any sense contributory

to his persuasiveness, we may practically lay it down as a general rule that there is no proof so effective as that of the character.[1]

Quintilian said of the importance of goodness, "Let the orator, then, whom I propose to form, be such a one as is characterized by the definition of Marcus Cato, *a good man skilled in speaking*." [2] Among the modern rhetoricians, William Norwood Brigance emphasized this element.

It is almost needless to say that a successful speaker must have a *strong moral character,* for "what you are speaks so loud I cannot hear what you say." No speaker can expect others to believe his words if they cannot trust him. . . . But you will notice that I spoke of the necessity not merely of a *good* moral character but of a *strong* moral character, which includes even more.[3]

James Albert Winans was another of modern times to discuss this subject.

Many writers upon the influence of speakers over audiences have emphasized simple goodness. . . . It is readily seen that a man of notoriously bad life cannot be an effective preacher of righteousness, though he plead like an angel of light. . . .
Nevertheless, we must take exception to Quintilian's "good man," as certain successful orators come to mind; or, indeed, to any sweeping statement of the sort. Honesty compels us to acknowledge that many men not good have been very successful speakers, even orators.[4]

[1] Aristotle, *Rhetoric* (J. E. C. Welldon, translator, *The Rhetoric of Aristotle,* London: Macmillan and Company, 1886, pp. 10–12, quoted by Lester Thonssen, *Selected Readings in Rhetoric and Public Speaking,* New York: The H. W. Wilson Company, 1942, p. 37), Book I, Chap. ii, Pars. 3–6.

[2] Quintilian, *Institutes of Oratory* (John Selby Watson, translator, *Quintilian's Institutes of Oratory,* London: George Bell & Sons, 1895, Vol. II, p. 391), Book XII, Chap. 1, Par. 1.

[3] William Norwood Brigance, *Speech Composition* (New York: F. S. Crofts & Co., 1937), p. 141.

[4] James Albert Winans, *Public Speaking* (New York: The Century Co., 1923), pp. 314–15. Copyright, 1915, 1917 by James A. Winans.

Although an exhaustive survey of the leading rhetoricians, both ancient and modern, was not attempted, it was apparent in the writings of the ten who were consulted that the element of goodness or character was not given as high a degree of emphasis among secular rhetoricians as it was among the Yale lecturers. At this point it is possible to detect what is likely the most important difference between secular and religious speakers. While the political orator, as both Brigance [5] and Winans [6] say, may display, with seeming impunity, certain weaknesses such as carelessness with money, addiction to drink, and love for gambling, the minister of Christ would be utterly ineffective if such weaknesses were known to be a part of his make-up. The pulpit demands a greater degree of goodness upon the part of the speaker than do the rostrum, the bar, and the legislative hall. This difference was pointed out by Campbell:

. . . it plainly appears that there is a certain delicacy in the character of a preacher which he is never at liberty totally to overlook, and to which, if there appear anything incongruous, either in his conduct or in his public performances, it will never fail to injure their effect. On the contrary, it is well known that as, in the other professions, the speaker's private life is but very little minded, so there are many things which, though they would be accounted nowise unsuitable from the bar or in the senate, would be deemed altogether unbefitting the pulpit.[7]

2. *In order to achieve his maximum effectiveness (and in addition to the possession of a genuine Christian character), the preacher must be sincere, must be earnest, must be original, must be well informed and studious, must possess a strong, healthy body, and must possess a good mind.*

There was almost complete agreement between the rhetoricians and the Yale lecturers concerning the qualifications

[5] Brigance, *op. cit.,* p. 141.

[6] Winans, *op. cit.,* p. 315.

[7] George Campbell, *The Philosophy of Rhetoric* (New York: Harper & Brothers, 1851), p. 123.

which the successful speaker should possess. For example, every one of the qualifications set forth in the Yale lectures, as summarized above, was listed by Winans.[8] The list of Brigance [9] was not quite as extended as that of Winans, though it contained most of the qualifications mentioned above. Most of the lists of qualifications followed the same general trend, some omitting one item, and some another. Even the ancient rhetoricians covered approximately the same area as did the modern writers. The following paragraph sets forth the main qualifications as Cicero saw them:

A knowledge of a vast number of things is necessary, without which volubility of words is empty and ridiculous; speech itself is to be formed, not merely by choice, but by careful construction of words; and all the emotions of the mind, which nature has given to man, must be intimately known; for all the force and art of speaking must be employed in allaying or exciting the feelings of those who listen. To this must be added a certain portion of grace and wit, learning worthy of a well-bred man, and quickness and brevity in replying as well as attacking, accompanied with a refined decorum and urbanity. Besides, the whole of antiquity and a multitude of examples is to be kept in the memory; nor is the knowledge of laws in general, or of the civil law in particular, to be neglected. And why need I add any remarks on delivery itself, which is to be ordered by action of body, by gesture, by look, and by modulation and variation of the voice, the great power of which, alone and in itself, the comparatively trivial art of actors and the stage proves, on which though all bestow their utmost labor to form their look, voice, and gesture, who knows not how few there are, and have ever been, to whom we can attend with patience? What can I say of that repository for all things, the memory, which unless it be the keeper of the matter and words that are the fruits of thought and invention, all the talents of the orator, we see, though they

8 Winans, *op. cit.*, pp. 185–348.
9 Brigance, *op. cit.*, pp. 120–96.

be of the highest degree of excellence, will be of no avail?
Let us then cease to wonder what is the cause of the
scarcity of good speakers, since eloquence results from
all those qualifications. . . .[10]

With but few exceptions, the qualifications which were recommended by secular rhetoricians to equip a person for secular speaking were the same qualifications which were recommended by sacred rhetoricians to equip a person for pulpit
speaking.

3. *The preacher must be confident in his own ability, yet
not conceited, must have a high respect and genuine love for
his audience, and must possess a strong liking for all of the
work of the ministry.*

Although there was a passage in Cicero's writings which
seemed to recommend a certain merit in timidity, the general
consensus of opinion was that the speaker should appear confident and sure of himself. Cicero said:

To me, those who speak best, and speak with the utmost ease and grace, appear, if they do not commence
their speeches with some timidity, and show some con-
fusion in the exordium, to have almost lost the sense of
shame, though it is impossible that such should not be
the case; for the better qualified a man is to speak, the
more he fears the difficulties of speaking, the uncertain
success of a speech, and the expectation of the audience.
But he who can produce and deliver nothing worthy of
his subject, nothing worthy of the name of an orator,
nothing worthy the attention of his audience, seems to
me, though he be ever so confused while he is speaking,
to be downright shameless; for we ought to avoid a character for shamelessness, not by testifying shame, but by
not doing that which does not become us.[11]

[10] Marcus Tullius Cicero, *De Oratore* (J. S. Watson, translator, *Cicero on
Oratory and Orators,* London: George Bell and Sons, 1884, pp. 146–47), Book I,
Chap. 5.
[11] Cicero, *op cit.* (Watson, p. 173), Book I, Chap. 26.

Brigance and Immel admonished the underconfident speaker to *"Try deliberately to think of yourself as worthy."* [12] A few sentences later the same authors suggested, *". . . act as if you had complete self-respect and confidence."* [13] Their final word was, *". . . be careful not to overdo self-respect!"* [14] This was exactly the same advice as that given in the Yale lectures.

Winans said, "Courtesy should not be merely assumed, but should rest upon fairness of spirit and also genuine respect for one's audience. . . . The humblest audience deserves respect." [15] Brigance [16] mentioned the need for the speaker to have a respect for his audience, and to possess the qualities of courtesy, fairness and tact. Nowhere, however, did the secular rhetoricians go so far as to suggest that the speaker have a genuine love for his audience. This seems to be a distinctive necessity of the preacher. It grows out of the intimate nature of his work with the people, and out of the deep seriousness of the subjects with which he deals.

Likewise, the secular writers did not mention the need for a love of the work, as the Yale lecturers did. However, they did mention the need for a willingness to labor long at the task of becoming a good speaker, which is akin to the love of the work.

4. *In order to reach its peak of effectiveness, the sermon must be presented in a style which is clear, concrete, interesting, original, and coherent. Sensationalism and elegance are undesirable elements. The style may profit from the judicious use of appropriate illustrations. Its language must be simple, familiar, and precise.*

Among the topics most fully discussed in the writings of the ancient rhetoricians was that of style. Whole chapters, and

---

[12] William Norwood Brigance and Ray Keeslar Immel, *Speechmaking; Principles and Practice* (New York: F. S. Crofts & Co., 1938), p. 32.

[13] *Ibid.*, p. 33.

[14] *Loc. cit.*

[15] Winans, *op. cit.*, p. 318.

[16] Brigance, *op. cit.*, p. 120.

even entire books, were written on the various elements of style. It is beyond the scope or the need of this chapter to give the complete picture of these lengthy discussions. A reading of the suggestions offered by the different rhetoricians in the different ages indicated that style runs in cycles. Cicero [17] designated three distinct styles which are sometimes described as the grand style, the moderate style, and the plain style. One of these styles will be in the ascendancy during one period of time, only to be replaced by another in a later period. Eventually the cycle is completed and the pendulum swings in the opposite direction. So far as the style commended in the Yale lectures is concerned, it can be said that it was the typical style of the times. The grand or oratorical style had already begun to give way to the moderate or more conversational style. This tendency progressed through the more than seventy-year period. Of course, certain elements, such as clearness, force, and beauty, are always desirable in style. No distinctive style was introduced as having peculiar advantages for the pulpit.

5. *After thorough preparation, the sermon is most effective when delivered extemporaneously.*

The advantages and disadvantages of extempore speaking have been discussed since the time of the early Greeks. One stage of the world's history finds this mode of speaking the leading type. Another period finds the manuscript method or the memoriter method in vogue. The Yale lecturers analyzed the temper of their own time and found the extempore method of delivery more desirable than either of the other methods. Had the series of lectures started fifty years earlier, such would not have been the case. Today, the extemporaneous method is still the most popular type of delivery.

6. *The order of the service, and the physical setting in*

[17] Marcus Tullius Cicero, *The Orator* (C. D. Yonge, *The Orations of Marcus Tullius Cicero*, London: G. Bell and Sons, 1911, Vol. IV, pp. 403–10), Chaps. XXIII–XXVIII.

*which the sermon is delivered must be so planned as to aid
the sermon in accomplishing its purpose.*

Very little was said among the ancients concerning the setting for their speeches. This may have been a result of the
speaker's inability to change the speech setting, even had he so
desired. Conditions in the forum, the law courts, and the as-
sembly were beyond the speaker's control. In the writings of
modern rhetoricians, however, the subject is discussed, although somewhat briefly even here. A rather full discussion of
the auditorium, the seating, and the ritual was given by Brigance.[18] His suggestions were exactly in line with those offered
in the Yale lectures.

7. *The sermon must have a definite purpose, the selection
of which is determined by the needs of the congregation.*

From the time of Aristotle to the present, rhetoricians have
consistently given attention to the ends or purposes of speaking. The following paragraph indicates the approach which
Aristotle made to the subject.

> There are three kinds of Rhetoric, corresponding to
> the three kinds of audience to which speeches are nat-
> urally addressed. For a speech is composed of three ele-
> ments, viz. the speaker, the subject of the speech and the
> persons addressed; and the end *or object* of the speech
> is determined by the last, viz. by the audience. . . .
> It follows that there must necessarily be three kinds of
> rhetorical speeches, the deliberative, the forensic and
> the epideictic.[19]

Cicero indicated his own consideration of the speech purpose
in these words:

> When, after hearing and understanding the nature of
> a cause, I proceed to examine the subject matter of it, I
> settle nothing until I have ascertained to what point my

---

[18] Brigance, *op. cit.,* pp. 151–54.
[19] Aristotle, *op. cit.* (Welldon, p. 22, Thonssen, p. 39), Book I, Chap. iii,
Par. 1.

whole speech, bearing immediately on the question and case, must be directed.[20]

Quintilian [21] followed Aristotle in dividing all speaking occasions into three groups according to their purposes—the epideictic, the deliberative, and the judicial. He made a real contribution, however, when he said, "There are also three objects which an orator must accomplish, to *inform,* to *move,* to *please* . . ." [22] Campbell, who is generally cited as the turning point between the Aristotelian and the modern view of speech purposes, summarized the matter in a single sentence: "All the ends of speaking are reducible to four: every speech being intended to enlighten the understanding, to please the imagination, to move the passions, or to influence the will." [23]

Outstanding among the modern writers on this subject was Arthur Edward Phillips. Speaking of the speech purpose, he said, "The first requisite to effectiveness is a knowledge of the purposes of speech—a clear understanding of its General Ends." [24] His listing of the general ends of speech was as follows: "The speaker wishes the listener to see—*Clearness,* or to feel—*Impressiveness,* or to accept—*Belief,* or to do—*Action,* or to enjoy—*Entertainment.*" [25] Much later in his book he spoke of the more specific purposes of speech.

The Statement of Aim is the statement of the *precise thing sought.* It resolves the General Subject into a specific assertion of what the listener is to believe; what he is to do; what he is to see, feel or enjoy.[26]

[20] Cicero, *De Oratore* (Watson, p. 252), Book II, Chap. 27.
[21] Quintilian, *op. cit.* (Watson, Vol. I, pp. 182–83), Book III, Chap. 4, Pars. 11, 12, 15.
[22] *Ibid.* (Watson, p. 183), Book III, Chap. 5, Par. 2.
[23] Campbell, *op. cit.,* p. 23.
[24] Arthur Edward Phillips, *Effective Speaking* (Chicago: The Newton Company, 1938), p. 17. Used by permission of The Geographical Publishing Co., Chicago.
[25] *Ibid.,* p. 19.
[26] *Ibid.,* p. 214.

Following Phillips, Brigance spoke of the General Ends of speaking, and of the Specific Ends of speaking. Concerning the latter, he said:

The four general purposes of speech are useful to start from, but never to stop with. Shooting at a hillside usually bags no game. After settling upon the general purpose of the speech, the speaker's next task is to choose, carefully and definitely, *just what particular response he wants from his audience.*[27]

There was very little in the Yale lectures about general or specific ends or purposes of speech. The speakers at Yale contented themselves with pointing out the need for each sermon to be built around a definite purpose, for each sermon to aim at a specific response. Brigance came closest of all the secular writers to expressing the same thought as did the Yale lecturers. He said:

No speaker can justify himself in consuming the time of any audience, be it large or small, unless he aims at winning some definite verdict, at attaining some definite goal. The lack of a definite goal is probably the cause of more failures than all other reasons combined.[28]

The Yale lecturers focused attention upon the necessity of a purpose behind each sermon. Their dealing with the subject was practical rather than analytical.

8. *In order to persuade men, the preacher must possess a thorough understanding of his own congregation and of men in general.*

Again, from ancient times until the present, the leading writers in the speech field have emphasized the need of audience analysis. For example, Aristotle wrote page after page upon the ends of human action,[29] the causes of action,[30] the

[27] Brigance, *op. cit.,* p. 63.
[28] *Ibid.,* p. 53.
[29] Aristotle, *op. cit.* (Welldon, pp. 30–31, Thonssen, p. 40), Book I, Chap. v, Par. 1.
[30] *Ibid.* (Welldon, pp. 72–73, Thonssen, p. 43), Book I, Chap. x, Par. 8.

analysis of the emotions,[31] and the analysis of people according to age.[32] Cicero,[33] likewise, wrote freely of the results of his own audience analysis. Campbell mentioned the need of understanding the nature of people.

> Rhetoric, as was observed already, not only considers the subject, but also the hearers and the speaker. The hearers must be considered in a twofold view, as men in general, and as such men in particular.[34]

A quotation from Brigance will serve to show the modern view on this subject.

> No two audiences are identical. Each has its special interests, attitudes, presumptions, and convictions, which make it different from any other. Differences in age, in occupation, in creed, in purpose, make it impossible to treat one audience precisely as another. Before planning a speech for any new audience the speaker must ask himself, What people will compose this audience? Why will they be there? What are their occupations? their age? creed? interests? Only after considering these factors can a speaker answer the vital question: *What response can I reasonably expect to get from this audience?* [35]

There was a feeling of unanimity among the rhetoricians, ancient and modern, and among the Yale lecturers that the speaker must study his audience with great care. That this unanimous opinion is true is not to be doubted.

9. *The most effective approach to the audience is the one which begins with the preacher and audience "en rapport," which appeals judiciously both to the reason and to the emotions, which makes use of indirect rather than direct appeals, which is audience-centered rather than subject-matter-centered, which is positive rather than negative, which appeals to*

[31] *Ibid.* (Welldon, pp. 114, 158–61, Thonssen, pp. 44–46), Book II, Chap. i, Par. 9; Chap. x.
[32] *Ibid.* (Welldon, pp. 164–70, Thonssen, pp. 46–49), Book II, Chap. xii–xiv.
[33] Cicero, *op cit.* (Watson, pp. 270–73), Book II, Chaps. 42, 43, 44.
[34] Campbell, *op. cit.*, p. 93.
[35] Brigance, *op. cit.*, p. 54.

man's basic motives, which repeats the chief elements to be graspead, and which includes the sparing use of humor.

Not a single persuasion technique or method of approach suggested in the Yale lectures is unique. Each suggestion can also be found among the secular rhetoricians, ancient or modern, and sometimes in both.

Cicero was undoubtedly speaking of that happy situation designated above by the term, "en rapport," when he said:

> For there is nothing . . . of more importance in speaking than that the hearer should be favourable to the speaker, and be himself so strongly moved that he may be influenced more by impulse and excitement of mind, than by judgment or reflection.[36]

Brigance recommended beginning upon common ground.

> Every young speaker will find it valuable to pay careful attention to this matter of common ground, for common ground emphasizes the agreements between speaker and audience and minimizes the differences. It therefore promotes good will and a sympathetic contact.[37]

Winans spoke in similar language: "Not only should we avoid awakening hostility; we should seek an alliance with our audience by getting on common ground with them." [38]

The discussion of the reason-emotion approach has continued from the earliest times. Although taking in more than this one element, the following paragraph shows Aristotle's view of this matter. It also serves to show his view of the importance of the speaker's own personal power, which was discussed earlier.

> The proofs provided through the instrumentality of the speech are of three kinds, consisting either in the moral character of the speaker or in the production of a certain disposition in the audience or in the speech itself

---

[36] Cicero, *op. cit.* (Watson, p. 270), Book II, Chap. 42.
[37] Brigance, *op. cit.*, p. 70.
[38] Winans, *op. cit.*, p. 260.

by means of real or apparent demonstration. The instrument of proof is the moral character, when the delivery of the speech is such as to produce an impression of the speaker's credibility; for we yield a more complete and ready credence to persons of high character not only ordinarily and in a general way, but in such matters as do not admit of absolute certainty but necessarily leave room for difference of opinion, without any qualification whatever. . . . For so far from following the example of some authors of rhetorical handbooks, who in their "art" of Rhetoric regard the high character of the speaker as not being itself in any sense contributory to his persuasiveness, we may practically lay it down as a general rule that there is no proof so effective as that of the character. *Secondly,* proof may be conveyed through the audience, when it is worked up by the speech to an emotional state. For there is a wide difference in our manner of pronouncing decisions, according as we feel pleasure or pain, affection or hatred; and indeed *the power of working upon the emotions* is, as we assert, the one end or object to which our present professors of the rhetorical art endeavor to direct their studies. This is a part of the subject which will be elucidated in detail, when we come to discuss the emotions. *Lastly,* the instrument of proof is the speech itself, when we have proved a truth or an apparent truth from such means of persuasion as are appropriate to a particular subject.[39]

Cicero expressed his view in these words, some of which were quoted above:

When, after hearing and understanding the nature of a cause, I proceed to examine the subject matter of it, I settle nothing until I have ascertained to what point my whole speech, bearing immediately on the question and case, must be directed. I then very diligently consider two other points; the one, how to recommend myself, or those for whom I plead; the other, how to sway the minds of those before whom I speak to that which I desire. Thus the whole business of speaking rests upon

[39] Aristotle, *op. cit.* (Welldon, pp. 10–12, Thonssen, p. 37), Book I, Chap. ii, Pars. 3–6.

three things for success in persuasion; that we prove
what we maintain to be true; that we conciliate those
who hear; that we produce in their minds whatever feeling our cause may require.[40]

Although he spent much more time discussing logical proof,
Quintilian did say, "Throughout the whole of any cause, as I
remarked, there is room for addresses to the feelings." [41]
Campbell showed the interrelation between reason and emotion.

Finally, as that kind, the most complex of all, which
is calculated to influence the will, and persuade to a certain conduct, is in reality an artful mixture of that which
proposes to convince the judgment, and that which interests the passions, its distinguishing excellence results
from these two, the argumentative and the pathetic incorporated together. These, acting with united force,
and, if I may so express myself, in concert, constitute that
passionate eviction, that *vehemence* of contention, which
is admirably fitted for persuasion, and hath always been
regarded as the supreme qualification in an orator. It
is this which bears down every obstacle, and procures
the speaker an irresistible power over the thoughts and
purposes of his audience. It is this which hath been so
justly celebrated as giving one man an ascendant over
others. . . .[42]

Later, the same writer designated the exact parts which argumentative and emotional appeals play in the persuasive process.

But if so much depend on passion, where is the scope
for argument? Before I answer this question, let it be
observed, that, in order to persuade, there are two things
which must be carefully studied by the orator. The first
is, to excite some desire or passion in the hearers; the
second is, to satisfy their judgment that there is a con-

40 Cicero, *op. cit.* (Watson, pp. 252–53), Book II, Chap. 27.
41 Quintilian, *op. cit.* (Watson, Vol. I, p. 421), Book VI, Chap. 2, Par. 2.
42 Campbell, *op. cit.*, pp. 26–27.

nexion between the action to which he would persuade
them, and the gratification of the desire or passion which
he excites. This is the analysis of persuasion. The former
is effected by communicating lively and glowing ideas
of the object; the latter, unless so evident of itself as to
supersede the necessity, by presenting the best and most
forcible arguments which the nature of the subject ad-
mits. In the one lies the pathetic, in the other the argumentative.[43]

Richard Whately also included both elements in his view of
persuasion.

Persuasion, therefore, depends on, first, *Argument,*
(to prove the expediency of the Means proposed,) and
secondly, what is usually called *Exhortation,* i. e., the excitement of men to adopt those Means, by representing
the End as sufficiently desirable.[44]

The modern treatment of this subject was amply set forth
by Brigance and Immel.

Where do reason and argument enter the picture?
What part do they play in human behavior? A very impelling part indeed. For one thing, people desire generally to know the truth, to recognize quackery, to avoid
being gullible, to resist animal urges—in short, to be
rational beings maintaining self-respect. To satisfy these
desires intelligent people must turn to reason. For another thing, although the mass of people, to be sure, avoid
reasoning so long as there is smooth sailing—they dislike
the strenuous effort which it demands—yet they resort
to it the instant they get into a jam, or must solve a per-
plexing problem, or must find a way out. Reason, in other
words, is the instrument for solving our problems, for
satisfying our desires, for obtaining the higher values of
life. Argument, of course, is reasoning set forth in print
or in spoken words. We may not "argue a man into a
desire," but we can, by argument and reason, enable our-

43 *Ibid.,* p. 100.
44 Richard Whately, *Elements of Rhetoric* (Boston: James Munroe and Company, 1851), p. 118.

selves and others to solve our problems and so advance toward attaining our desires.

. . . .

It follows, therefore, that, although argument plays an important part in persuasion, arguments are not equally persuasive simply because they are equally logical. The persuasive speaker must be able to unite argument with the springs of action in human beings. He must be able to premise logic upon impelling wants—self-preservation, progress, honor, and the like. His argument must not only impel the hearers to accept his logic as true, it must also arouse them to *want* what their minds have proclaimed as true. This is not mere appeal to passions or mere play on emotions. It is *loaded logic*. And rest assured that no other kind of logic—no appeal to reason which does not interweave an appeal to want—will seriously influence human behavior.[45]

The Yale lecturers were, therefore, on solid ground when they found it legitimate to appeal to the reason and to the emotions in persuading men.

Among the ancients, Aristotle pointed out the importance of appealing to desires. He spoke of the ends of human action in this fashion:

It may be said that all men both individually and collectively have a certain object at which they aim in all that they choose and in all that they avoid. This object may be summarily defined as happiness and the constituents of happiness.[46]

Some pages later he named seven causes of action: "To sum up then; all our actions are necessarily due to seven causes, viz. chance, nature, compulsion, habit, reasoning, passion and desire." [47] Campbell also spoke of appealing to desires:

[45] Brigance and Immel, *op. cit.*, pp. 268–69.
[46] Aristotle, *op. cit.* (Welldon, pp. 30–31, Thonssen, p. 40), Book I, Chap. v, Par. 1.
[47] *Ibid.* (Welldon, pp. 72–73, Thonssen, p. 43), Book I, Chap. x, Par. 8.

. . . there are two things which must be carefully studied by the orator. The first is, to excite some desire or passion in the hearers; the second is, to satisfy their judgment that there is a connexion between the action to which he would persuade them, and the gratification of the desire or passion which he excites.[48]

Among modern writers on the subject, Brigance and Immel gave an important place in the process of persuasion to the same appeal.

It was not, however, until modern psychologists, with the accumulation of knowledge behind them and the newest techniques at their disposal, began to investigate human behavior, that the full import of this aspect of persuasion was realized. R. S. Woodworth gives us perhaps its best summary: "So far as it is possible for us to influence other people and control their behavior, it is by controlling their desires and purposes." [49]

Their definition of persuasion was, "PERSUASION IS A PROCESS OF VITALIZING OLD DESIRES, PURPOSES, OR IDEALS. . . . PERSUASION IS A PROCESS OF SUBSTITUTING NEW DESIRES, PURPOSES, OR IDEALS IN THE PLACE OF OLD ONES." [50]

Of the other suggestions found in the Yale lectures concerning the most persuasive approach to an audience, Winans mentioned indirection,[51] repetition,[52] and humor.[53] In covering another point, Brigance[54] insisted that the speech subject must be adapted to the audience. Alan H. Monroe[55] discussed the positive-negative approach in the persuasion process, covering still another point of the Yale lectures. Thus, it is true that the preachers who delivered the Lyman Beecher

[48] Campbell, op. cit., p. 100.
[49] Brigance and Immel, op. cit., pp. 266–67.
[50] Ibid., pp. 269–70.
[51] Winans, op. cit., p. 228.
[52] Ibid., p. 212.
[53] Ibid., p. 327.
[54] Brigance, op. cit., pp. 26–27.
[55] Alan H. Monroe, Principles and Types of Speech (revised edition; New York: Scott, Foresman and Company, 1939), p. 207.

series of lectures brought forth no new techniques of persuasion. It may be said, therefore, that the pulpit has no peculiar, distinctive persuasion techniques of its own.

A comparison of the recommendations of the preachers who delivered the Lyman Beecher Lectures to the young men of the Yale Divinity School, with the admonitions of secular rhetoricians of all ages to prospective secular orators, leads to the conclusion that there is no distinctive set of rules which applies only to pulpit speaking. With but few exceptions, the principles underlying all effective speaking are the same. Certain modifications of the suggestions of the rhetoricians are sometimes made necessary by the peculiar pulpit situation and subject matter, but the basic principles remain the same.

Among the modifications of the rules of secular speaking made necessary by the special requirements of pulpit speaking are these:

The major difference is found in the pulpit's heightened demand for character and personal righteousness on the part of its occupant. This grows out of the fact that every speaker must exemplify in his own person the truth which he sets forth, and the preacher's truth is a gospel of righteousness.

Another difference between the two fields of speaking is to be found in the closer and more intimate relationship which exists between the minister and his congregation and that which exists between the average secular speaker and his audience. When the preacher is known to be a man of exceptional piety and godly character, and when he sustains to his congregation the role of loving friend, his hearers make less rigorous demands on points of style, delivery, language, technique, and other similar elements. He can be eminently successful, without possessing the finer techniques of the speaking art. This is certainly less true of the secular orator, for he seldom has quite the same sympathetic feeling from his audience as has the beloved minister.

In a study such as this, when the opinions of a number of men are tabulated and totals are drawn, there is a temptation to put too much confidence in those totals. Sometimes the survey is of such a nature that such conclusions are valid and fully reliable. In this study such conclusions must be examined with care. The total number of lecturers who mentioned each of the basic factors of effective preaching is indicative of the relative importance of these factors, but this criterion cannot be considered an infallible guide. The reason is obvious when the following paragraph from Brooks is read:

> He who is called upon to give these lectures cannot but remember that they are given every year, and that he has had very able and faithful predecessors. There are certainly, therefore, some things which he may venture to omit without being supposed to be either ignorant or careless of them. There are certain first principles, of primary importance, which he may take for granted in all that he says. They are so fundamental, that they must be always present, and their power must pervade every treatment of the work which is built upon them. But they need not be deliberately stated anew each year.[56]

The main emphasis of this volume has been upon the art and technique of preaching. The words of many eminent men have been quoted. It seems fitting, however, that the final words should be those of the Holy Scriptures themselves. Listen, first, to the charge of the apostle Paul:

> I charge thee in the sight of God, and of Christ Jesus, who shall judge the living and the dead, . . . preach the word; be urgent in season, out of season; reprove, rebuke, exhort, with all longsuffering and teaching. . . .

[56] Brooks, *op. cit.*, p. 3.

be thou sober in all things, suffer hardship, do the work of an evangelist, fulfil thy ministry.[57]

Listen finally to Christ's Great Commission:

Go ye into all the world, and preach the gospel to the whole creation.[58]

[57] II Timothy 4:1-2, 5, from the American Standard Version of the Revised Bible (copyrighted by the International Council of Religious Education) and used by permission.

[58] *Ibid.,* Mark 16:15.

BIBLIOGRAPHY

A. THE LYMAN BEECHER LECTURES
ON PREACHING

Abbott, Lyman, *The Christian Ministry*. Boston: Houghton Mifflin and Company, 1905. 317 pp.

Beecher, Henry Ward, *Yale Lectures on Preaching*. 3 vols.; New York: Fords, Howard, & Hulbert, 1892.

Behrends, A. J. F., *The Philosophy of Preaching*. New York: Charles Scribner's Sons, 1890. 234 pp.

Bowie, Walter Russell, *The Renewing Gospel*. New York: Charles Scribner's Sons, 1935. 296 pp.

Broadus, John, *A Treatise on the Preparation and Delivery of Sermons*. Revised edition; New York: Richard R. Smith, Inc., 1930. 562 pp.

Brooks, Phillips, *Lectures on Preaching*. New York: E. P. Dutton & Company, 1898. 281 pp.

Brown, Charles Reynolds, *The Art of Preaching*. New York: The Macmillan Company, 1922. 250 pp.

————, *The Social Message of the Modern Pulpit*. New York: Charles Scribner's Sons, 1912. 293 pp.

Brown, John, *Puritan Preaching in England*. New York: Charles Scribner's Sons, 1900. 290 pp.

Burton, Nathaniel J., *In Pulpit and Parish*. [New York: The Macmillan Company, 1925.] 639 pp.

Buttrick, George A., *Jesus Came Preaching*. New York: Charles Scribner's Sons, 1931. 239 pp.

————, and others, *Preaching in These Times*. New York: Charles Scribner's Sons, 1940. 179 pp.

Calkins, Raymond, *The Eloquence of Christian Experience*. New York: The Macmillan Company, 1927. 232 pp.

Coffin, Henry Sloane, *In a Day of Social Rebuilding*. New Haven: Yale University Press, 1918. 176 pp.

Crosby, Howard, *The Christian Preacher*. New York: Anson D. F. Randolph & Company, 1879. 195 pp.

Dale, R. W., *Nine Lectures on Preaching*. London: Hodder & Stoughton, 1890. 302 pp.

Day, Albert Edward, *Jesus and Human Personality*. New York: The Abingdon Press, 1934. 269 pp.

Fairbairn, A. M., *The Place of Christ in Modern Theology*. London: Hodder & Stoughton, 1893. 556 pp.

Faunce, William Herbert Perry, *The Educational Ideal in the Ministry*. New York: The Macmillan Company, 1908. 286 pp.

Fitch, Albert Parker, *Preaching and Paganism*. New Haven: Yale University Press, 1920. 229 pp.

Forsyth, P. T., *Positive Preaching and Modern Mind*. New York: Hodder & Stoughton [1907]. 374 pp.

Fosdick, Harry Emerson, *The Modern Use of the Bible*. New York: The Macmillan Company, 1924. 291 pp.

Freeman, James Edward, *The Ambassador*. New York: The Macmillan Company, 1928. 212 pp.

Gladden, Washington, *Social Salvation*. Boston: Houghton Mifflin and Company, 1902. 240 pp.

————, *Tools and the Man*. Boston: Houghton Mifflin Company, 1893. 308 pp.

Gordon, George A., *Ultimate Conceptions of Faith*. Boston: Houghton Mifflin and Company, 1903. 399 pp.

Greer, David H., *The Preacher and His Place*. New York: Edwin S. Gorham, 1904. 263 pp.

Gunsaulus, Frank W., *The Minister and the Spiritual Life*. New York: Fleming H. Revell Company, 1911. 397 pp.

Hall, John, *God's Word Through Preaching*. New York: Dodd & Mead, Publishers, 1875. 274 pp.

Henson, H. Hensley, *The Liberty of Prophesying*. New Haven: Yale University Press, 1910. 293 pp.

Horne, Charles Silvester, *The Romance of Preaching*. New York: Fleming H. Revell Company, 1914. 302 pp.

Horton, Robert F., *Verbum Dei*. New York: Macmillan and Co., 1893. 300 pp.

Hyde, William DeWitt, *The Gospel of Good Will*. New York: The Macmillan Company, 1916. 245 pp.

Jacks, L. P., *Elemental Religion*. New York: Harper & Brothers, 1934. 143 pp.

Jefferson, Charles E., *The Building of the Church*. New York: The Macmillan Company, 1911. 306 pp.

Jowett, J. H., *The Preacher: His Life and Work*. New York: Hodder & Stoughton, 1912. 239 pp.

Kelman, John, *The War and Preaching*. London: Hodder & Stoughton [1919]. 286 pp.

McConnell, Francis J., *The Prophetic Ministry*. New York: The Abingdon Press, 1930. 308 pp.

McDowell, William Fraser, *Good Ministers of Jesus Christ*. New York: The Abingdon Press, 1918. 307 pp.

Merrill, William Pierson, *The Freedom of the Preacher*. New York: The Macmillan Company, 1922. 147 pp.

Morrison, Charles Clayton, *What Is Christianity?* Chicago: Willett, Clark & Company, 1940. 324 pp.

Mouzon, Edwin DuBose, *Preaching with Authority*. Garden City, New York: Doubleday, Doran & Company, Inc., 1929. 245 pp.

Noyes, Morgan Phelps, *Preaching the Word of God*. New York: Charles Scribner's Sons, 1943. 213 pp.

Oxnam, G. Bromley, *Preaching in a Revolutionary Age*. New York: Abingdon-Cokesbury Press, 1944. 207 pp.

Park, John Edgar, *The Miracle of Preaching*. New York: The Macmillan Company, 1936. 184 pp.

Parkhurst, Charles H., *The Pulpit and the Pew*. New Haven: Yale University Press, 1913. 195 pp.

Peabody, Francis Greenwood, *Jesus Christ and the Christian Character*. New York: Hodder & Stoughton, 1910. 304 pp.

Pepper, George Wharton, *A Voice from the Crowd*. New Haven: Yale University Press, 1915. 207 pp.

Robinson, E. G., *Lectures on Preaching*. New York: Henry Holt and Company, 1883. 214 pp.

Scherer, Paul, *For We Have This Treasure*. New York: Harper & Brothers, Publishers, 1944. 212 pp.

Sclater, J. R. P., *The Public Worship of God*. New York: George H. Doran Company, 1927. 199 pp.

Simpson, Matthew, *Lectures on Preaching*. New York: Phillips & Hunt, 1879. 336 pp.

Smith, George Adam, *Modern Criticism and the Preaching of the Old Testament*. London: Hodder & Stoughton, 1902. 325 pp.

Sockman, Ralph W., *The Highway of God*. New York: The Macmillan Company, 1942. 228 pp.

Sperry, Willard L., *We Prophesy in Part*. New York: Harper & Brothers, Publishers, 1938. 201 pp.

Stalker, James, *The Preacher and His Models*. London: Hodder & Stoughton, 1891. 284 pp.

Taylor, William M., *The Ministry of the Word*. London: T. Nelson and Sons [1876]. 318 pp.

———, *The Scottish Pulpit*. New York: Harper & Brothers, 1887. 287 pp.

Tittle, Ernest Fremont, *Jesus After Nineteen Centuries*. New York: The Abingdon Press, 1932. 217 pp.

Trumbull, H. Clay, *The Sunday School: Its Origin, Mission, Methods, and Auxiliaries*. Philadelphia: John D. Wattles, 1888. 415 pp.

Tucker, William Jewett, *The Making and the Unmaking of the Preacher*. Boston: Houghton Mifflin and Company, 1898. 224 pp.

Van Dyke, Henry, *The Gospel for an Age of Doubt*. New York: The Macmillan Company, 1897. 457 pp.

Watson, John [Maclaren, Ian], *The Cure of Souls*. New York: Dodd, Mead & Company, 1896. 301 pp.

Williams, Charles D., *The Prophetic Ministry for Today*. New York: The Macmillan Company, 1921. 184 pp.

B.   OTHER SOURCES

Aristotle, *Rhetoric*. J. E. C. Welldon, translator, *The Rhetoric of Aristotle*. London: Macmillan and Company, 1886. 306 pp. Quoted by Lester Thonssen, *Selected Readings in Rhetoric and Public Speaking*. New York: The H. W. Wilson Company, 1942. 324 pp.

Brigance, William Norwood, *Speech Composition*. New York: F. S. Crofts & Co., 1937. 385 pp.

———, and Ray Keeslar Immel, *Speechmaking; Principles and Practice*. New York: F. S. Crofts, 1938. 385 pp.

Campbell, George, *The Philosophy of Rhetoric*. New York: Harper & Brothers, 1851. 435 pp.

Cicero, Marcus Tullius, *De Oratore*. J. S. Watson, translator, *Cicero on Oratory and Orators*. London: George Bell and Sons, 1884. 522 pp.

————, *The Orator*. C. D. Yonge, *The Orations of Marcus Tullius Cicero*. 4 vols.; London: G. Bell and Sons, 1911.

Monroe, Alan H., *Principles and Types of Speech*. Revised edition; New York: Scott, Foresman and Company, 1939. 546 pp.

Phillips, Arthur Edward, *Effective Speaking*. Revised edition; Chicago: The Newton Company, 1938. 384 pp.

Quintilian, *Institutes of Oratory*. John Selby Watson, translator, *Quintilian's Institutes of Oratory*. 2 vols.; London: George Bell & Sons, 1892.

Whately, Richard, *Elements of Rhetoric*. Boston: James Munroe and Company, 1851. 347 pp.

Winans, James Albert, *Public Speaking*. New York: The Century Co., 1923. 526 pp.

APPENDIX

THE LYMAN BEECHER LECTURES
ON PREACHING

1871–1872 Henry Ward Beecher, *Yale Lectures on Preaching*. First series; New York: J. B. Ford & Company, 1872.

1872–1873 Henry Ward Beecher, *Yale Lectures on Preaching*. Second series; New York: J. B. Ford & Company, 1873.

1873–1874 Henry Ward Beecher, *Yale Lectures on Preaching*. Third series; New York: J. B. Ford & Company, 1874. A one-volume edition, *Yale Lectures on Preaching,* as is published by Fords, Howard, & Hulbert, New York, in 1892.

1874–1875 John Hall, *God's Word Through Preaching*. New York: Dodd & Mead, Publishers, 1875.

1875–1876 William M. Taylor, *The Ministry of the Word*. London: T. Nelson and Sons [1876].

1876–1877 Phillips Brooks, *Lectures on Preaching*. New York: E. P. Dutton & Company, 1898.

1877–1878 R. W. Dale, *Nine Lectures on Preaching*. London: Hodder & Stoughton, 1890.

1878–1879 Matthew Simpson, *Lectures on Preaching*. New York: Phillips & Hunt, 1879.

1879–1880 Howard Crosby, *The Christian Preacher*. New York: Anson D. F. Randolph & Company, 1879.

1880–1881 Joseph Tuthill Duryea, George Harris, Samuel E. Herrick, Nathaniel Judson Burton, and Llewelyn David Bevan. Lectures not published.

1881–1882 E. G. Robinson, *Lectures on Preaching*. New York: Henry Holt and Company, 1883.

1882–1883 No lectures.

1883–1884 Nathaniel J. Burton, *In Pulpit and Parish*. [New York: The Macmillan Company, 1925.]

1884–1885 Henry Martin Storrs, *The American Preacher*. Not published.

1885–1886 William M. Taylor, *The Scottish Pulpit*. New York: Harper & Brothers, 1887.

1886–1887 Washington Gladden, *Tools and the Man*. Boston: Houghton Mifflin Company, 1893.

1887–1888 H. Clay Trumbull, *The Sunday School: Its Origin, Mission, Methods, and Auxiliaries*. Philadelphia: John D. Wattles, 1888.

1888–1889 John Broadus, *A Treatise on the Preparation and Delivery of Sermons*. Revised edition; New York: Richard R. Smith, Inc., 1930.

1889–1890 A. J. F. Behrends, *The Philosophy of Preaching*. New York: Charles Scribner's Sons, 1890.

1890–1891 James Stalker, *The Preacher and His Models*. London: Hodder & Stoughton, 1891.

1891–1892 A. M. Fairbairn, *The Place of Christ in Modern Theology*. London: Hodder & Stoughton, 1893.

1892–1893 Robert F. Horton, *Verbum Dei*. New York: Macmillan and Co., 1893.

1893–1894 No lectures.

1894–1895 David H. Greer, *The Preacher and His Place*. New York: Edwin S. Gorham, 1904.

1895–1896 Henry van Dyke, *The Gospel for an Age of Doubt*. New York: The Macmillan Company, 1897.

1896–1897 John Watson [Ian Maclaren], *The Cure of Souls*. New York: Dodd, Mead & Company, 1896.

1897–1898 William Jewett Tucker, *The Making and the Unmaking of the Preacher*. Boston: Houghton Mifflin and Company, 1898.

1898–1899 George Adam Smith, *Modern Criticism and the Preaching of the Old Testament*. London: Hodder & Stoughton, 1902.

1899–1900 John Brown, *Puritan Preaching in England*. New York: Charles Scribner's Sons, 1900.

1900–1901 No lectures.

1901–1902 Washington Gladden, *Social Salvation*. Boston: Houghton Mifflin and Company, 1902.

1902–1903 George A. Gordon, *Ultimate Conceptions of Faith.* Boston: Houghton Mifflin and Company, 1903.

1903–1904 Lyman Abbott, *The Christian Ministry.* Boston: Houghton Mifflin and Company, 1905.

1904–1905 Francis Greenwood Peabody, *Jesus Christ and the Christian Character.* New York: Hodder & Stoughton, 1910.

1905–1906 Charles Reynolds Brown, *The Social Message of the Modern Pulpit.* New York: Charles Scribner's Sons, 1912.

1906–1907 P. T. Forsyth, *Positive Preaching and Modern Mind.* New York: Hodder & Stoughton [1907].

1907–1908 William Herbert Perry Faunce, *The Educational Ideal in the Ministry.* New York: The Macmillan Company, 1908.

1908–1909 H. Hensley Henson, *The Liberty of Prophesying.* New Haven: Yale University Press, 1910.

1909–1910 Charles E. Jefferson, *The Building of the Church.* New York: The Macmillan Company, 1911.

1910–1911 Frank W. Gunsaulus, *The Minister and the Spiritual Life.* New York: Fleming H. Revell Company, 1911.

1911–1912 J. H. Jowett, *The Preacher: His Life and Work.* New York: Hodder & Stoughton, 1912.

1912–1913 Charles H. Parkhurst, *The Pulpit and the Pew.* New Haven: Yale University Press, 1913.

1913–1914 Charles Silvester Horne, *The Romance of Preaching.* New York: Fleming H. Revell Company, 1914.

1914–1915 George Wharton Pepper, *A Voice from the Crowd.* New Haven: Yale University Press, 1915.

1915–1916 William DeWitt Hyde, *The Gospel of Good Will.* New York: The Macmillan Company, 1916.

1916–1917 William Fraser McDowell, *Good Ministers of Jesus Christ.* New York: The Abingdon Press, 1918.

1917–1918 Henry Sloane Coffin, *In a Day of Social Rebuilding.* New Haven: Yale University Press, 1918.

1918–1919 John Kelman, *The War and Preaching.* London: Hodder & Stoughton [1919].

1919–1920 Albert Parker Fitch, *Preaching and Paganism*. New Haven: Yale University Press, 1920.

1920–1921 Charles D. Williams, *The Prophetic Ministry for Today*. New York: The Macmillan Company, 1921.

1921–1922 William Pierson Merrill, *The Freedom of the Preacher*. New York: The Macmillan Company, 1922.

1922–1923 Charles Reynolds Brown, *The Art of Preaching*. New York: The Macmillan Company, 1922.

1923–1924 Harry Emerson Fosdick, *The Modern Use of the Bible*. New York: The Macmillan Company, 1924.

1924–1925 William Ralph Inge, *The Preaching of the Kingdom of God in History*. Lectures not published.

1925–1926 Raymond Calkins, *The Eloquence of Christian Experience*. New York: The Macmillan Company, 1927.

1926–1927 J. R. P. Sclater, *The Public Worship of God*. New York: George H. Doran Company, 1927.

1927–1928 James Edward Freeman, *The Ambassador*. New York: The Macmillan Company, 1928.

1928–1929 Edwin DuBose Mouzon, *Preaching with Authority*. Garden City, New York: Doubleday, Doran & Company, Inc., 1929.

1929–1930 Francis J. McConnell, *The Prophetic Ministry*. New York: The Abingdon Press, 1930.

1930–1931 George A. Buttrick, *Jesus Came Preaching*. New York: Charles Scribner's Sons, 1931.

1931–1932 Ernest Fremont Tittle, *Jesus After Nineteen Centuries*. New York: The Abingdon Press, 1932.

1932–1933 L. P. Jacks, *Elemental Religion*. New York: Harper & Brothers, 1934.

1933–1934 Albert Edward Day, *Jesus and Human Personality*. New York: The Abingdon Press, 1934.

1934–1935 Walter Russell Bowie, *The Renewing Gospel*. New York: Charles Scribner's Sons, 1935.

1935–1936 John Edgar Park, *The Miracle of Preaching*. New York: The Macmillan Company, 1936.

1936–1937 No lectures.

1937–1938 Willard L. Sperry, *We Prophesy in Part*. New York: Harper & Brothers Publishers, 1938.

1938–1939 Charles Clayton Morrison, *What Is Christianity?* Chicago: Willett, Clark & Company, 1940.

1939–1940 George Arthur Buttrick, Edwin McNeill Poteat, Arthur Howe Bradford, Elmore McNeill McKee, Wyatt Aiken Smart, and Ernest Fremont Tittle, *Preaching in These Times*. New York: Charles Scribner's Sons, 1940.

1940–1941 Ralph W. Sockman, *The Highway of God*. New York: The Macmillan Company, 1942.

1941–1942 Morgan Phelps Noyes, *Preaching the Word of God*. New York: Charles Scribner's Sons, 1943.

1942–1943 Paul Scherer, *For We Have This Treasure*. New York: Harper & Brothers, Publishers, 1944.

1943–1944 G. Bromley Oxnam, *Preaching in a Revolutionary Age*. New York: Abingdon-Cokesbury Press, 1944.

INDEX